POCKET NATURE

AND MOTHS

POCKET NATURE
BUTTERFLIES
AND MOTHS

PAUL STERRY
ANDREW MACKAY

DK

DORLING KINDERSLEY

DK

LONDON, NEW YORK, MUNICH,
MELBOURNE, AND DELHI

DK LONDON
Senior Art Editor Ina Stradins
Project Art Editor Vanessa Thompson
Senior Editor Angeles Gavira
Editor Georgina Garner
DTP Designer Adam Shepherd
Picture Editor Neil Fletcher
Illustrator Andrew Mackay
Production Controllers
Elizabeth Cherry, Melanie Dowland
Managing Art Editor Phil Ormerod
Managing Editor Liz Wheeler
Art Director Bryn Walls
Category Publisher Jonathan Metcalf

DK DELHI
Designers Kavita Dutta,
Malavika Talukder, Indrani Parker,
Angshuman De
Editors Sheema Mookherjee,
Dipali Singh, Glenda Fernandes
Editorial Consultant Anita Roy
Editorial Support Chumki Sen,
Bhavna Seth
DTP Designers Balwant Singh,
Sunil Sharma, Jessica Subramanian
DTP Co-ordinator Pankaj Sharma
Cartographers Ashwani Tyagi,
Suresh Kumar
Managing Art Editor Aparna Sharma

This edition published in 2010
First published in Great Britain in 2004 by
Dorling Kindersley Limited
80 Strand, London WC2R 0RL
A Penguin Company

Copyright © 2004
Dorling Kindersley Limited

ISBN 978 1 4053 4995 6

Reproduced by Colourscan, Singapore
Printed and bound by Sheck Wah Tong, China

see our complete catalogue at
www.dk.com

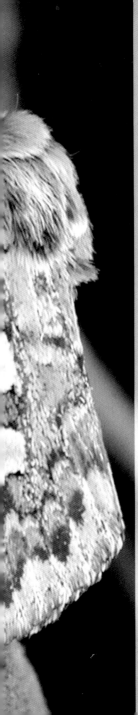

CONTENTS

RSPB a million voices for nature

The Royal Society for the Protection of Birds (RSPB) speaks out for birds and wildlife, tackling the problems that threaten our environment. It works with bird and habitat conservation organizations in a global partnership called BirdLife International. Nature is amazing – help us keep it that way.

THE AUTHORS

Paul Sterry studied zoology at Imperial College. He has written more than 30 books on natural history.

Andrew Mackay is a freelance natural history artist, writer, and editor, who has studied moths for many years.

How this book works

This guide covers the 320 most commonly seen butterfly and moth species in northwest Europe. At the beginning of the book is a short introduction, which focuses on the process of species identification in the field. The guide is then divided into two chapters: Butterflies, and Moths. Within the butterfly chapter, the species are arranged by colour and broadly by family so that similar looking species appear close together for ease of comparison. The moths are arranged by family.

CHAPTER HEADING
In the butterflies chapter, this is followed by the colour category.

▽ **GROUP INTRODUCTIONS**
Each of the two chapters opens with an introductory page describing the group's shared characteristics. Photographs of representative species show the diversity in the group.

COMMON NAME

SCIENTIFIC NAME

DESCRIPTION
Conveys the main distinguishing features and characteristics of the butterfly or moth.

VARIATIONS
Additional photographs illustrate any significant differences between upper and undersides, males and females.

SCALE DRAWING
To give an indication of the species' wingspan, a drawing representing the butterly or moth is set next to a drawing of this guide. See panel top right.

CATERPILLARS
Artworks show the larval stage of the butterfly or moth; caterpillar size is not well documented so sizes given are estimates of maximum length.

Moths

Over 8,000 species of moths, nearly 95% of the continent's Lepidoptera, occur in Europe, yet they are generally less well known than butterflies. Although most fly at night, there are many day-flying species, and almost any moth may be seen by day if disturbed from its resting place. Moths range in size from tiny 'micro-moths' with wingspans of just a few millimetres, to the large hawk-moths, such as the Elephant Hawk-moth shown below. Moths are often unfairly thought of as rather dull, while some are indeed mainly brown or grey to provide camouflage, many are just as brightly coloured as butterflies.

Purple-ed

Lycaena hippothoe (

In bright sunlight, the of this species, display edges – an excellent cl upperwings are orange orange band on the hi the brightest colours.

dark spots

orange band

up to 2cm long

Nettle-tre

Libythea celtis (Libyt

This interesting butter wing shape and by the mouthpart appendages orange-buff and brown is also distinctive – the the upperwings being mirrored on the unde The species is relativel long-lived as an adult, hibernating during the winter months.

grey-brown ground colour

up to 3.5cm long

▷ **SINGLE-PAGE ENTRIES**
Species that exhibit greater or more complex features, or are of special interest, are given a full page.

NOTES
Describe striking or unique features or behaviours that will aid identification, and may also provide interesting background information.

Garden Tiger
Arctia caja (Arctiidae)

The large and strikingly marked Garden Tiger has declined dramatically in many parts of its range in recent years, possibly due to climate change. The complex pattern of dark brown and cream on the forewings varies from north to south. The contrasting hindwings are usually bright orange, with prominent black spots. Also orange, the abdomen is marked with black bars. The caterpillar of the Garden Tiger is sometimes known as the "woolly bear" since it is covered with many long brown hairs. These contain an irritant poison and should never be handled.

▽ SPECIES ENTRIES

The typical page describes two butterfly or moth species. Each entry follows the same easy-to-access structure. All have one main photograph of the species, which is taken in its natural setting in the wild. This is supported by one or more detail pictures of different views or sexes. Annotations, a scale artwork, a distribution map, and a concise data box add key information and complete the entry.

SCALE MEASUREMENTS

Two small scale drawings are placed next to each other in every entry as a rough indication of the wingspan of the species. The drawing of the book represents this guide, which is 19cm high. The butterfly or moth illustration is a stylized representation of the species in silhouette.

Species wingspan 10cm | Book Height 19cm

FAMILY NAME

FLIES:ORANGE **61**

opper

…perwings of the male …urple sheen along the …y. The female's …th a submarginal …rctic females have

INHABITS *damp areas in meadows and grassland, occurring in foothills and lower mountain slopes up to 2,000m.*

…ur ♂♀

…eaks …g edge

…cm.
…une–July.
T *Bistort (Persicaria)* and

…*Large Copper* (p.58); …r (left), which has a larger …upperwings. …ad but local.

…erfly

…gnized by its jagged …jection of its …nottled

snout-like projection

FOUND *on wooded slopes, maquis, parks, and gardens, the common factor being the presence of the larval foodplant.*

orange-buff patches

♂♀

jagged wing margin

WINGSPAN *4.5cm.*
FLIGHT PERIOD *June–September and, after hibernation, March–April.*
LARVAL FOODPLANT *Nettle tree (Celtis).*
SIMILAR SPECIES *Comma (p.75), which has a similar wing outline.*
STATUS *Widespread and fairly common in southern Europe.*

HABITAT PICTURE
Shows the type of habitat in which you are most likely to find the species.

HABITAT CAPTION
Describes the habitat or range of habitats in which you are likely to find the butterfly or moth.

PHOTOGRAPHS
Illustrate the species in its natural setting and characteristic pose.

ANNOTATION
Characteristic features of the species are picked out in the annotation.

MAPS
The shading on the map indicates the potential occurrence of the species in the region, although the species may be occasional in some areas of the range and more prolific in others. While there is detailed distribution information available for butterflies, the data available for moths only states the countries in which the species has been recorded. The shading on the maps reflects this level of detail in each case.

COLOUR BANDS
Bands are colour-coded, with a different colour for each of the two chapters.

SYMBOLS
For clarity, symbols are used to denote males and females (where these are visually distinct) and for the different views.

Female ♀   Male ♂

Upperside view ◖   Underside view ◗

OTHER KEY INFORMATION
These panels provide consistent information on the following points:
WINGSPAN: *the span of the wings, from tip to tip, with the wings spread open.*
FLIGHT PERIOD: *the months during which the butterfly or moth is active and may be observed. May also state whether there is more than one brood, where known, and if the species hibernates.*
TIME OF FLIGHT: *given for moths only, this states whether the species is night- or day-flying.*
LARVAL FOODPLANT: *lists the plants the larva (caterpillar) feeds on; for clarity, the scientific name of the plant is also given.*
SIMILAR SPECIES: *lists species that look similar to the featured butterfly or moth, often describing distinguishing features.*
STATUS: *states how common or rare the species is in the region.*

Anatomy

Butterflies and moths are insects, forming the group – or order – Lepidoptera. A literal translation of Lepidoptera is 'scale wings' and, indeed, the wings of almost all species in this group are entirely cloaked in scales, which give the wings their colours and patterns. Like other adult insects, the body of a butterfly or moth is divided into three sections: the head, on which are found the eyes, mouthparts, and antennae; the thorax, to which the wings and legs are attached by powerful internal muscles; and the abdomen, which contains many of the vital organs, including the digestive and reproductive systems.

antenna

eye

thorax

abdomen

basal area of wing

vein

leading edge

forewing

hindwing

eyespot

tail streamer

Butterfly Upperside

When feeding or basking in sunshine, some butterflies rest with their wings held flat. From above, the hindwings are partially concealed by the forewings, but the degree to which they are hidden varies between species, and factors such as the intensity of the sun may also affect the basking position of individuals within a species. The wings are held rigid by a network of veins, often emphasised by bold markings. The upperwings of a butterfly are generally more colourful than the underwings.

FLIGHT TIME
Like all butterflies, the Swallowtail (pictured) is strictly diurnal. By contrast, the majority of moths are nocturnal, although some are day flying and others may be active at dawn or twilight

Butterfly Underside

Almost all butterflies – some skipper species prove the exception – rest with their wings folded together above the abdomen, the upper surfaces lying face to face. In this position, the three pairs of legs characteristic of adult insects can be seen and the hindwings conceal the forewings to varying degrees, often depending upon the state of wariness or torpor of the individual. Some butterflies never reveal the upper surface of the wing except in flight; they feed, bask, and rest with wings folded.

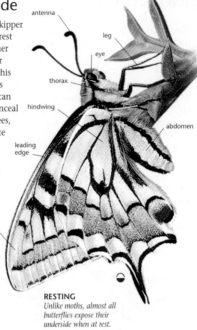

antenna
leg
eye
thorax
hindwing
abdomen
leading edge
forewing

RESTING
Unlike moths, almost all butterflies expose their underside when at rest.

trailing edge
wing margin

CLUBBED OR TAPERED?
Moths' antennae taper to a point or, in males of some species, they are branched and feathery; a butterfly's antennae are clubbed or swollen toward the tip.

head
antenna
leg
thorax
abdomen
forewing

Moth

Most moths rest with their wings held in a tent-like manner, concealing the abdomen. From above, the hindwings are hidden by the forewings, only becoming visible when the insect is disturbed. A few moth species will spread their wings out flat when, for example, resting on tree bark: the upper surface of the moths' forewings is often beautifully patterned to afford the insect camouflage. Some moths resemble fallen leaves; others are a close match for lichen-covered tree bark.

Identification

Some butterfly and moth species are easy to identify: think of the
Peacock (p.90), whose unique upperwing colours and markings are
unmistakable. Yet, within some groups – notably Browns, Blues, and
Skippers – there are species that are bafflingly similar to one another.
By observing physical features, however, such as colours, markings,
and wing shape, along with habitat preferences and geographical
range, almost all species can be identified by a persistent beginner.

Colour and Markings

The wings are generally the most striking part of a butterfly or moth, and their
colour and markings offer vital clues to identification. Some features, such as
eyespots or contrasting bands, are easy to discern in the field and to relate to
images in this book; others are subtler and require close scrutiny and a degree of
experience. Look at the shape and position of markings and how these vary
from upperside to underside and hindwing to forewing.

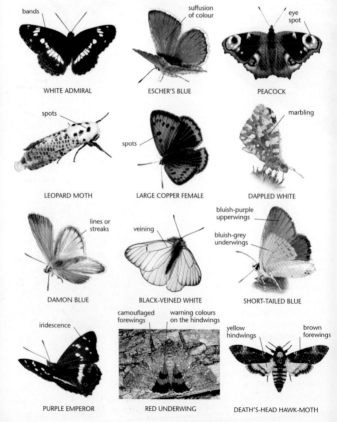

bands

WHITE ADMIRAL

suffusion
of colour

ESCHER'S BLUE

eye
spot

PEACOCK

spots

LEOPARD MOTH

spots

LARGE COPPER FEMALE

marbling

DAPPLED WHITE

lines or
streaks

DAMON BLUE

veining

BLACK-VEINED WHITE

bluish-purple
upperwings

bluish-grey
underwings

SHORT-TAILED BLUE

iridescence

PURPLE EMPEROR

camouflaged
forewings

warning colours
on the hindwings

RED UNDERWING

yellow
hindwings

brown
forewings

DEATH'S-HEAD HAWK-MOTH

Wing Shape

Butterfly and moth wing shape varies remarkably given that their primary role – flight – is purely functional. Some species have broad and rounded wings that permit extended gliding flight; others have narrow and rather angular wings, typically associated with a buzzing flight pattern. A peculiar wing outline may also enhance the camouflage of the underwing, for example, a resting Brimstone (p.54) is a good match for a fresh ivy leaf, in outline shape as well as colour.

tail streamers

jagged margin

angular margin

scalloped hindwing

TWO-TAILED PASHA **COMMA** **SMALL TORTOISESHELL** **MELEAGER'S BLUE**

broad and narrow

angular forewing

rounded

broad and pointed

HUNGARIAN GLIDER **SMALL SKIPPER** **WOOD WHITE** **THE DRINKER**

long thin forewings (round-ended)

feathery plumes

small and transparent

long thin forewings (square-ended)

DIAMOND-BACK MOTH **SIX-SPOT BURNET** **TWENTY-PLUME MOTH** **HORNET MOTH**

Size

Size can be a useful way of distinguishing two superficially similar species. It may not always be possible to make precise measurements in the field, but size can be estimated for comparative purposes.

WINGSPAN 3cm

WINGSPAN 4.4–4.8cm

DUKE OF BURGUNDY FRITILLARY
This species looks like a Fritillary, but is much smaller and not a true member of the group.

HEATH FRITILLARY
Much larger and more active than the Duke of Burgundy, this species is representative of the Fritillary family.

Variations

Some species exhibit little variation: for example, almost all individual Peacocks appear identical. In other species, different broods appear entirely dissimilar, and strikingly different colour forms are found side by side.

DIFFERENT BROODS
The upperwings of the first and second broods of the Map Butterfly differ greatly.

WEAR AND TEAR
Older specimens of the Light Emerald appear faded beside fresh individuals.

VARIABLE FORMS
The Riband Wave is notoriously variable and occurs in a wide range of forms.

Sex

In some species, obvious differences in colour or markings distinguish the sexes; in others, look for subtler identifying features. For example, males of some moth species, such as the Brindled Beauty, may vary in colour, but can always be identified by their feathery antennae; the females have non-feathered antennae.

COMMON BLUE

BRINDLED BEAUTY

Resting Position

Considering how a species holds its wings while at rest can aid identification. Some butterflies never reveal their upperwings at rest; some hold the wings out flat; others may keep them angled. Moths typically hold the forewings angled or rolled, concealing the hindwings and abdomen.

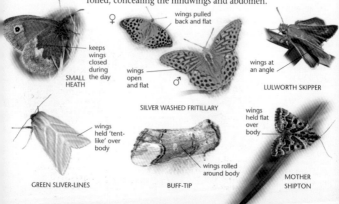

SMALL HEATH

SILVER WASHED FRITILLARY

LULWORTH SKIPPER

GREEN SLIVER-LINES

BUFF-TIP

MOTHER SHIPTON

Habitat

Although a few butterfly and moth species will inhabit a broad range of habitats, most have very specific living requirements: habitat choice may be determined by the range of plant species eaten by the larva. This can be an important identification clue in cases where the species in question is extremely habitat-specific.

LOWLANDS
The Silver-studded Blue is associated with lowland heathland areas.

UPLANDS
The similar Zephyr Blue is more typically found in upland meadows.

UPPER SLOPES
The Peak White is seldom found away from upland slopes.

Two-tailed Pasha

FOOTHILLS
The Dappled White is found on lower mountain slopes.

FRUIT
Rotting fruit may provide a useful source of fluids and nutrients.

Small Tortoiseshell

Peacock

Red Admiral

FLOWERS
Flower-rich habits provide abundant nectar to feed on.

SHELTER
Small Tortoiseshells often hibernate in attics and outhouses during winter.

Distribution

Similar species may be differentiated by the difference in their distribution. In a number of cases, ranges are entirely distinct and contained, separated by thousands of miles.

SOUTHERN
Shepherd's Fritillary is found in southern European ranges.

NORTHERN
Superficially similar, Frejya's Fritillary occurs in Scandinavia.

Butterflies

The Order Lepidoptera is made up of over 165,000 species worldwide, of which around 12 per cent are butterflies. Several hundred butterfly species occur in Europe, and representatives can be found in almost all regional habitats. The majority of butterflies have wings adorned with stunning colours or striking markings, which may aid camouflage or scare off predators. Members of the same butterfly family often share similar characters. For example, the upperwings of the male Reverdin's Blue (below) immediately identify it as a member of the Blue family. Butterflies are diurnal, sun-loving insects, and seldom fly on overcast, cold, or wet days.

TURQUOISE BLUE   GREEN HAIRSTREAK   LULWORTH SKIPPER   SOUTHERN GATEKEEPER

Short-tailed Blue

Cupido argiades (Lycaenidae)

This active, low-flying butterfly has a short hindwing tail, which may not always be visible in the field. Males have bluish purple upperwings; in females they are mainly brown. Both sexes have blue-grey underwings with a row of dark-centred orange spots along the hindwing margin.

In warm seasons, its range extends northwards and migrants have occurred in southern England.

FAVOURS *meadows, verges, and other flower-rich grassy places from sea level to foothills.*

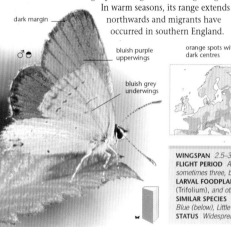

dark margin

bluish purple upperwings

bluish grey underwings

spots on forewing

orange spots with dark centres

short tail ♂●

up to 1cm long

♂●

WINGSPAN *2.5–3cm.*
FLIGHT PERIOD *April–September, in two, sometimes three, broods.*
LARVAL FOODPLANT *Trefoil (Lotus), clover (Trifolium), and other pea family members.*
SIMILAR SPECIES *Provençal Short-tailed Blue (below), Little Blue (p.17).*
STATUS *Widespread and often common.*

Provençal Short-tailed Blue

Cupido alcetas (Lycaenidae)

This butterfly frequently basks in the sun, making it easy to observe well. The small hindwing tail can be hard to discern in the field. Only males have bluish upperwings; female upperwings are dark brown. In both sexes the pale grey underwings are suffused blue at the base and adorned with black dots.

FOUND *in open, sunny meadows and flowery verges from sea level to 1,250m.*

pale grey ground colour

dark margin

uniform bluish colour

♂●

♂●

up to 1cm long

white fringe

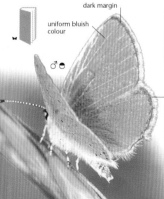

WINGSPAN *3-3.2cm.*
FLIGHT PERIOD *April–September, usually in two or more broods.*
LARVAL FOODPLANT *Crown vetch (Coronilla varia) and other pea family plants.*
SIMILAR SPECIES *Short-tailed Blue (above), Little Blue (p.17).*
STATUS *Locally common.*

Eastern Short-tailed Blue

Cupido decoloratus (Lycaenidae)

Careful attention to subtle details will be needed in order to identify this species. A lack of orange on the underwings and the presence of a tiny hindwing tail, which is not easy to see in the field, distinguish it from most other Blues. A small dark line or spot at the centre of the upper forewing separates the male from its close relatives.

FAVOURS *grassy places with flowers, including verges and hillside meadows, in low-lying areas below 500m.*

dark mark on forewing

blackish veins

grey-blue ground colour

black spots

Caterpillar not sufficiently known

♂

tiny tail-like projection

WINGSPAN *2.5cm.*
FLIGHT PERIOD *April–September, in successive broods.*
LARVAL FOODPLANT *Medick (Medicago) and lucerne (M. sativa).*
SIMILAR SPECIES *Short-tailed Blue (p.15), Provençal Short-tailed Blue (p.15).*
STATUS *Locally common.*

Osiris Blue

Cupido osiris (Lycaenidae)

This butterfly is usually seen warming itself in the sun. The males have bluish purple upperwings, while those of females are dark brown, sometimes almost black. Both sexes have pale bluish grey underwings marked by small black spots and suffused with blue at the wing base. The larvae feed on the flowerheads of the foodplant.

LIVES *in flowery meadows on hills and lower mountain slopes from 500m–2,000m.*

bluish purple upperwings

bluish grey underwings

black dots

♂

bluish wing base

up to 1.5cm long

WINGSPAN *2.5–3cm.*
FLIGHT PERIOD *May–September, in one or two broods.*
LARVAL FOODPLANT *Sainfoin (Onobrychis).*
SIMILAR SPECIES *Little Blue (right), Holly Blue (p.23), and Mazarine Blue (p.28).*
STATUS *Local, often forming small and discrete colonies.*

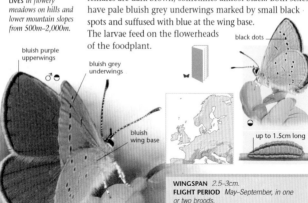

Little Blue

Cupido minimus (Lycaenidae)

This tiny butterfly is extremely active on sunny days. It can be difficult to follow on the wing because of its small size and buzzing flight. In both sexes, the ground colour of the upperwings is sooty brown, only the males showing a dusting of blue near the wing base. The pale grey underwings of both sexes are spotted with black. Both the slug-like larvae and the pupae are usually attended by ants. The larvae feed on the flowerheads of the foodplant.

FOUND in flower-rich grassland, usually on areas of chalk and limestone. Typically favours warm and sunny slopes.

wing base suffused blue

sooty brown ground colour

♂

white fringe

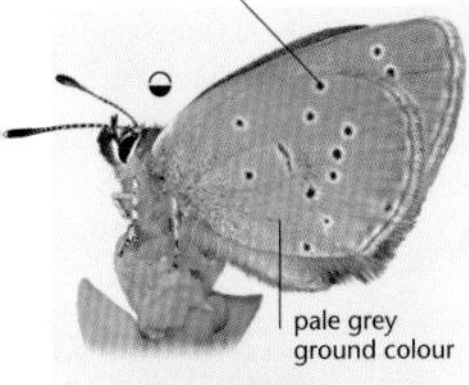

white-ringed black dots

pale grey ground colour

no blue at wing base

sooty brown wings

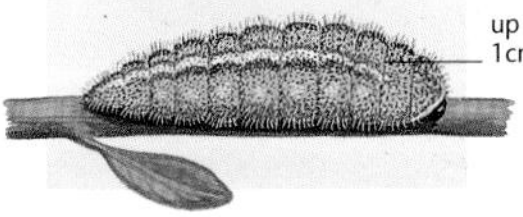

♀

up to 1cm long

NOTE

On warm and sunny days, the Little Blue can be found drinking from puddles on the ground. If water is in short supply, then a dozen or more will sometimes be found together. On occasions it is even attracted to human sweat, and can hover extremely close to the observer's face and neck.

WINGSPAN 2–2.5cm.
FLIGHT PERIOD May–August, in one or two broods.
LARVAL FOODPLANT Mainly kidney-vetch (Anthyllis vulneraria).
SIMILAR SPECIES Short-tailed Blue (p.15), Osiris Blue (left).
STATUS Widespread and locally common.

Black-eyed Blue

Glaucopsyche melanops (Lycaenidae)

This butterfly is an active and sun-loving species. The male has blue upperwings, while those of the female are dark brown, sometimes almost black, and suffused with blue at the wing base. The larvae, which feed on flowers, are often attended by ants.

FAVOURS *heathland and maquis scrubland with sunny clearings and plenty of larval foodplants, from sea level to 1,200m.*

deep blue upperwings

crescent of dark spots

grey wings

dark margin

blue suffusion at wing base

dark brown ground colour

♂●

♀●

up to 1cm long

WINGSPAN *2.5–3cm.*
FLIGHT PERIOD *April–May.*
LARVAL FOODPLANT *Broom (Genista), Dorycnium, and other members of the pea family.*
SIMILAR SPECIES *Holly Blue (p.23), Green-underside Blue (p.25).*
STATUS *Local, but not uncommon.*

Baton Blue

Scolitantides baton (Lycaenidae)

This upland butterfly has pale bluish purple upperwings in the male; those of the female are dark brown, variably suffused with bluish purple at the wing base. A sluggish species, it is sometimes discovered walking over vegetation. The adult is fond of the flowers of wild thyme.

PREFERS *sunny, grassy slopes with short vegetation, from sea level to 1,500m.*

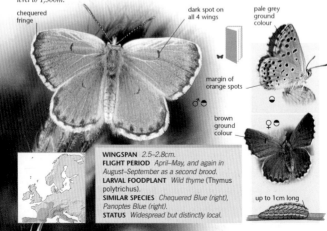

chequered fringe

dark spot on all 4 wings

pale grey ground colour

margin of orange spots

♂●

brown ground colour

♀●

up to 1cm long

WINGSPAN *2.5–2.8cm.*
FLIGHT PERIOD *April–May, and again in August–September as a second brood.*
LARVAL FOODPLANT *Wild thyme (Thymus polytrichus).*
SIMILAR SPECIES *Chequered Blue (right), Panoptes Blue (right).*
STATUS *Widespread but distinctly local.*

Panoptes Blue

Scolitantides panoptes (Lycaenidae)

Subtle colour differences distinguish this Iberian species from the Baton Blue (left). The male's upperwings are a deeper shade of violet-blue than its relative's but the dark margins are narrower and better defined. In the female, the upperwings are brown and in both sexes, the underwing is darker grey. The wing colours emphasize the contrasting fringe.

FOUND *on upland grassy slopes, between 1,000m and 2,000m; often where grazing limits vegetation.*

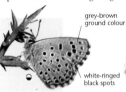

grey-brown
ground colour

♂ ●

violet-blue
ground colour

white-ringed
black spots

*Caterpillar not
sufficiently known*

chequered
fringe

WINGSPAN *2.5cm.*
FLIGHT PERIOD *May–July.*
LARVAL FOODPLANT *Thyme (Thymus).*
SIMILAR SPECIES *Baton Blue (left), which typically has paler blue upperwings and displays sluggish movements.*
STATUS *Relatively common, although its range is restricted to Iberia.*

Chequered Blue

Scolitantides orion (Lycaenidae)

A distinctive species, the Chequered Blue's underwings are more attractive than the upper. Both sexes have dingy grey-brown upperwings, and the male has a bluish purple suffusion towards the wing base, this being more extensive in Scandinavian males. By contrast, the soft grey underwings are adorned with conspicuous black spots and have an orange-yellow band on the hindwing.

INHABITS *dry, stony mountainsides and cliffs with short vegetation.*

blue tinge at
wing base

♂ ●

dull brown
ground
colour

striking black
spots

orange-
yellow
band

sooty
brown
wings

♀ ●

up to 1.5cm long

WINGSPAN *3cm.*
FLIGHT PERIOD *May–July.*
LARVAL FOODPLANT *Stonecrop (Sedum).*
SIMILAR SPECIES *Baton Blue (left), Silver-studded Blue (p.20), Magpie Moth (p.173).*
STATUS *Distinctly local and patchily distributed, due in part to its precise habitat requirements.*

Silver-studded Blue

Plebejus argus (Lycaenidae)

On sunny days, this beautiful little butterfly seems active all the time, flitting between flowerheads and resting on each only momentarily. Males have purplish blue upperwings. However, the extent of this colour, as well as the dark margin, varies across the species' geographical range. Females have mainly brown upperwings. Both sexes have pale grey-brown underwings (generally darker in females than males), and there are numerous spots and a submarginal orange band on both wings; the marginal black spots on the hindwing have shiny greenish centres.

PREFERS *dry, open habitats including heathland, grassy hillsides, and coastal dunes. Occurs from sea level to 2,000m.*

purplish blue ground colour

♂●

orange band with black spots

greyish brown ground colour

shiny green or blue centres

♂●

rich brown ground colour

♀●

crescent of orange spots

up to 1cm long

pale fringe

dark margin, variable in extent

NOTE

The Silver-studded Blue usually suns itself in the early morning and late afternoon. These are the times of day when you will get the best and most prolonged views of this fast-flying butterfly. This butterfly is often seen resting on the very tips of clumps of heather (Calluna).

WINGSPAN *2.4–3cm.*
FLIGHT PERIOD *May–August, with a second brood extending the season to September in the south.*
LARVAL FOODPLANT *Heather (Calluna) and gorse (Ulex) on heathland; elsewhere rock-rose (Helianthemum) and trefoil (Lotus).*
SIMILAR SPECIES *Chequered Blue (p.19), Zephyr Blue (p.26), Idas Blue (p.26), Reverdin's Blue (p.27).*
STATUS *Widespread and locally very common.*

Alpine Argus

Plebejus orbitulus (Lycaenidae)

Very much an upland species, the Alpine Argus has its European stronghold in the Alps. The males have conspicuous, shiny blue upperwings with dark margins. However, the extent of colour is variable in individuals. The upperwing in females is rich brown. Both sexes have pale grey underwings, with pale spots on the hindwing.

dark margin

RESTRICTED *to upland grassland between 1,000m and 3,000m, where damp conditions favour the larval foodplant.*

shiny blue

♂●

pale grey ground colour

white spots

WINGSPAN *2.5–3cm.*
FLIGHT PERIOD *June–August.*
LARVAL FOODPLANT *Alpine milk-vetch (Astragalus alpinus).*
SIMILAR SPECIES *Adonis Blue, in upperwings only (p.32).*
STATUS *Fairly common within its restricted European range.*

up to 1.5cm long

Glandon Blue

Plebejus glandon (Lycaenidae)

As is the case with many upland butterflies, the Glandon Blue takes every opportunity to bask in the sun, opening its wings wide in order to warm itself. The female's upperwings are brown, while those of the male have limited sky-blue patches. In both sexes the underwings are grey-brown, marked with black and white spots.

FAVOURS *slopes with montane vegetation, which is typically very short and snow-covered in winter.*

♂●

dark spot on each wing

blue on inner wing

white-ringed dark spots

wide dark margin

WINGSPAN *2.5–3cm.*
FLIGHT PERIOD *July–August.*
LARVAL FOODPLANT *Alpine snowbell (Soldanella alpina) and rock jasmine (Androsace).*
SIMILAR SPECIES *None within its range, and given its preference for high altitudes.*
STATUS *Locally fairly common.*

●

up to 1cm long

Eros Blue

Polyommatus eros (Lycaenidae)

BREEDS *exclusively on mountain slopes, up to 2,500m, where the vegetation is typically short and sparse.*

This high-altitude species drinks at puddles and spends time sunbathing with its wings open, offering good observation opportunities. Males have shiny sky-blue upperwings, while those of females are brown. In both sexes, the underwings are pale grey-brown, with black and orange spots.

shiny sky-blue upperwings

♂●

black and orange spots

grey-brown underwings

up to 1cm long

distinct dark border

WINGSPAN *2.5–3cm.*
FLIGHT PERIOD *June–August.*
LARVAL FOODPLANT *Mainly milk-vetches (Astragalus).*
SIMILAR SPECIES *Turquoise Blue (p.29), Common Blue (p.30), False Eros Blue (P. eroides), which is usually smaller.*
STATUS *Local and seldom very common.*

Amanda's Blue

Polyommatus amandus (Lycaenidae)

INHABITS *flower-rich grassland, typically in upland meadows, but sometimes found at sea level.*

The male of this active and sun-loving species has sky-blue upperwings, but those of the female are mainly brown. In both sexes the underwings are grey-brown with black and orange spots. Like many other Blue butterflies, the Amanda's Blue is often seen drinking at puddles and even fresh cow pats.

arc of black spots

♂●

white fringe

sky-blue ground colour

grey base

up to 2.5cm long

♂●

WINGSPAN *4cm.*
FLIGHT PERIOD *June–July.*
LARVAL FOODPLANT *Tufted vetch (Vicia cracca) and sainfoin (Onobrychis).*
SIMILAR SPECIES *Escher's Blue (p.29), Turquoise Blue (p.29), Chalk-hill Blue (p.31).*
STATUS *Locally fairly common, especially in the hills.*

Holly Blue

Celastrina argiolus (Lycaenidae)

For many people, the Holly Blue is a familiar species as it is often found in gardens where holly and ivy – the two plants with which it is most closely associated – are common. Both sexes have blue upperwings although they are paler in females than males. The dark wing margins are more extensive in females, and more so in the second brood of the year. The pale bluish white underwings of both sexes are adorned with small black spots.

FOUND *in diverse habitats such as woodland, inland cliffs, and gardens – the common factor being larval foodplants.*

narrow dark margin

violet-blue ground colour

faintly chequered pale fringe

♂●

small dark spots

bluish white wings

sky-blue base

♀●

variable dark margin

up to 1cm long

NOTE

Holly Blues drink honeydew, rather than nectar, and while doing so, they seem quite oblivious to onlookers. Excellent close-up views of the butterfly can be obtained at such moments as it walks over foliage.

WINGSPAN *3cm.*
FLIGHT PERIOD *April–May and August–September, in two distinct broods.*
LARVAL FOODPLANT *Mainly holly (Ilex) for first brood larvae but ivy (Hedera) for second brood larvae.*
SIMILAR SPECIES *Osiris Blue, male (p.16), which lacks the subtly chequered fringe.*
STATUS *Generally common and widespread.*

Long-tailed Blue

Lampides boeticus (Lycaenidae)

OCCURS *in a variety of flower-rich grassy habitats appearing almost anywhere due to its migratory habits.*

Despite its small size, the migratory Long-tailed Blue is a powerful flier. In most years, it spreads north beyond its usual range and on occasion has been known to reach southern England. When resting, it seldom exposes its upper wings, which are violet-blue in males and sooty brown in females. The more commonly viewed brownish underside has grey-white bars on the forewing and a broad pale band and twin eyespots on the hindwing in both the sexes. The hindwings also have long tails.

pale band

♂♀

twin eyespots

whitish barring

♀♀

up to 1.5cm long

NOTE
Keep in mind that the tail streamer sometimes breaks off in older, worn out specimens. On seeing the brownish underwings only, an inexperienced observer could mistake such a resting individual for a Hairstreak.

sooty brown ground colour

♀♀

violet-blue flush at wing base

long tail on hindwing

WINGSPAN *3.5cm.*
FLIGHT PERIOD *May–October, in two or three broods.*
LARVAL FOODPLANT *A wide range of members of the pea family (Fabaceae).*
SIMILAR SPECIES *Lang's Short-tailed Blue (right), which does not have the pale band on the underside hindwings.*
STATUS *Common and widespread within its given range; occasional elsewhere.*

Lang's Short-tailed Blue

Leptotes pirithous (Lycaenidae)

This powerful flier is a strong migrant. It rarely reveals its upperwings, which are mainly violet-blue in the male and more brown in the female. In both sexes, the barred underwings are marked by two colourful eyespots and a long tail.

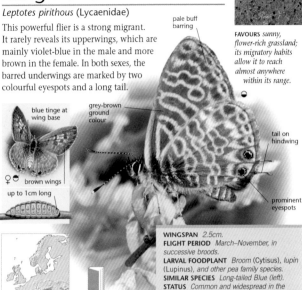

pale buff barring

FAVOURS *sunny, flower-rich grassland; its migratory habits allow it to reach almost anywhere within its range.*

grey-brown ground colour

tail on hindwing

prominent eyespots

blue tinge at wing base

♀ ♂ brown wings

up to 1cm long

WINGSPAN *2.5cm.*
FLIGHT PERIOD *March–November, in successive broods.*
LARVAL FOODPLANT *Broom (Cytisus), lupin (Lupinus), and other pea family species.*
SIMILAR SPECIES *Long-tailed Blue (left).*
STATUS *Common and widespread in the south of its range; scarce further north.*

Green-underside Blue

Glaucopsyche alexis (Lycaenidae)

This distinctive Blue species has grey-brown underwings marked with white-ringed black spots and suffused with green at the base. The upperwings are violet-blue in the male but dark brown in the female. They are rarely seen, since the Green-underside Blue seldom rests with its wings spread out.

black margin

FOUND *in flower-rich grassland and open maquis; in foothills and lower mountain slopes, also at sea level.*

violet-blue ground colour

♂ ●

greenish suffusion

♂ ♀ ●

grey-brown wings

dark brown wings

♀ ♂ blue tinge

up to 1.5cm long

WINGSPAN *3.5cm.*
FLIGHT PERIOD *April–May.*
LARVAL FOODPLANT *Broom (Cytisus), lucerne (Medicago sativa), and other pea family species.*
SIMILAR SPECIES *Holly Blue (p.23), Mazarine Blue (p.28).*
STATUS *Widespread and generally common.*

Zephyr Blue

Plebejus pylaon (Lycaenidae)

FLIES *low over flower-rich grassy habitats, most commonly on mountain slopes.*

The sun-loving Zephyr Blue has a distinct preference for upland habitats. Males in particular are quite variable in appearance across the species' range although typically the upperwings are a shade of violet-blue. Females have dark brown upperwings, and the underwings of both sexes are pale grey-brown and patterned with dark spots.

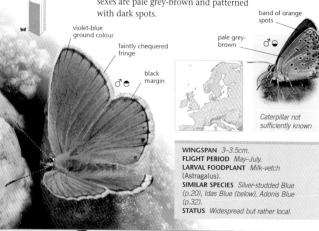

violet-blue ground colour

faintly chequered fringe

black margin

♂●

band of orange spots

pale grey-brown

♂●

Caterpillar not sufficiently known

WINGSPAN *3–3.5cm.*
FLIGHT PERIOD *May–July.*
LARVAL FOODPLANT *Milk-vetch (Astragalus).*
SIMILAR SPECIES *Silver-studded Blue (p.20), Idas Blue (below), Adonis Blue (p.32).*
STATUS *Widespread but rather local.*

Idas Blue

Plebejus idas (Lycaenidae)

BREEDS *in a variety of open grassy habitats, from sea level to lower mountain slopes.*

This attractive little butterfly flies low over the ground and is often seen sunning itself. Males are rather variable across the species' range but typically they have violet-blue upperwings; in females, these are rich brown. Both sexes have pale grey-brown underwings, with black spots and an orange band.

variable black margin

violet-blue ground colour

orange band with arrow-shaped black spots

white fringe

up to 1.5cm long

♂●

WINGSPAN *3cm.*
FLIGHT PERIOD *June–July.*
LARVAL FOODPLANT *Pea family members, including trefoil (Lotus) and vetch (Vicia); sea buckthorn (Hippophae) in the Alps.*
SIMILAR SPECIES *Silver-studded Blue (p.20), Reverdin's Blue (right).*
STATUS *Widespread and common.*

Reverdin's Blue

Plebejus argyrognomon (Lycaenidae)

This colourful butterfly is similar to Idas Blue (below left) and difficult to distinguish in the field. A direct comparison of the two reveals Reverdin's Blue to have marginally paler underwings, the orange submarginal band being slightly more intense, lined by rounded rather than pointed black spots. Males have violet-blue upperwings while those of females are brown.

FAVOURS *flower-rich grassy places from sea level to low mountain slopes at 1,500m.*

orange band on hindwing

rich brown

♀⬤

pale grey-brown

♀⬤

orange band flanked by black spots

up to 2cm long

violet-blue ground colour

narrow black margin

♂⬤

WINGSPAN *3–3.2cm.*
FLIGHT PERIOD *June–July.*
LARVAL FOODPLANT *Crown vetch (Coronilla varia) and other pea family members.*
SIMILAR SPECIES *Silver-studded Blue (p.20), Idas Blue (left).*
STATUS *Widespread and locally common; seldom as numerous as the similar Idas Blue.*

Cranberry Blue

Plebejus optilete (Lycaenidae)

It is comparatively easy to get good views of this species because of its sluggish, low-flying habits and its propensity to pose with its wings open. Only the male has violet-blue upperwings, those of the female being a rich brown colour. Both sexes have grey-brown underwings, studded with dark spots.

FOUND *in moors and bogs with acid soil, up to 2,500m in the Alps, but even at sea level in the north of its range.*

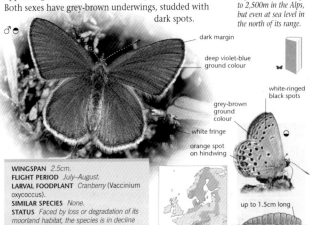

♂⬤

dark margin

deep violet-blue ground colour

grey-brown ground colour

white fringe

orange spot on hindwing

white-ringed black spots

⬤

up to 1.5cm long

WINGSPAN *2.5cm.*
FLIGHT PERIOD *July–August.*
LARVAL FOODPLANT *Cranberry (Vaccinium oxycoccus).*
SIMILAR SPECIES *None.*
STATUS *Faced by loss or degradation of its moorland habitat, the species is in decline and is now distinctly local.*

Mazarine Blue

Polyommatus semiargus (Lycaenidae)

The relative lack of markings on the underwings assists in the identification of this widespread species. The upperwings, which are violet-blue in males but brown in females, are easily observed since it frequently sunbathes with its wings spread out. On sunny days, sizeable groups gather at puddles to drink.

FOUND *in flower-rich fields and verges at sea level, to meadows up to 2,000m.*

dark margin

violet-blue ground colour

♂ 👓

few dark spots

pale grey-brown wings

♀ 👓

violet-blue suffusion at wing base

rich brown wings

up to 1.5cm long

WINGSPAN *3cm.*
FLIGHT PERIOD *June–July.*
LARVAL FOODPLANT *Clover (Trifolium), kidney-vetch (Anthyllis vulneraria), and other pea family members.*
SIMILAR SPECIES *Osiris Blue (p.16), which has darker markings on the underwings.*
STATUS *Widespread and generally common.*

Chapman's Blue

Polyommatus thersites (Lycaenidae)

This sun-loving butterfly has a southerly distribution in Europe. The male has violet-blue upperwings while those of the female are rich brown with orange spots on the hindwing. In both sexes, the grey-brown underwings have black and orange spots and there is a whitish streak on the hindwing. Unlike the similar Common Blue (p.30), it has no spot on the underside forewing cell.

PREFERS *grassy places with flowers, from verges at sea level to meadows on lower mountain slopes.*

darker at margin

violet-blue ground colour

white fringe

grey-brown with black spots

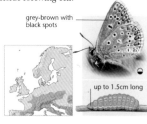

up to 1.5cm long

♂ 👓

WINGSPAN *3–3.2cm.*
FLIGHT PERIOD *May–August, in two or more broods.*
LARVAL FOODPLANT *Sainfoin (Onobrychis).*
SIMILAR SPECIES *Common Blue (p.30), which has a spot on the forewing underside.*
STATUS *Widespread and generally common in the south of its range.*

Escher's Blue

Polyommatus escheri (Lycaenidae)

Males of this southern species, with their bright blue upperwings, are a dazzling sight basking in the sunshine. By contrast, the females' upperwings are a sombre brown, although this emphasizes the orange margins. Both sexes have grey-brown underwings marked with black and orange spots.

dark margin

INHABITS *hills up to 2,000m, hay meadows, and flower-rich grassy places at low levels.*

grey-brown with dark spots

bright blue upperwings

orange marginal spots

♀

rich brown

up to 2cm long

WINGSPAN *3.5–4cm.*
FLIGHT PERIOD *June–August.*
LARVAL FOODPLANT *Milk-vetch (Astragalus) and sainfoin (Onobrychis).*
SIMILAR SPECIES *Amanda's Blue (p.22); Common Blue (p.30), which has a forewing spot on its underwing.*
STATUS *Widespread and common.*

Turquoise Blue

Polyommatus dorylas (Lycaenidae)

The Turquoise Blue is a butterfly with a distinctly upland distribution, a fact that is an aid to accurate identification. The male has sky-blue upperwings whereas those of the female are a rich brown colour. In both sexes, the underwings are pale grey-brown, marked with conspicuous black spots, which are largest on the forewing, and rather insignificant orange ones.

SEEN *on sunny and flowery hillsides and lower mountain slopes, typically between 1,000m and 2,000m.*

sky-blue ground colour

large dark spots on forewing

orange band

up to 1.5cm long

♂

dark margin

white fringe

WINGSPAN *3.2cm.*
FLIGHT PERIOD *May–August.*
LARVAL FOODPLANT *Clover (Trifolium) and medick (Medicago).*
SIMILAR SPECIES *Eros Blue (p.22), Amanda's Blue (p.22).*
STATUS *Widespread and often common in the right altitudinal range.*

Common Blue

Polyommatus icarus (Lycaenidae)

This is one of the region's commonest butterflies, and most natural or semi-natural areas of meadow and grassland support populations of it. In some places, and in good seasons, it can even be locally abundant. Despite a degree of variability in appearance, most males have blue upperwings tinged with a hint of violet; female upperwings are brown with orange spots and a variable amount of violet-blue at the wing base. Underwings of both sexes are grey-brown with orange and black white-ringed spots.

FOUND *in a wide variety of grassy places from sea level to more than 2,000m, wherever the larval foodplant grows abundantly.*

black and orange spots

dark spot on forewing cell

rich brown ground colour

orange submarginal spots

bright violet-blue ground colour

♂

♀

up to 1.5cm long

white fringe

narrow dark margin

WINGSPAN 3.2cm.
FLIGHT PERIOD *April–October, in successive broods.*
LARVAL FOODPLANT *Bird's-foot trefoil (Lotus corniculatus) and other pea family members.*
SIMILAR SPECIES *Eros Blue (p.22), Chapman's Blue (p.28), Escher's Blue (p.29) lacks the black spot on the underside forewing cell; Adonis Blue (p.32) has a white wedge-like mark on the underside hindwing.*
STATUS *Widespread and common.*

NOTE

If you find the Blue butterflies confusing, get to know the Common Blue well before you attempt identification of the more tricky species. It is the commonest of its kind and will serve as a benchmark.

Chalk-hill Blue

Polyommatus coridon (Lycaenidae)

A sun-loving butterfly that is characteristic of chalky grassland, the Chalk-hill Blue is a particularly attractive species. The male has bright sky-blue upperwings, which are often revealed when it is feeding or basking in the sunshine. The female is more subdued in appearance and has mainly dark brown upperwings; the hindwings are adorned with a submarginal row of orange, white, and black eyespots. In common with many other Blue butterflies, the larvae of the Chalk-hill Blue are attended by ants.

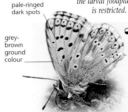

ASSOCIATED with flower-rich chalk and limestone grassland – habitats to which the larval foodplant is restricted.

pale-ringed dark spots

grey-brown ground colour

NOTE

The species is notoriously variable, particularly in the extent of the dark margin on the male upperwing. However, the sky-blue upperwing ground colour, and the favoured habitat are good clues to identity, of males at least.

brown ground colour

chequered fringe

orange spots

♀ ☉

up to 1.5cm long

broad, dark brown margin

♂ ☉

bright sky-blue ground colour

WINGSPAN *4cm.*
FLIGHT PERIOD *July–August.*
LARVAL FOODPLANT *Horseshoe vetch (Hippocrepis comosa).*
SIMILAR SPECIES *Amanda's Blue (p.22), which has a prominent black spot on the underside forewing; Provençal Chalk-hill Blue (p.32), which has a different flight period.*
STATUS *Widespread and often locally common, given its specific habitat requirements.*

Provençal Chalk-hill Blue

Polyommatus hispana (Lycaenidae)

This butterfly is very similar to the Chalk-hill Blue (p.31), but the two species have different flight periods so should be distinguished fairly easily. Males have particularly pale blue upperwings while those of females are dark brown with orange submarginal spots. The grey-brown underwings of both sexes are marked with black and orange spots.

FAVOURS *sunny meadows and grassy slopes with flowers, typically on chalky soils, from sea level to 1,000m.*

orange spots ♀●

black spots

white-ringed dark spots

sooty margin

♂●

pale blue ground colour

♂●

up to 1.5cm long

WINGSPAN *4cm.*
FLIGHT PERIOD *April–May and September, in two broods.*
LARVAL FOODPLANT *Crown vetch (Coronilla varia) and other pea family members.*
SIMILAR SPECIES *Chalk-hill Blue (p.31), which flies in July and August.*
STATUS *Locally common in its small range.*

Adonis Blue

Polyommatus bellargus (Lycaenidae)

The male Adonis Blue has eye-catching electric blue upperwings offset by a chequered border. The female, however, has brown upperwings, with orange spots and a variable blue suffusion. Both sexes have grey-brown underwings with orange and black spots.

FOUND *in flower-rich grassland on limestone or chalk, where grazing maintains relatively short turf.*

♂●

wedge-shaped mark on hindwing

♂●

chequered border

♀

blue suffusion on brown wings

electric blue upperwings

crescent-shaped orange spots

up to 1.5cm long

WINGSPAN *3.2cm.*
FLIGHT PERIOD *May–June and July–August, in two broods.*
LARVAL FOODPLANT *Horseshoe vetch (Hippocrepis comosa).*
SIMILAR SPECIES *None.*
STATUS *Locally common, but affected by changed land use and habitat loss.*

Furry Blue

Polyommatus dolus (Lycaenidae)

Like many other butterflies, the Furry Blue's body is covered in silky hairs. However, the presence of a furry patch on the silvery white to pale blue forewings sets the male apart from its relatives; the female has brown upperwings. The underwings are grey in males but brown in females; both are marked with dark spots, and a pale streak is sometimes visible on the hindwing.

FLIES *over flowery, rough grassland, from lowland areas to hills around 1,500m.*

♂●

furry patch

dark margin

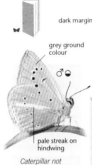

grey ground colour

♂●

white fringe

pale streak on hindwing

Caterpillar not sufficiently known

WINGSPAN *3.5cm.*
FLIGHT PERIOD *July–August.*
LARVAL FOODPLANT *Lucerne (Medicago sativa) and sainfoin (Onobrychis).*
SIMILAR SPECIES *Chalk-hill Blue (p.31), which lacks the male's furry forewing patch.*
STATUS *Local and rather scarce within its limited southern range.*

Dusky Large Blue

Maculinea nausithous (Lycaenidae)

Although they are rarely displayed, the upperwings of the male Dusky Large Blue are violet blue with a wide dark margin; in the female, they are a rich brown colour. The undersides of both sexes are dusky dark brown with pale brown margins and small dark spots. As with other members of the genus, the larvae are attended by ants, without which the life cycle cannot be completed.

RESTRICTED *to wetland areas, where the larval foodplant and a particular ant species are present.*

●

black spots

brown ground colour

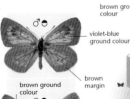

♂●

violet-blue ground colour

brown ground colour

brown margin

♀●

Caterpillar not sufficiently known

WINGSPAN *4cm.*
FLIGHT PERIOD *June–July.*
LARVAL FOOD *Great burnet (Sanguisorba officinalis); larvae of red ants (Myrmica).*
SIMILAR SPECIES *Large Blue (p.34).*
STATUS *Local and declining, due to habitat destruction and degradation.*

Large Blue

Maculinea arion (Lycaenidae)

This is one of the larger and more distinctive species among the Blue butterflies. It also has an intriguing life cycle – the larva resides in the nest of a red ant species for the latter part of its life, feeding on the grubs of its host. Both sexes have light blue upperwings. However, in females, the margins are broader, there are dark spots on both wings, and the hindwing spots are larger than in males. In both sexes, the underwings are grey-brown with dark spots that are fringed white, and have a blue suffusion at the base of the hindwing.

RESTRICTED *to dry grassland, often on chalky soil, where wild thyme or marjoram and red ants are abundant.*

pale grey-brown ground colour

bold dark spots

bluish suffusion at base of hindwing

♂ ●

up to 1.5cm long

NOTE

Changes in land use are adversely affecting this species' favoured habitat. A correct balance between too much and too little grazing is critical to ensure the survival of this fascinating butterfly. Following its extinction in England in the latter part of the 20th century, it has been re-introduced successfully.

♀ ●

dark spots on forewing

pale blue ground colour

white fringe

broad dark margin

WINGSPAN *4cm.*
FLIGHT PERIOD *July.*
LARVAL FOOD *Wild thyme (Thymus polytrichus) and marjoram (Origanum) in the larva's early stages; subsequently feeds on larvae of red ants (Myrmica).*
SIMILAR SPECIES *Alcon Blue (Maculinea alcon), which typically has far fewer dark markings on the upperwings.*
STATUS *Widespread but generally scarce and declining.*

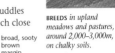

Damon Blue

Polyommatus damon (Lycaenidae)

On sunny days, Damon Blues gather to drink at puddles alongside other upland Blue butterflies. During such close encounters, the pale grey-brown underwings, common to both sexes, can be seen clearly, together with the species' distinctive markings. Only the male has blue upperwings, those of the female being brown.

BREEDS *in upland meadows and pastures, around 2,000–3,000m, on chalky soils.*

broad, sooty brown margin

sky-blue ground colour

♂ ●

pale grey-brown ground colour

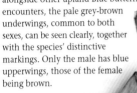

white streak on hindwing

white fringe

●

up to 1.5cm long

WINGSPAN *3.3cm.*
FLIGHT PERIOD *July–August.*
LARVAL FOODPLANT Sainfoin *(Onobrychis).*
SIMILAR SPECIES *Ripart's Anomalous Blue, female (p.125).*
STATUS *Distinctly local, partly because of precise habitat requirements.*

Meleager's Blue

Polyommatus daphnis (Lycaenidae)

The main clue to this species' identity is the scalloped rear margin of its hindwing. A unique feature for a butterfly of this size, it is most pronounced in females and emphasized by the markings on the wings. Both sexes have blue upperwings, the female having a dark leading edge on the forewing. The underwings of both sexes are grey-brown with black spots.

FAVOURS *undisturbed sunny, flower-rich grassland in hills up to 1,500m, but also seen in low-lying areas.*

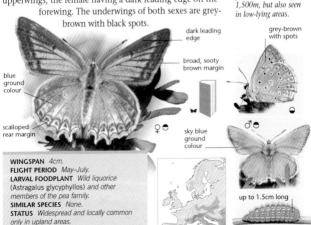

dark leading edge

broad, sooty brown margin

blue ground colour

scalloped rear margin

♀ ●

grey-brown with spots

●

♂ ●

sky blue ground colour

up to 1.5cm long

WINGSPAN *4cm.*
FLIGHT PERIOD *May–July.*
LARVAL FOODPLANT Wild liquorice *(Astragalus glycyphyllos) and other members of the pea family.*
SIMILAR SPECIES *None.*
STATUS *Widespread and locally common only in upland areas.*

Green Hairstreak

Callophrys rubi (Lycaenidae)

In spite of its bright underside ground colour, this active butterfly can be very difficult to spot. At rest it looks exactly like a green leaf. In flight, its colours blend with the surroundings so well that it is almost impossible to follow its movements. The Green Hairstreak seldom exposes its uniformly brown upperwings when resting, usually only showing its underwings, which are a bright leaf green. Both the underside wings are marked by a broken white line. However, this line is more pronounced on the hindwings than the forewings.

INHABITS *a wide variety of scrubby habitats, from heath and woodland margins to hedgerows and rough grassland.*

brown ground colour

up to 1.5cm long

NOTE

Males are territorial and use favoured prominent perches. Stand motionless beside one of these, and with time, the owner should return, giving you an excellent view.

faint, broken white line on forewing

clear, broken white line on hindwing

bright green ground colour

WINGSPAN 2.5cm.
FLIGHT PERIOD *March–July in south of range, April–June in north of range; in a number of broods.*
LARVAL FOODPLANT *Gorse (Ulex), Bird's-foot trefoil (Lotus corniculatus), ling (Calluna), and other low-growing plants.*
SIMILAR SPECIES *Chapman's Green Hairstreak (C. avis), which has bold, broken white lines on its underwings.*
STATUS *Widespread and locally common.*

Dappled White

Euchloe ausonia (Pieridae)

This subtly marked butterfly is often seen drinking nectar on sunny days, when it is comparatively easy to observe. On the predominantly white upperside, the hindwings are faintly dappled, while the forewings bear striking black markings. On the underside, the wings are dappled with yellow marbling on the hindwing, while the forewing is mainly white.

bold black tip

FOUND *in grassy places in foothills and lower mountain slopes of S. Europe, at 1,000–2,000m.*

white ground colour

black spot on forewing

yellow-green marbling

up to 3cm long

WINGSPAN *3.5cm.*
FLIGHT PERIOD *April–June.*
LARVAL FOODPLANT *Wild Candytuft (Iberis) and other cabbage family members (Brassicaceae).*
SIMILAR SPECIES *Peak White (p.42), Bath White (p.44).*
STATUS *Fairly common and widespread.*

Fenton's Wood White

Leptidea morsei (Pieridae)

Similar to the Wood White (p.38), this delicate butterfly's wings are even more rounded. It is usually slightly larger than its relative although, confusingly, first-brood individuals are typically smaller than the second brood. The male's white wings show a dark tip on the upper surface of the forewing that is darker in the second brood. The female has mainly white wings with just a suggestion of the male's dark markings.

FAVOURS *woodland rides and clearings, and is seldom seen in more open habitats frequented by the Wood White.*

rounded wings

♂○

white ground colour

grey marbling

WINGSPAN *4–4.5cm.*
FLIGHT PERIOD *April–July, in two broods.*
LARVAL FOODPLANT *Spring vetch (Lathyrus verna) and other related pea family members.*
SIMILAR SPECIES *Wood White (p.38).*
STATUS *Locally common in wooded hills in the east.*

Caterpillar not sufficiently known

Wood White

Leptidea sinapis (Pieridae)

FAVOURS *grassy places, including woodland rides and meadows; however, it is always restricted to extremely sheltered sites.*

With its broad and rounded wings, the Wood White is relatively easy to identify by shape alone. Its delicate appearance is matched by its rather feeble flight – it may have difficulty flying at all on windy days. When it does take to the wing, its fluttery flight pattern is another good clue to its identity. The whitish upperwings are variably tipped with smoky grey, more pronounced in males than females. First broods are greyer overall than subsequent generations. The underwings of both sexes are variably flushed yellow and streaked with grey.

broad, rounded wings

yellowish white ground colour

grey streaks

dark smudge at wing tip

white wings ♂

up to 2cm long

NOTE

The Wood White spends a lot of time sitting on sheltered plant stems. Even when it does fly on calm, sunny days, it keeps low to the ground, often flitting through, rather than over, vegetation.

WINGSPAN *4cm.*
FLIGHT PERIOD *Variable: May–June, as a single brood, in the north; April–September, with up to three broods, in the south.*
LARVAL FOODPLANT *Meadow Vetchling (Lathyrus pratensis) and other pea family members.*
SIMILAR SPECIES *Fenton's Wood White (p.37), which is larger.*
STATUS *Generally local, with a patchy distribution, but fairly common where it does occur.*

Orange-tip

Anthocharis cardamines (Pieridae)

The Orange-tip is one of the most distinctive spring
butterflies in the region and can often be seen flitting
along flowery verges and woodland rides. The male is
particularly striking, with bright orange tips on its white
upper forewings, which can also be seen on its
underwings. The tips of the female's forewings
are black rather than orange, making it quite
subdued in appearance. The underside of the
hindwing in both sexes is white with subtle
greenish marbling.

FLIES *along flowery
roadside verges,
woodland rides, and
meadows; sometimes
appears in gardens.*

green
marbling

♂ ◖

faint
grey tip

dark
spot

white
ground
colour

♀ ◖

NOTE

*A female Orange-tip
could be mistaken
for a Bath White
(p.44), so note the
Orange-tip's paler
appearance with
fewer dark spots,
and delicate flight.*

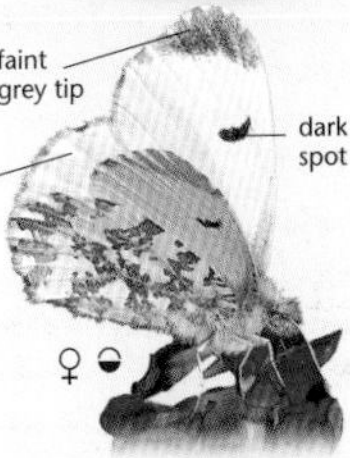

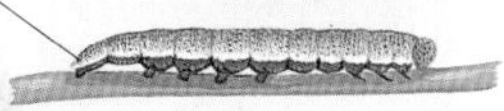

up to 2.5cm
long

bright orange
wing tip

dark spot on
forewing

white ground
colour

♂ ◖

WINGSPAN *4cm.*
FLIGHT PERIOD *April–June.*
LARVAL FOODPLANT *Garlic mustard
(Alliaria petiolata), Cuckoo flower
(Cardamine pratensis), and other
cabbage family members.*
SIMILAR SPECIES *Bath White (p.44).*
STATUS *Widespread and common.*

Small Apollo

Parnassius phoebus (Papilionidae)

FOUND exclusively in alpine meadows, seldom below 2,000m, and typically on damp, stony ground where its larval foodplants grow abundantly.

A hardy mountain species, the Small Apollo survives at high altitudes where even in the summer months it may be cold. Its creamy white wings are patterned with black and red spots and there is a dark grey suffusion at the wing base. The upperside and the underside of the wings are very similar. However, females tend to show a greater extent of grey on the wings than males.

black spots on forewing

creamy white ground colour

red spots

♂♀

up to 4.5cm long

dark wing base

WINGSPAN *7.5–8cm.*
FLIGHT PERIOD *June–August.*
LARVAL FOODPLANT *Various species of saxifrage (Saxifraga) and houseleek (Sempervivum).*
SIMILAR SPECIES *Apollo (p.45), which has a greater extent of grey suffusion on its wings.*
STATUS *Local and seldom common.*

Clouded Apollo

Parnassius mnemosyne (Papilionidae)

FAVOURS grassy places and meadows, at low levels in the north of its range, and from 1,500m to 2,000m in the south of its range.

This upland species has almost transparent forewing tips. The wings themselves, which are broad, rounded, and white with black veins, often look waxy, especially in older specimens. The absence of red spots on the wings separates this species from other Apollos. The underwing pattern and colour are similar to those of the upperwing.

underside similar to upperside

♂♀

two black spots on forewing

creamy white ground colour

up to 4cm long

♂♀

black veins

WINGSPAN *6cm.*
FLIGHT PERIOD *May–July.*
LARVAL FOODPLANT *Corydalis (Corydalis).*
SIMILAR SPECIES *Black-veined White (p.46), which lacks the twin black spots on the forewing.*
STATUS *Locally common.*

Small White

Pieris rapae (Pieridae)

This is a typical small white butterfly, and one of the commonest and most widespread species in Europe, if not the world. The larva is a pest of cultivated plants belonging to the cabbage family and can cause considerable damage in vegetable gardens and fields. By contrast, the adult butterfly is a welcome visitor to any garden border as it flits from flower to flower. Its white upperwings have a blackish tip and are marked with two black spots, one of which is much less distinct in males. The yellow and greyish white underwings are similarly marked.

INHABITS *areas with cabbage family plants; particularly common in gardens and on farmland.*

yellow and grey hindwing

NOTE

This species migrates north in spring and summer, accounting for the abundance in part of its range during those seasons. However, it is the most numerous White butterfly in much of Europe throughout the summer.

white ground colour

twin black spots

up to 2.5cm long

white ground colour

dark tip to forewing

dark spot on forewing

WINGSPAN *5cm.*
FLIGHT PERIOD *April–October, in successive broods.*
LARVAL FOODPLANT *Members of the cabbage family, especially the genus* Brassica; *nasturtium (*Tropaeolum majus*).*
SIMILAR SPECIES *Southern Small White (p.42), which has a darker, more extensive wing tip; Green-veined White (p.43), which has grey-green veins on the underwings; Large White (p.47).*
STATUS *Widespread and extremely common.*

Peak White

Pontia callidice (Pieridae)

This mountain species has white upperwings, with dark spots on the forewings and variable amounts of grey marbling on the hindwings; the dark markings are most extensive in females. The underwings are white and yellow with dark grey spots on the forewings and greenish grey veins on the hindwings.

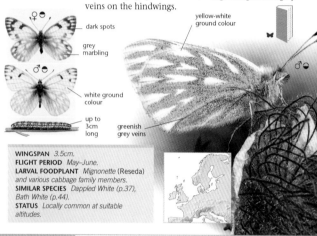

RESTRICTED *to mountains in the south, favouring alpine meadows and crags, typically at 2,000m.*

♀♂

— dark spots

— grey marbling

— white ground colour

— up to 3cm long

yellow-white ground colour

♂♀

greenish grey veins

WINGSPAN *3.5cm.*
FLIGHT PERIOD *May–June.*
LARVAL FOODPLANT *Mignonette (Reseda) and various cabbage family members.*
SIMILAR SPECIES *Dappled White (p.37), Bath White (p.44).*
STATUS *Locally common at suitable altitudes.*

Southern Small White

Pieris mannii (Pieridae)

This southern species is very similar to the Small White (p.41). It is hard to distinguish between the two by viewing the underwings alone, although the Southern Small White's yellow coloration is more intense. A reliable identification feature is the darker and more extensive black tip on the upper forewing of the Southern Small White.

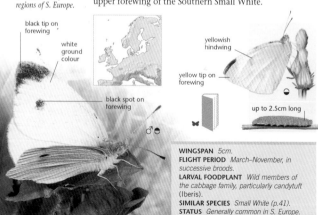

FLIES *over rough, grassy ground where wildflowers abound, in warm, sunny regions of S. Europe.*

black tip on forewing

white ground colour

black spot on forewing

yellowish hindwing

yellow tip on forewing

up to 2.5cm long

♂♀

WINGSPAN *5cm.*
FLIGHT PERIOD *March–November, in successive broods.*
LARVAL FOODPLANT *Wild members of the cabbage family, particularly candytuft (Iberis).*
SIMILAR SPECIES *Small White (p.41).*
STATUS *Generally common in S. Europe.*

Green-veined White

Pieris napi (Pieridae)

Once this butterfly's underwings have been seen clearly, there is usually no doubt about its identity. The well-defined network of greenish grey veins that criss-cross the yellow hindwings distinguishes it from related species. In most other respects, it is rather similar to the Small White (p.41), having white upperwings, the forewing showing a dark tip, and a single dark spot in males, with two in females. In both sexes the underside of the forewing is white with a yellow tip and twin grey spots; the females are marginally larger than males.

FOUND *in a wide range of flowery habitats, from roadside verges and gardens, to woodland rides and damp meadows.*

green-grey veins

black forewing tip

white ground colour

yellow ground colour

twin spots ♀●

♂●

dark veins

white ground colour

up to 2.5cm long

NOTE

Second or third generation Green-veined Whites (seen in late summer and early autumn) have less distinct veins on the underside of the hindwings. They can look confusingly similar to the Small White (p.41).

WINGSPAN *5cm.*
FLIGHT PERIOD *March–October in two or three broods; single-brooded in spring in the north of its range.*
LARVAL FOODPLANT *Garlic Mustard (Alliaria petiolata) and other wild cabbage family members.*
SIMILAR SPECIES *Small White (p.41), particularly later generations of Green-veined White.*
STATUS *Widespread and common.*

Bath White

Pontia daplidice (Pieridae)

This active and fast-flying butterfly is a well-known migrant, sometimes also appearing north of its given range. Its upperwings are white with grey marbling on the hindwing. The upper forewings, however, have variable dark markings, these being more pronounced in females than males. On the underside, the hindwing is beautifully marbled with greenish grey, while the forewing is white with a yellow tip.

FOUND *in flower-rich grassy places, this strong flyer, with a tendency to migrate and disperse, can turn up almost anywhere.*

forewing tipped with black

dark spot on forewing

♂ ⚲

faint grey marbling on hindwing

greenish marbling

white ground colour

up to 2.5cm long

NOTE

The Bath White is more likely to be encountered in low-lying meadows than other members of the genus Pontia. Also it is the only one where the dark spot on the underside of the forewing reaches the front margin.

WINGSPAN *5cm.*
FLIGHT PERIOD *March–November.*
LARVAL FOODPLANT *Mignonette* (Reseda) *and a wide range of cabbage family members, including rock cress* (Arabis).
SIMILAR SPECIES *Dappled White (p.37), which has yellow marbling on the wing underside; female Orange Tip (p.39); Peak White (p.42), which has grey marbling on the wing underside.*
STATUS *Widespread and common, especially in the south.*

Apollo

Parnassius apollo (Papilionidae)

With its large, rounded wings, the Apollo is the quintessential mountain butterfly. Its creamy upperwings are marked with three prominent black spots on the forewings, while the hindwings have several black-ringed red spots. The underside reflects the same pattern as the upperside. A variable grey suffusion colours the wings, and is more noticeable in females. Fortunately, the Apollo is rather lethargic and close views can be had when it is feeding, or sunbathing in the mornings or late afternoons.

RESTRICTED *to alpine meadows and stony mountain slopes, up to 2,000m in the Alps, but lower in the north of its range.*

NOTE

Older specimens that have been battered by the elements sometimes have nearly transparent wings that take on a waxy appearance, a far cry from the beauty of a pristine, newly emerged specimen.

variable grey suffusion

♂ ♀

creamy white ground colour

black-ringed red spots

black spots on forewing

♀

up to 5cm long

WINGSPAN *8cm.*
FLIGHT PERIOD *July–September.*
LARVAL FOODPLANT *Stonecrop (Sedum) and houseleek (Sempervivum).*
SIMILAR SPECIES *Small Apollo (p.40), which has a red spot on the forewing; Clouded Apollo (p.40), which has no red spots.*
STATUS *Locally common within its restricted high altitude range, but threatened by loss, or degradation, of its favoured habitats.*

Black-veined White

Aporia crataegi (Pieridae)

The Black-veined White must surely be one of the most straightforward European butterflies to identify. Not only is it quite large but it also has a distinctive shape and well-defined markings, common to both the upper and lower surfaces of the wings. An increasing use of insecticides is implicated in a decline seen in the species' range and abundance in certain parts of Europe; it seems likely that this factor contributed to its extinction in Britain.

FOUND *in a wide variety of flowery habitats, from meadows and roadside verges to scrub, orchards, and gardens.*

clearly defined black veins

♂●

black margin

white ground colour

♂●

rounded wings

up to 4cm long

NOTE

For the best views of Black-veined Whites, watch them while they drink at the edges of drying puddles. Dozens, sometimes even hundreds, of butterflies gather at these spots, jostling for the best drinking position.

WINGSPAN *6cm.*
FLIGHT PERIOD *Mainly July–August.*
LARVAL FOODPLANT *Blackthorn (Prunus spinosa) and other members of the genus, including cultivated species.*
SIMILAR SPECIES *Clouded Apollo (p.40), which has darker wing tips and dark spots on its forewings.*
STATUS *Widespread and common, especially in the hills and in the vicinity of orchards.*

Large White

Pieris brassicae (Pieridae)

Although the adult Large White is a charming sight in the garden, the species has achieved notoriety thanks to its gregarious larvae. It is not uncommon to find hordes of them demolishing the leaves of cabbages and other related plants in cultivation. In both sexes, the upperwings are creamy white and show a dark tip to the forewing; in females, two dark spots can also be seen on the forewing. On the underside in both sexes, the hindwing is yellowish grey while the forewing is white with two dark spots.

OCCURS *in a range of flowery places, from meadows and roadside verges to farmland and town gardens.*

yellow-grey ground colour

NOTE

As a bonus to gardeners, many Large White larvae are parasitized by a tiny wasp called Apanteles. *It lays its eggs in the caterpillar's body, then having consumed the internal organs, the wasp larvae emerge and pupate in yellow cocoons around the dried larval skin.*

creamy ground colour

dark tip

grey tip on forewing

twin dark spots on hindwing

♀ ⊖

up to 4cm long

white forewing

dark spot on forewing

SIMILAR SPECIES *Small White (p.41); in flight, male could be confused with female Brimstone (p.54).*

WINGSPAN *6cm.*
FLIGHT PERIOD *April–October, in successive broods.*
LARVAL FOODPLANT *Cabbage (Brassica) and other cultivated cabbage family members; also nasturtium (Tropaeolum majus).*
SIMILAR SPECIES *Small White (p.41); in flight, male could be confused with female Brimstone (p.54).*
STATUS *Widespread and common; migrant visitor in the north of its range.*

Clouded Yellow

Colias crocea (Pieridae)

This colourful butterfly is active and fast-flying, qualities that enable it to undertake long migrations north each year from its stronghold in southern Europe. The extent of the species' travels varies from year to year but in most seasons the range extends northwards as far as southern Britain. Unfortunately, its life cycle is not completed here because of the cold, wet weather in autumn. In flight, the dominant orange-yellow wing colour catches the eye. The upperwings have a broad, dark brown margin. However, resting individuals rarely, if ever, open their wings fully.

FAVOURS *all sorts of flowery, grassy places. Given the species' migratory nature, it can appear in a variety of habitats within its range.*

NOTE

Some female Clouded Yellows occur in a pale form that looks confusingly similar to a Pale Clouded Yellow (p.51). Pay attention to the upperwing colour and wing shape.

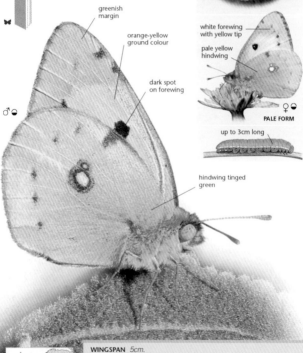

orange-yellow ground colour

broad, dark brown margin

♂●

greenish margin

orange-yellow ground colour

dark spot on forewing

♂●

white forewing with yellow tip

pale yellow hindwing

♀●　PALE FORM

up to 3cm long

hindwing tinged green

WINGSPAN *5cm.*
FLIGHT PERIOD *May–October.*
LARVAL FOODPLANT *Clover (Trifolium), lucerne (Medicago sativa), and other pea family members.*
SIMILAR SPECIES *Pale form resembles Mountain Clouded Yellow (right); Danube Clouded Yellow (right); Pale Clouded Yellow (p.51).*
STATUS *Common in southern and central Europe; variable further north.*

Mountain Clouded Yellow

Colias phicomone (Pieridae)

As Clouded Yellow species go, this butterfly is relatively straightforward to identify. Given its limited range and restriction to upland habitats, the pale, sooty greenish coloration is a useful guide. Unfortunately, as with other Clouded Yellows, resting and feeding individuals rarely open their wings, so their unusual colour can be fully appreciated only in flight.

RESTRICTED to sunny and grassy mountain slopes, around 2,000m, where foodplants are plentiful.

dark spot on forewing

pale spot on hindwing

greenish yellow ground colour

sooty green-grey ground colour

dark margin

♀ ⊖

up to 3.5cm long

WINGSPAN *4.5–5cm.*
FLIGHT PERIOD *June–August.*
LARVAL FOODPLANT *Vetch (Vicia) and other pea family members.*
SIMILAR SPECIES *Pale form of Clouded Yellow (left), Pale Clouded Yellow (p.51).*
STATUS *Distinctly local, but not uncommon in suitable locations.*

Danube Clouded Yellow

Colias myrmidone (Pieridae)

Although this species seldom rests with its wings open, keen-eyed observers can usually appreciate the upperwing colour when the butterfly is in flight: it is a richer shade of orange than in the superficially similar Clouded Yellow (left). The underwings too are a deeper shade of yellow and the dark spots are smaller and less intense.

FOUND only on low-lying grassland along the River Danube and in its catchment area.

yellow-orange ground colour

dark spots

⊖

red-ringed pale spot

dark central spot

♂ ♦ deep orange ground colour

dark margin with yellow spots

♀ ⊖

Caterpillar not sufficiently known

WINGSPAN *5cm.*
FLIGHT PERIOD *June–September.*
LARVAL FOODPLANT *Broom (Cytisus).*
SIMILAR SPECIES *Clouded Yellow (left), which has a lighter ground colour and greenish yellow underwings.*
STATUS *Locally common, but threatened by the spread of modern agriculture.*

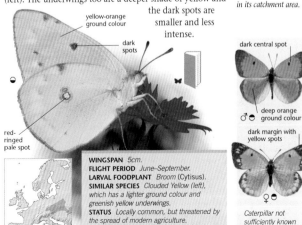

Moorland Clouded Yellow

FLIES *over upland moors and, at lower altitudes, on northern heaths.*

Colias palaeno (Pieridae)

Although the Moorland Clouded Yellow shows variability across its wide geographical range, its overall pale yellow coloration and well-defined, narrow and unbroken dark wing margins all help with identification. The precise foodplant requirements of the larva means that this butterfly is confined to moorlands and is seldom seen elsewhere.

pale yellow wings

light spot on hindwing

pale yellow ground colour

prominent dark margins

♂

whitish wings

♀

up to 3.5cm long

WINGSPAN *5cm.*
FLIGHT PERIOD *June–August.*
LARVAL FOODPLANT *Northern bilberry (Vaccinium uliginosum).*
SIMILAR SPECIES *Pale Clouded Yellow (right), which has a lighter ground colour and pointed forewing tip.*
STATUS *Common in suitable habitats.*

Northern Clouded Yellow

RESTRICTED *to grassy tundra on the fringes of the Arctic.*

Colias hecla (Pieridae)

Any orange-yellow butterfly sighted on the fringes of the Arctic is almost certain to be a Northern Clouded Yellow. In common with its relatives, it almost never rests or feeds with its wings open, so observers must be content with viewing the mainly greenish yellow underwings.

dark spot on forewing

greenish yellow hindwing

pale spot on hindwing

orange-yellow ground colour

dark margin ♂

up to 3.5cm long

WINGSPAN *4.5cm.*
FLIGHT PERIOD *July–August.*
LARVAL FOODPLANT *Alpine milk vetch (Astragalus alpinus).*
SIMILAR SPECIES *None within the range and habitat of this species.*
STATUS *Fairly common within its range; one of the very few butterflies found here.*

Pale Clouded Yellow

Colias hyale (Pieridae)

This species may look like a variation of the Clouded Yellow (p.49) in the field, and be difficult to identify. However, the shape of its forewing, which is rather pointed, and the overall pale lemon yellow coloration, help to distinguish between it and other Clouded Yellows. The female is much paler in colour than the male.

FOUND *in a variety of flowery, grassy places, this migratory species can occur anywhere within its range.*

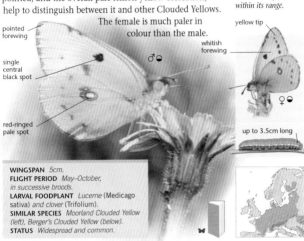

pointed forewing

single central black spot

red-ringed pale spot

♂♀

yellow tip

whitish forewing

♀♀

up to 3.5cm long

WINGSPAN *5cm.*
FLIGHT PERIOD *May–October, in successive broods.*
LARVAL FOODPLANT *Lucerne (Medicago sativa) and clover (Trifolium).*
SIMILAR SPECIES *Moorland Clouded Yellow (left), Berger's Clouded Yellow (below).*
STATUS *Widespread and common.*

Berger's Clouded Yellow

Colias alfacariensis (Pieridae)

This species is superficially very similar to the Pale Clouded Yellow (above), and it is difficult to distinguish between the two in the field. The wings of the male Berger's Clouded Yellow are brighter yellow; the dark markings on the wing tips and margins are less pronounced; and the upper hindwing spot is orange and not pinkish.

FAVOURS *flowery and grassy places; its migratory nature means that it could turn up anywhere within its range.*

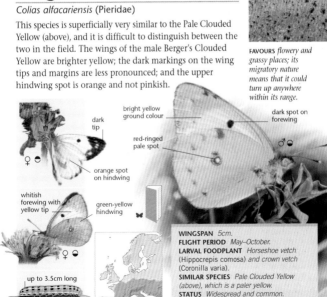

♀♀

dark tip

orange spot on hindwing

whitish forewing with yellow tip

green-yellow hindwing

bright yellow ground colour

red-ringed pale spot

dark spot on forewing

♂♀

up to 3.5cm long

WINGSPAN *5cm.*
FLIGHT PERIOD *May–October.*
LARVAL FOODPLANT *Horseshoe vetch (Hippocrepis comosa) and crown vetch (Coronilla varia).*
SIMILAR SPECIES *Pale Clouded Yellow (above), which is a paler yellow.*
STATUS *Widespread and common.*

Scarce Swallowtail

Iphiclides podalirius (Papilionidae)

FOUND *in flowery areas of grassy scrub, along woodland rides, gardens, and in orchards.*

The wings of this large butterfly are rather pale and strongly marked with dark bars. Its hindwings are characterized by eye-catching, long tail streamers. With experience, this species can even be identified on the wing: apart from its size, the effortless, floating flight pattern is distinctive. The Scarce Swallowtail is a frequent visitor to flowers, especially lavender. While feeding on them, it is often preoccupied enough to allow a close approach by observers.

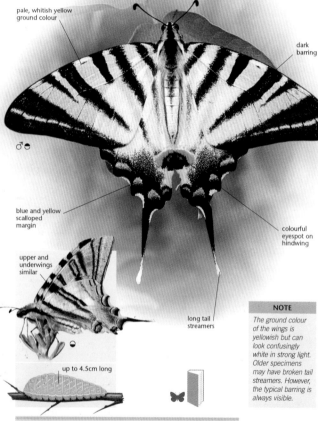

pale, whitish yellow ground colour

dark barring

♂ ●

blue and yellow scalloped margin

colourful eyespot on hindwing

upper and underwings similar

●

long tail streamers

up to 4.5cm long

NOTE

The ground colour of the wings is yellowish but can look confusingly white in strong light. Older specimens may have broken tail streamers. However, the typical barring is always visible.

WINGSPAN *8cm.*
FLIGHT PERIOD *April–May, and again in September as a second brood.*
LARVAL FOODPLANT *Blackthorn (Prunus spinosa) and cultivated members of the genus, such as plum (P. x domestica).*
SIMILAR SPECIES *Swallowtail (right), which can be distinguished by its more intricate wing markings.*
STATUS *Widespread and generally common, particularly in the south of its range.*

Swallowtail

Papilio machaon (Papilionidae)

This large and spectacular species is almost unmistakable. Although Swallowtails seem rather restless, they often remain relatively still when feeding, allowing observers excellent views of their beautiful markings. The overall colour of both surfaces of the wings is yellow, and they are patterned with a network of black veins and bands. The upperwings also reveal a marginal band of blue scaling and a colourful eyespot. Lastly, there is the trademark tail streamer on the hindwing. This characteristic feature is found in many members of this butterfly family and lends it the name "Swallowtail".

FAVOURS *flowery, often damp grassy areas, in mainland Europe. The British subspecies is confined to fens.*

similar upper and lower surface

eyespot fainter on underwing

up to 5cm long

NOTE

The Swallowtail's larvae are extremely colourful, a warning to birds that they are distasteful. They are quite easy to spot while feeding on the leaves of their foodplants.

network of black veins

yellow ground colour

♂♀

band of blue scaling

tail streamer

colourful eyespot

WINGSPAN *8–9cm.*
FLIGHT PERIOD *April–September, in successive broods, in the south; one or more broods further north, with a more limited flight period.*
LARVAL FOODPLANT *Fennel (Foeniculum), milk parsley (Peucedanum palustre), and other carrot family members.*
SIMILAR SPECIES *Scarce Swallowtail (left).*
STATUS *Widespread and common; local further north; in Britain it is restricted to East Anglia.*

Brimstone

Gonepteryx rhamni (Pieridae)

SEEN *in areas of scrub, woodland rides, and gardens, the common factor being the presence of the larval foodplant.*

For many naturalists, the sight of a Brimstone in early spring is a sign that winter has finally ended. On sunny mornings as early as February, this species emerges from hibernation in search of nectar sources. The male Brimstone's bright yellow colour is sufficient to identify even flying individuals. The typical wing shape found in both sexes, can only be seen in resting butterflies and is the best way to identify a female.

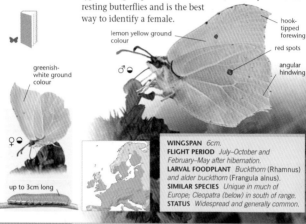

hook-tipped forewing

lemon yellow ground colour

red spots

angular hindwing

greenish-white ground colour

♂●

♀●

up to 3cm long

WINGSPAN *6cm.*
FLIGHT PERIOD *July–October and February–May after hibernation.*
LARVAL FOODPLANT *Buckthorn (Rhamnus) and alder buckthorn (Frangula alnus).*
SIMILAR SPECIES *Unique in much of Europe; Cleopatra (below) in south of range.*
STATUS *Widespread and generally common.*

Cleopatra

Gonepteryx cleopatra (Pieridae)

FOUND *in a variety of scrub habitats, including open maquis woodland typical of S. Europe.*

Although it resembles the Brimstone (above), the male Cleopatra is easy to recognize as its bright yellow wings show a deep orange flush on the forewings. The extremely pale females are less distinctive than males, and a view of a resting individual is required for identification – a faint orange stripe on the underside of the forewing is a useful clue to its identity.

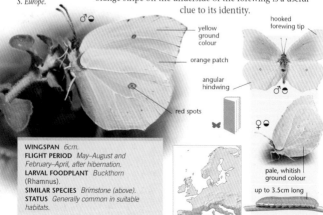

hooked forewing tip

yellow ground colour

orange patch

angular hindwing

♂●

red spots

♀●

pale, whitish ground colour

up to 3.5cm long

WINGSPAN *6cm.*
FLIGHT PERIOD *May–August and February–April, after hibernation.*
LARVAL FOODPLANT *Buckthorn (Rhamnus).*
SIMILAR SPECIES *Brimstone (above).*
STATUS *Generally common in suitable habitats.*

Small Copper

Lycaena phlaeas (Lycaenidae)

Despite its small size, the Small Copper catches the eye due to its bright markings. Although some of the upperwing surface is brown, this relatively sombre background serves to highlight the vivid orange markings. The underwings have more subdued colours than the upperwings although the pattern of markings is broadly similar. A subtle variation in wing markings exists across the species' range; in particular, the extent of the orange submarginal band on the hindwing shows considerable variation.

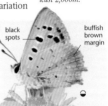

FLIES *over all kinds of flowery, grassy places, from roadside verges to meadows and cliffs, from sea level to at least 2,000m.*

black spots

buffish brown margin

up to 1.5cm long

NOTE

Male Small Coppers are strongly territorial and it can be interesting to watch them defend their "home patch" against intruding rivals. They even attack male butterflies belonging to other species on occasion.

orange-red forewing

brown margin

brown spots

brown hindwing

pointed rear margin

submarginal orange band

WINGSPAN *3–3.8cm.*
FLIGHT PERIOD *April–October, in successive broods.*
LARVAL FOODPLANT *Sorrel and dock (*both* Rumex).*
SIMILAR SPECIES *Violet Copper (p.57).*
STATUS *Widespread and one of the commonest butterflies in the region.*

Duke of Burgundy

Hamearis lucina (Riodinidae)

The beautifully intricate wing patterns of this rather small species certainly merit close scrutiny. Fortunately, this is often possible because it tends to sunbathe just above the ground, allowing observers to get surprisingly close. The rich brown ground colour of the upperwings is studded with orange-buff spots while the tawny lower surface is adorned with dark spots on the forewing and white spots on the hindwing. The entire effect is offset by a uniformly chequered fringe. Broadly speaking, the sexes are similar, although the orange upperwing spots and white underwing spots are larger and brighter in females.

ASSOCIATED *with meadows and woodland margins, where the larval foodplants grow.*

chequered fringe

orange-buff spots

rich brown ground colour

dark spots on forewing

rufous-brown ground colour

white spots on hindwing

up to 1.5cm long

NOTE

The Duke of Burgundy bears a superficial resemblance to the true Fritillary species (family Nymphalidae). However, all of these are much larger and generally more active butterflies.

WINGSPAN *3cm.*
FLIGHT PERIOD *May–June; sometimes a second brood in August–September in the south.*
LARVAL FOODPLANT *Primrose (Primula vulgaris) and cowslip (P. veris).*
SIMILAR SPECIES *None.*
STATUS *Locally common, forming discrete colonies associated with an abundance of larval foodplants.*

Provence Hairstreak

Tomares ballus (Lycaenidae)

At first glance, this brownish species could be mistaken for one of the Coppers. To confuse matters further, the green scaling on the underside of the hindwing resembles that of a Green Hairstreak (p.36). However, no other butterfly of this size has the extent of orange and green on its underwings and so identification should be easy.

FAVOURS *open scrub- and maquis-covered slopes with a Mediterranean climate.*

orange ground colour on forewing

brown ground colour

orange forewing with brown margin

brown hindwing

up to 1.5cm long

green scaling on hindwing

WINGSPAN *2.5–3cm.*
FLIGHT PERIOD *January–April.*
LARVAL FOODPLANT *Vetch (Anthyllis), trefoil (Lotus), and other pea family members.*
SIMILAR SPECIES *Green Hairstreak (p.36), Small Copper (p.55).*
STATUS *Fairly common.*

Violet Copper

Lycaena helle (Lycaenidae)

This species has a passing resemblance to a miniature Blue or a tiny Hairstreak. However, a close view of the male's upperwings reveals a distinctive violet sheen. By contrast, the female has orange and brown upperwings. Both sexes have brown underwings, with black spots and a submarginal orange band on both wings.

RESTRICTED *to wetland habitats, including marshes, river margins, and moors, from sea level to 1,500m.*

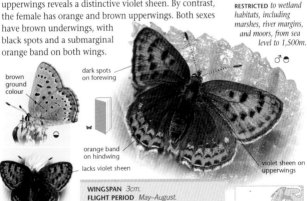

brown ground colour

dark spots on forewing

orange band on hindwing

lacks violet sheen

violet sheen on upperwings

up to 1.5cm long

WINGSPAN *3cm.*
FLIGHT PERIOD *May–August.*
LARVAL FOODPLANT *Knotgrass (Polygonum), bistort (Polygonum bistorta), and sorrel (Rumex sp).*
SIMILAR SPECIES *None.*
STATUS *Widespread but very local; declining due to habitat destruction.*

Large Copper

Lycaena dispar (Lycaenidae)

Seen sunning itself on waterside vegetation, a Large Copper is a spectacular sight. Males are particularly attractive, the upperwings being largely bright coppery orange with a well-defined margin. The females are relatively subdued, with more dark brown markings than the male. The underwings of the two sexes are broadly similar, showing extensive pale blue-grey on the hindwing and orange on the forewing; both wings are studded with several black spots.

RESTRICTED to areas of damp grassland, often in marshes or beside drainage ditches and slow-flowing rivers.

dark margin

dark spot on forewing

♂ ☻

bright coppery orange ground colour

dark spots on orange forewing

♀ ☻

dark brown hindwing

orange margin

orange forewing ground colour

blue-grey hindwing

orange band

black spots

☻

up to 2cm long

NOTE

The pale blue-grey undersurface of the hindwing, studded with black spots, helps to distinguish this butterfly from other superficially similar species. The underside of the forewing, however, is orange in colour; typically, the colour is more intense than its close relatives.

WINGSPAN *3.5–5cm.*
FLIGHT PERIOD *May–September, in two broods in the south, one brood in the north.*
LARVAL FOODPLANT *Dock (Rumex).*
SIMILAR SPECIES *Scarce Copper (right), Purple-shot Copper (p.60), and Purple-edged Copper (p.61).*
STATUS *Local and declining in much of its range as a result of habitat degradation and destruction.*

Scarce Copper

Lycaena virgaureae (Lycaenidae)

This stunning butterfly often basks in the sun, so observers can usually get good views of the open upperwings. In males these are shiny orange with neat black margins; southern forms are adorned with a few dark spots. In females, the upperwings are orange-brown and dark brown. In both sexes, the forewings are mainly orange-buff underneath, while the hindwings are greyish buff.

black indented margin on hindwing

shiny orange ground colour

FAVOURS *flower-rich, grassy places. Most common in hills, up to 2,000m, but also occurs near the coast.*

♂

brown spots on forewing

♀

white spots

up to 2cm long

WINGSPAN *3–4cm.*
FLIGHT PERIOD *July–August.*
LARVAL FOODPLANT *Different varieties of dock (Rumex).*
SIMILAR SPECIES *Large Copper (left), which has blue-grey hindwing undersides.*
STATUS *Widespread but seldom particularly common.*

Sooty Copper

Lycaena tityrus (Lycaenidae)

Rather sombre in appearance, the Sooty Copper has largely brown and orange-buff wings. Females have orange forewings and more rounded wings, not unlike the Blues. Males have narrower wings, with the pointed hindwing seen in many Coppers, giving them an almost Hairstreak-like outline.

orange spots

FOUND *mostly in flowery meadows in low-lying areas; also in the hills.*

grey-buff ground colour

submarginal orange spots

dark spots on orange forewing

sooty brown ground colour

row of orange spots

♀

up to 2cm long

♂

WINGSPAN *3–3.5cm.*
FLIGHT PERIOD *April–May, with a second brood in August–September.*
LARVAL FOODPLANT *Dock and sorrel (both Rumex).*
SIMILAR SPECIES *Some female members of the Blue butterflies.*
STATUS *Widespread and fairly common.*

Purple-shot Copper

Lycaena alciphron (Lycaenidae)

Confusingly, two distinct subspecies of this butterfly occur in the region. The coppery, dark-spotted upperwings of the males from the east of the region (*L. a. alciphron*) have a purple sheen and the females have mainly dark brown upperwings. Their counterparts from mountains in the southwest (*L. a. gordius*) have upperwings that are coppery orange and dark-spotted in males, but orange-brown with dark spots in females. All forms have underwings that are mainly grey on the hindwings and orange buff on the forewings, both adorned with black spots.

FREQUENTS *flower-rich, grassy meadows in low-lying country;* L. a. gordius *found in mountains.*

orange-buff forewing

submarginal orange spots

greyish hindwing

♀ ☻

orange-brown wings

L. a. gordius

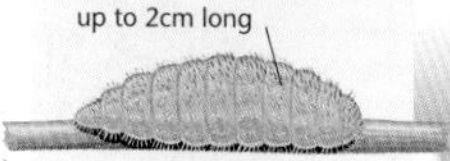

up to 2cm long

dark spots

narrow dark border

coppery ground colour with violet sheen

♂ ☻

NOTE

Look for L. a. alciphron *in low-lying meadows in the east of the region;* L. a. gordius *is seldom seen below 1,000m, and is confined to mountain meadows in the Alps, Pyrenees, and other neighbouring ranges.*

WINGSPAN *4cm.*
FLIGHT PERIOD *June–July.*
LARVAL FOODPLANT *Dock and sorrel (both Rumex).*
SIMILAR SPECIES *Large Copper (p.58); the mountain form (L. a. gordius) could be confused with a Purple-edged Copper (right).*
STATUS *Both subspecies are locally common, given their distinct ranges and altitudinal preferences; although L. a. gordius does tend to occur in smaller, more well-defined colonies.*

Purple-edged Copper

Lycaena hippothoe (Lycaenidae)

In bright sunlight, the orange-red upperwings of the male of this species, display an attractive purple sheen along the edges – an excellent clue to its identity. The female's upperwings are orange and brown with a submarginal orange band on the hindwings; sub-Arctic females have the brightest colours.

INHABITS *damp areas in meadows and grassland, occurring in foothills and lower mountain slopes up to 2,000m.*

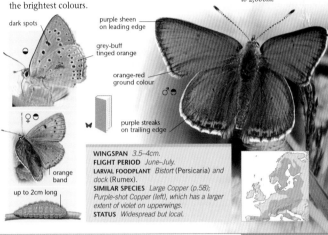

dark spots

purple sheen on leading edge

grey-buff tinged orange

orange-red ground colour ♂●

purple streaks on trailing edge

♀●

orange band

up to 2cm long

WINGSPAN *3.5–4cm.*
FLIGHT PERIOD *June–July.*
LARVAL FOODPLANT *Bistort (Persicaria) and dock (Rumex).*
SIMILAR SPECIES *Large Copper (p.58); Purple-shot Copper (left), which has a larger extent of violet on upperwings.*
STATUS *Widespread but local.*

Nettle-tree Butterfly

Libythea celtis (Libytheidae)

This interesting butterfly can be recognized by its jagged wing shape and by the snout-like projection of its mouthpart appendages (palps). The mottled orange-buff and brown on the wings is also distinctive – the pattern on the upperwings being more-or-less mirrored on the underwings. The species is relatively long-lived as an adult, hibernating during the winter months.

FOUND *on wooded slopes, maquis, parks, and gardens, the common factor being the presence of the larval foodplant.*

snout-like projection

orange-buff patches

♂●

grey-brown ground colour

●

jagged wing margin

up to 3.5cm long

WINGSPAN *4.5cm.*
FLIGHT PERIOD *June–September and, after hibernation, March–April.*
LARVAL FOODPLANT *Nettle tree (Celtis).*
SIMILAR SPECIES *Comma (p.75), which has more extensive orange markings.*
STATUS *Widespread and fairly common in S. Europe.*

Shepherd's Fritillary

Boloria pales (Nymphalidae)

RESTRICTED *to high alpine meadows, typically at altitudes of 2,000–3,000m.*

A true mountain butterfly typically found above the tree line, Shepherd's Fritillary has many subspecies across its range. The orange upperwings are marked with black spots, and have dark scaling towards the wing base, which varies in subspecies. The forewing underside is orange-brown while the hindwing has a mosaic-like pattern of reddish brown, creamy yellow, and white.

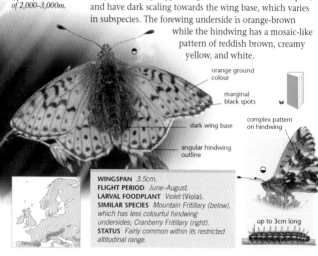

orange ground colour

marginal black spots

dark wing base

complex pattern on hindwing

angular hindwing outline

up to 3cm long

WINGSPAN 3.5cm.
FLIGHT PERIOD June–August.
LARVAL FOODPLANT Violet (Viola).
SIMILAR SPECIES Mountain Fritillary (below), which has less colourful undersides; Cranberry Fritillary (right).
STATUS Fairly common within its restricted altitudinal range.

Mountain Fritillary

Boloria napaea (Nymphalidae)

FAVOURS *damp alpine or sub-Arctic meadows but lower altitudes and wetter habitats in the south of its range.*

This species is similar to Shepherd's Fritillary (above), but the two prefer subtly different habitats and their ranges overlap only in the south of the region. The Mountain Fritillary's marginally larger size can seldom be appreciated in the field but its underwing markings are fainter on the forewings and less complex and colourful on the hindwings.

yellow-buff tip

dark grey wing base

2 rows of dark spots

dull mosaic of brown patches

orange ground colour

brownish orange ground colour

up to 3.5cm long

WINGSPAN 4cm.
FLIGHT PERIOD July–August.
LARVAL FOODPLANT Alpine bistort (Polygonum viviparum).
SIMILAR SPECIES Shepherd's Fritillary (above), which has darker underwings.
STATUS Local in mountains in S. Europe; more widespread in Scandinavia.

Cranberry Fritillary

Boloria aquilonaris (Nymphalidae)

The upperwings of the Cranberry Fritillary are orange with black spots, some of which link to form jagged lines. On the underside, the ground colour is orange-buff with black markings and particularly striking white spots on the hindwing. The precise habitat requirement of this colourful species is a useful pointer in its identification.

FOUND *in bogs and damp heaths on acid soils where cranberries flourish; its altitudinal range decreases in the north of its range.*

white spots on hindwing

orange ground colour

2 rows of black spots

jagged black lines

up to 3cm long

WINGSPAN *3.5cm.*
FLIGHT PERIOD *June–August.*
LARVAL FOODPLANT *Cranberry (Vaccinium).*
SIMILAR SPECIES *Shepherd's Fritillary (left), which is not restricted to boggy habitats and whose larvae feed on violet.*
STATUS *Local but not uncommon.*

Bog Fritillary

Boloria eunomia (Nymphalidae)

The markings on the upperwings and on the underside of the hindwing confirm the identity of this species. A dark margin, lined with pale spots, and an inner row of black spots that runs parallel to this are features of the upper surface. Below, a pale patch in the centre of the hindwing and marginal white spots are key features.

OCCURS *in wetland areas, including bogs in the south and damp tundra in the north.*

orange ground colour

jagged black lines

central group of white spots

small dark spots

dark margin with orange spots

up to 2cm long

WINGSPAN *3.5–4.5cm.*
FLIGHT PERIOD *June–July.*
LARVAL FOODPLANT *Bistort (Polygonum).*
SIMILAR SPECIES *Pearl-bordered Fritillary (p.65), which does not occur in bogs or wetland areas.*
STATUS *Locally fairly common.*

Small Pearl-bordered Fritillary

FOUND *in a variety of habitats where larval foodplants grow, from open woodland to low mountain slopes, up to 2,000m in the south.*

Boloria selene (Nymphalidae)

It would be difficult to separate this species from some of its close relatives – notably the Pearl-bordered Fritillary (right) – by simply looking at its upperwings; they all appear confusingly similar. What distinguishes them are the markings on the underside of the hindwing. In addition to the seven white pearl-like spots along the margin, which are strongly defined by black lines along their inner edge, there are several silvery white spots at the centre and towards the base of the wing. In contrast, the Pearl-bordered Fritillary has just one central white spot, with another smaller one close to the wing base.

7 white spots on hindwing margin

several white spots

up to 2cm long

NOTE

To get the best views for identification, choose a partly sunny day when occasional clouds obscure the sun. During the brief, dull periods, the butterflies will stop flying and rest on flowerheads and stems with their wings shut.

orange ground colour

numerous black spots

WINGSPAN *4cm.*
FLIGHT PERIOD *June–July.*
LARVAL FOODPLANT *Violet (Viola).*
SIMILAR SPECIES *Pearl-bordered Fritillary (right), which has a single silvery spot at the centre of its hindwing undersides.*
STATUS *Widespread and locally common, although habitat loss is affecting its numbers.*

Pearl-bordered Fritillary

Boloria euphrosyne (Nymphalidae)

For the beginner, many smaller Fritillary species look bafflingly similar to one another. Although geographical location and habitat help distinguish them, a close view of the underwing pattern is the surest way of identification. Fortunately, the Pearl-bordered Fritillary has colours and patterns on the underside of its hindwings that are diagnostic. The key is the combination of seven silvery white pearl-like spots along the margin, a single central white spot on the hindwing, and a smaller one near the wing base.

FREQUENTS *woodland rides and clearings, often doing best where traditional woodland practices, such as coppicing, encourage the larval foodplants.*

black spots often link to form jagged lines

orange-brown ground colour

parallel rows of black spots along margins

central silvery white spot

7 white spots on hindwing

single basal white spot

up to 2.5cm long

NOTE

The low-flying Pearl-bordered Fritillary is fond of alighting on the flower spikes of bugle (*Ajuga reptans*). With some care, individuals can be observed at close range while feeding or resting on these flowers.

WINGSPAN *4–4.5cm.*
FLIGHT PERIOD *Mainly May–June; sometimes a second brood in August in the south.*
LARVAL FOODPLANT *Violet (Viola).*
SIMILAR SPECIES *Small Pearl-bordered Fritillary (left).*
STATUS *Widespread and locally common.*

Freija's Fritillary

Boloria freija (Nymphalidae)

A hardy butterfly, this Fritillary occurs at sub-Arctic and Arctic latitudes and is tolerant of bouts of harsh weather. Given its northerly range, and its restriction to moorland habitat, there are few species with which it could be confused. To rule out mistaken identity, look for the distinct black zig-zag marking on the underside of the hindwing.

RESTRICTED to tundra-like moor, often on lower mountain slopes, where the larval foodplants flourish.

zig-zag line on underwing

black spots

black area near wing base

Caterpillar not sufficiently known

orange-buff ground colour

WINGSPAN *3.5–4cm.*
FLIGHT PERIOD *May–June.*
LARVAL FOODPLANT *Cloudberry (Rubus chamaemorus) and bilberry (Vaccinium).*
SIMILAR SPECIES *Thor's Fritillary (right).*
STATUS *Locally common but easily overlooked, except on sunny days.*

Weaver's Fritillary

Boloria dia (Nymphalidae)

This is a relatively small and delicate-looking species. However, as Fritillaries go, it is rather distinctive, particularly in the shape of the hindwing: the leading edge is almost square-cut where it reaches the margin. The undersurface is marbled with violet. The orange upperwings, adorned with black spots, are similar to those of many close relatives.

LIVES in wooded heathland areas and open, grassy woodland where flowers and bramble flourish.

square-cut corner

violet-brown patch

up to 2.5cm long

black spots

orange ground colour

WINGSPAN *3.5cm.*
FLIGHT PERIOD *May–August, in two or more broods.*
LARVAL FOODPLANT *Violet (Viola) and possibly bramble (Rubus).*
SIMILAR SPECIES *None.*
STATUS *Widespread and locally common within its range.*

Thor's Fritillary

Boloria thore (Nymphalidae)

This northern and upland butterfly has a fragmented distribution in Europe and the species varies in appearance across its range. However, a common feature is the crescent of yellow markings on the underside of the hindwing. In the Alps, specimens of Thor's Fritillary are dark reddish brown, with the yellow crescent especially prominent. On the other hand, in Scandinavia they have a paler, buffish orange ground colour overall, with the yellow pattern on the lower hindwing appearing relatively indistinct. Specimens from this region also tend to be smaller than their Alpine relatives.

FOUND *in open woodland habitats, typically at around 1,500m in the Alps but closer to sea level in Scandinavia.*

dark spots

crescent of linked yellow spots

NOTE

In Scandinavia, older specimens of other small Fritillaries resemble the pale northerly race of Thor's Fritillary that occurs there, and may confuse identification. Look for the crescent of yellow spots on the underside hindwing to ascertain the identity of this species.

---

up to 2.5cm long

orange-brown ground colour

extensive brown spots

dark suffusion on hindwing

WINGSPAN *4.5cm.*
FLIGHT PERIOD *June–July.*
LARVAL FOODPLANT *Violet (Viola).*
SIMILAR SPECIES *Freija's Fritillary (left); Small Pearl-bordered Fritillary (p.64) and Heath Fritillary (p.71) when old and worn, may also resemble the pale race.*
STATUS *Locally fairly common within its restricted range in birch forests of the Alps.*

Glanville Fritillary

Melitaea cinxia (Nymphalidae)

FAVOURS *a variety of grassy places, from coastal undercliffs to verges and hill slopes up to 2,000m or more.*

Both the upper and lower surfaces of this butterfly's wings offer good clues to its identity. The upper hindwing has four or five black spots, arranged in a crescent within the orange submarginal band. The concentric bands of orange and creamy white on the underside of the hindwing are also distinctive. In Britain this species occurs only in a few spots on the Isle of Wight.

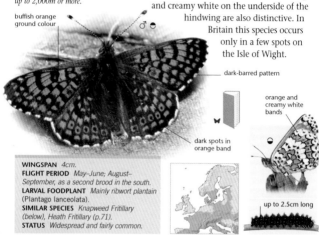

buffish orange ground colour

♂ ●

dark-barred pattern

orange and creamy white bands

dark spots in orange band

up to 2.5cm long

WINGSPAN *4cm.*
FLIGHT PERIOD *May–June; August–September, as a second brood in the south.*
LARVAL FOODPLANT *Mainly ribwort plantain (Plantago lanceolata).*
SIMILAR SPECIES *Knapweed Fritillary (below), Heath Fritillary (p.71).*
STATUS *Widespread and fairly common.*

Knapweed Fritillary

Melitaea phoebe (Nymphalidae)

FOUND *in flowery meadows and on slopes from low-lying areas up to 1,500m or more.*

This attractive species' wings are adorned with a mosaic of orange, yellow, and black markings, but the intensity and extent of each colour is extremely variable. In many specimens, the upperwing pattern is vaguely reminiscent of the Marsh Fritillary (p.81) while the underwing pattern recalls the Glanville Fritillary (above). The wing shape is usually more angular than with related species.

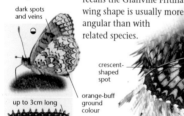

dark spots and veins

●

crescent-shaped spot

orange-buff ground colour

up to 3cm long

♂ ●

orange, yellow, and black mosaic

WINGSPAN *4.5–5cm.*
FLIGHT PERIOD *April–September, in successive broods.*
LARVAL FOODPLANT *Knapweed (Centaurea) and plantain (Plantago).*
SIMILAR SPECIES *Glanville Fritillary (above), Marsh Fritillary (p.81).*
STATUS *Widespread and locally common.*

Spotted Fritillary

Melitaea didyma (Nymphalidae)

This beautiful species is extraordinarily variable, exhibiting differences between the sexes, across its range, and between broods. Fortunately, the majority of males are distinctive, having strikingly bright orange upperwings, as bright as those of a fresh Comma (p.75) that are adorned with very distinct black spots. However, the extent of the black spotting and the intensity of the ground colour vary across the species' range and, to a lesser degree, according to which brood is involved. Females have overall greyer upperwings, so much so that some forms look like a different species.

OCCURS *in flower-rich grassy habitats from lowland meadows and roadside verges to lower mountain slopes up to 2,000m.*

bright orange ground colour

variable black spots

♂♀

chequered fringe

orange-buff forewing

orange and cream bands on hindwing

greyish forewings with dark lines

orange leading edge on hindwing

♀

up to 2.5cm long

NOTE

Thankfully, some Spotted Fritillary features are more constant than others: in all specimens, the wings are relatively broad and rounded and the underwing markings are far less variable than those of the upperwings.

WINGSPAN *3.5–5cm.*
FLIGHT PERIOD *May–August, in broods.*
LARVAL FOODPLANT *Plantain (Plantago), toadflax (Linaria), and speedwell (Veronica).*
SIMILAR SPECIES *Lesser Spotted Fritillary (p.70).*
STATUS *Widespread and generally common.*

Lesser Spotted Fritillary

Melitaea trivia (Nymphalidae)

FOUND *in flower-rich meadows across a range of altitudes but usually associated with hilly country, at 1,000–1,500m.*

This butterfly can look very similar to the Spotted Fritillary (p.69). However, compared to its relative, the Lesser Spotted Fritillary is typically much smaller, its upperwing colour is a duller orange, and the black marginal spots on the underside hindwing are angular rather than rounded in shape. The orange-buff forewing underside has a hint of a pale tip.

orange-brown ground colour

orange-buff forewing

♂♀

variable black spots

chequered fringe

concentric orange and white bands

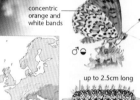

♂♀

up to 2.5cm long

WINGSPAN *2.5–3cm.*
FLIGHT PERIOD *June–August, in two successive broods.*
LARVAL FOODPLANT *Mulleins (Verbascum).*
SIMILAR SPECIES *Spotted Fritillary (p.69), which is larger and more striking in appearance.*
STATUS *Locally common.*

False Heath Fritillary

Melitaea diamina (Nymphalidae)

ASSOCIATED *with open woodland or damp, shady grassland along rides in scrub; most common in the hills.*

Although this species is slightly variable, generally it is rather dark in appearance. This is particularly noticeable on the upper surface of the hindwings, which are sometimes almost uniformly dark brown. In specimens where paler spots are present, these are typically of a similar size across the wing surface, and arranged in line with the white elements of the chequered fringe.

orange forewing

♂♀

up to 2.5cm long

pale crescent-shaped band

orange-brown ground colour

uniform pale spots

variable black markings

♂♀

dark brown hindwing

WINGSPAN *4–4.8cm.*
FLIGHT PERIOD *Mainly June–July, but sometimes as a later second brood.*
LARVAL FOODPLANT *Plantain (Plantago) and cow wheat (Melampyrum).*
SIMILAR SPECIES *Heath Fritillary (right), which is more orange.*
STATUS *Distinctly local.*

Heath Fritillary

Melitaea athalia (Nymphalidae)

As may be expected from so widespread a species, the Heath Fritillary's appearance is variable across its range; this is in addition to subtle and varied differences that exist between the sexes. However, in most specimens the orange upperwings are adorned with a network of black markings, creating a mosaic effect. The hindwings are overall darker than the forewings. They have a dark margin and usually show at least two concentric rows of orange spots. The underside of the hindwing has concentric bands of creamy white and orange-brown; the central pale band is usually the lightest and stands out.

FREQUENTS *wooded heathland and along open woodland rides; the common factor being the presence of larval foodplants.*

network of black markings

orange ground colour

♂●

dark margin

concentric rows of orange spots

orange-buff ground colour

♂●

pale central band

up to 2.5cm long

NOTE

Individuals from the southwest of the Heath Fritillary's range have very bright upperwings: sometimes the orange markings appear almost yellow-buff. On the other hand, Scandinavian specimens are small and often dull.

WINGSPAN *4.4–4.8cm.*
FLIGHT PERIOD *May–September, in successive broods; single-brooded in the north.*
LARVAL FOODPLANT *Common cow wheat (Melampyrum pratense) and ribwort plantain (Plantago lanceolata).*
SIMILAR SPECIES *Glanville Fritillary (p.68), False Heath Fritillary (left).*
STATUS *Widespread and locally common, except margins of its range, where its distribution is patchy, verging on scarce.*

Meadow Fritillary

Melitaea parthenoides (Nymphalidae)

FAVOURS *open, flowery meadows from lowlands to lower mountain slopes at around 2,000m.*

The colourful upperwings of this small butterfly are adorned with black markings. The dark line running across the centre of the forewing, slanting sharply towards the body near the trailing edge of the wing, is distinctive. The females are less colourful than the males, with a paler central band.

prominent dark line on forewing

orange ground colour

orange and white bands

♂♀

chequered fringe

up to 2cm long

WINGSPAN *4cm.*
FLIGHT PERIOD *May–June, with a second brood August–September in the lowlands.*
LARVAL FOODPLANT *Plantain (Plantago) and cow wheat (Melampyrum).*
SIMILAR SPECIES *Heath (p.71), Nickerl's (below), and Grison's (right) Fritillaries.*
STATUS *Locally common, especially in hills.*

Nickerl's Fritillary

Melitaea aurelia (Nymphalidae)

FOUND *in meadows and pastures with flowers, from low-lying terrain to altitudes of 1,200m.*

The richly marked, deep orange and black upperwings of Nickerl's Fritillary have an almost chequerboard pattern. The wing margins are very dark, especially in males, contrasting with the white in the chequered fringe. On the underside, the forewing has a few dark spots, while the hindwing has orange-brown and creamy white bands.

orange-buff ground colour

♂♀

rich orange ground colour

bands of orange and cream

chequered fringe

♀♀

network of black markings

up to 2.5cm long

WINGSPAN *3.5cm.*
FLIGHT PERIOD *July–August.*
LARVAL FOODPLANT *Plantain (Plantago) and cow wheat (Melampyrum).*
SIMILAR SPECIES *Heath Fritillary (p.71), Meadow Fritillary (above), Grison's Fritillary (right).*
STATUS *Widespread and fairly common.*

Grison's Fritillary

Melitaea varia (Nymphalidae)

This species' upland distribution helps to narrow the field when it comes to identification. Its upperwings are predominantly orange, a duller shade in females, and show a limited extent of dark markings when compared to some of its relatives. Towards the middle of the trailing edge of the forewing, there is a dark mark, often shaped like a thighbone; this is mirrored, less distinctly, on the under surface.

RESTRICTED *to upland grassy slopes with comparatively sparse vegetation, from 2,000m to 2,500m.*

dark marking on forewing

bands of orange and cream

orange ground colour

up to 2.5cm long

WINGSPAN *3–3.5cm.*
FLIGHT PERIOD *July–August.*
LARVAL FOODPLANT *Mainly gentian (Gentiana and Gentianella).*
SIMILAR SPECIES *Meadow Fritillary (left), Nickerl's Fritillary (left); both of which are found at lower altitudes.*
STATUS *Local within its restricted range.*

Assmann's Fritillary

Melitaea britomartis (Nymphalidae)

This species is the eastern counterpart of the Meadow Fritillary (left). Fortunately, the geographical ranges of the two extremely similar species hardly overlap, ruling out confusion over their identity. A reasonably constant feature of Assmann's Fritillary is that the pale bands, particularly the marginal one, on the underside of its hindwing are duller and darker than in the Meadow Fritillary.

FLIES *low over flower-rich meadows, usually in low-lying areas and shaded open woodland.*

few black markings

up to 2cm long

dark markings on orange ground colour

chequered buff margin

WINGSPAN *3.5cm.*
FLIGHT PERIOD *May–June, and July–August as a second brood.*
LARVAL FOODPLANT *Common cow wheat (Melampyrum pratense) and plantain (Plantago).*
SIMILAR SPECIES *Meadow Fritillary (left).*
STATUS *Widespread and common.*

Small Tortoiseshell

Nymphalis urticae (Nymphalidae)

The Small Tortoiseshell is one of Europe's most familiar and attractive butterflies. The colourful upperwings are mainly orange, but are boldly marked with black, yellow, and dark brown; discrete blue markings around the wing margins complete the mosaic effect. By contrast, the underwings are rather sombre and afford the butterfly a degree of camouflage when resting with its wings shut. Small Tortoiseshells appear in two or three successive broods each year; adults from the last generation of autumn hibernate over the winter months, often using attics and outhouses; they emerge again in early spring.

INHABITS *a variety of flowery wayside places, from fields, verges, and gardens in lowlands, to meadows on lower mountain slopes.*

yellow and black markings on forewing

buffish yellow markings

orange ground colour

blue spots in margin

smoky brown ground colour

up to 2.5cm long

NOTE

If you want to attract Small Tortoiseshells to your garden, not only should you grow nectar-rich plants such as buddleia (Buddleia) and iceplant (Sedum spectabile) for the adults, but you must also include patches of nettle (Urtica) for the larvae.

WINGSPAN *4.2–4.5cm.*
FLIGHT PERIOD *March–October, in a number of successive broods.*
LARVAL FOODPLANT *Nettle (Urtica).*
SIMILAR SPECIES *Underwings could be mistaken for the much bigger Large Tortoiseshell (p.86).*
STATUS *Widespread and common.*

Comma

Nymphalis c-album (Nymphalidae)

This is one of the most distinctive European butterflies. The colours and shape of its wings, with ragged margins, allow recognition even in silhouette. The sombre underwings, marked with a white comma-like shape, contrast with the orange upperwings.

FOUND *in a wide range of flower-rich and wayside habitats, from verges and woodland to meadows and gardens.*

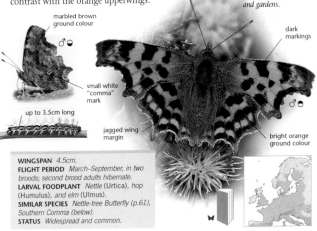

marbled brown ground colour

♂♀

small white "comma" mark

up to 3.5cm long

jagged wing margin

dark markings

♂♀

bright orange ground colour

WINGSPAN 4.5cm.
FLIGHT PERIOD *March–September, in two broods; second brood adults hibernate.*
LARVAL FOODPLANT *Nettle (Urtica), hop (Humulus), and elm (Ulmus).*
SIMILAR SPECIES *Nettle-tree Butterfly (p.61), Southern Comma (below).*
STATUS *Widespread and common.*

Southern Comma

Nymphalis egea (Nymphalidae)

Although superficially similar to the Comma (above), this southern species is identifiable with care. The jagged wing margins are even more angular than those of its relative and the white marking on the underside hindwing is small and Y-shaped, rather than like a comma. The orange-yellow upperwings are adorned with fewer dark spots, mainly on the forewing.

FAVOURS *sunny and, stony slopes in areas with a Mediterranean climate.*

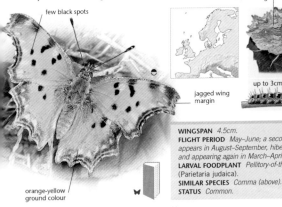

few black spots

buff and smoky brown wings

jagged wing margin

up to 3cm long

orange-yellow ground colour

WINGSPAN 4.5cm.
FLIGHT PERIOD *May–June; a second brood appears in August–September, hibernating and appearing again in March–April.*
LARVAL FOODPLANT *Pellitory-of-the-Wall (Parietaria judaica).*
SIMILAR SPECIES *Comma (above).*
STATUS *Common.*

Queen of Spain Fritillary

Issoria lathonia (Nymphalidae)

FOUND *in a wide range of grassy places with flowers. Its fast flight and migratory habits mean that it can turn up almost anywhere within the given range.*

For its size, the Queen of Spain Fritillary must be one of the fastest-flying butterflies, and this characteristic is reflected in its tendency to migrate and disperse over long distances. It is one of the most distinctive of European Fritillaries. The outline of the wings is rather angular, unlike the more rounded-winged appearance of many of its relatives of a similar size. However, its best distinguishing feature is the number of large silvery spots found on the underside of the hindwing.

bold black spots on forewing

♂●

orange ground colour

marbled brown hindwing

large silver spots

angular wing margin

numerous black spots

up to 3.5cm long

NOTE

When the urge takes them, or when disturbed, Queen of Spain Fritillaries switch in an instant from idle feeding to incredibly fast and direct flight. Within a matter of seconds, they will have disappeared from view. So if you want to obtain a close view, be extremely stealthy when approaching a feeding individual.

WINGSPAN 4.2cm.
FLIGHT PERIOD February–October.
LARVAL FOODPLANT Violet (Viola).
SIMILAR SPECIES None – the large silvery spots on the hindwing underside are unique to this species and diagnostic.
STATUS Widespread and common; in some summers, it extends beyond its given range, sometimes reaching as far as S. England.

Niobe Fritillary

Argynnis niobe (Nymphalidae)

The upper surface of this broad-winged butterfly is rich orange and beautifully marked with black lines and spots. However, the Niobe Fritillary occurs in two different forms that can be told apart from the pattern on their underwings: *A. n. niobe* has pale silvery white spots on the hindwings, while *A. n. eris*, which is more widespread, has yellow-buff spots on the hindwings.

FAVOURS *a wide range of flower-rich grassy habitats from lowland meadows to hillside slopes up to 2,000m.*

orange ground colour

pattern of black lines and spots

broad wings

buff-spots on hindwings

A. n. eris ♂ ●

up to 4cm long

♂ ●

WINGSPAN *4.5–5.5cm.*
FLIGHT PERIOD *June–July.*
LARVAL FOODPLANT *Violet (Viola).*
SIMILAR SPECIES *High Brown Fritillary (p.85), which has paler underwing veins.*
STATUS *Buff-spotted form is common and widespread; silver-spotted form is common only in C. France.*

Twin-spot Fritillary

Brenthis hecate (Nymphalidae)

Although the Twin-spot Fritillary's underwing ground colour is variable, it has a set of features that make identification relatively straightforward. First, look for two parallel rows of black spots of more-or-less uniform size on the upperwings. Then, check if this pattern is mirrored on the underwings. If it is, you can be sure about the identity of the butterfly.

INHABITS *upland meadows and grassy hillside slopes, typically around 1,000–1,500m.*

double row of black spots

twin row of spots as on upperside

orange ground colour

♂ ●

up to 3.5cm long

WINGSPAN *4.5–5cm.*
FLIGHT PERIOD *May–June.*
LARVAL FOODPLANT *Trefoil (Lotus) and other pea family members.*
SIMILAR SPECIES *Marbled Fritillary (p.78), which has a large yellow band on the hindwing underside.*
STATUS *Widespread and fairly common.*

Marbled Fritillary

Brenthis daphne (Nymphalidae)

FOUND *on warm slopes with plenty of scrub and woodland cover, typically in low-lying areas of S. Europe.*

The relatively broad, rounded wings of this species, with twin rows of black spots on the orange upperwing, offer initial clues to its identity. However, the underside of the hindwing is the best identification feature. It has a purple tinge to the marbled outer half, inside of which is a broad pale band.

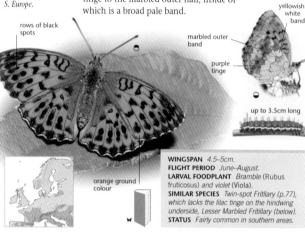

rows of black spots

yellowish white band

marbled outer band

purple tinge

up to 3.5cm long

orange ground colour

WINGSPAN *4.5–5cm.*
FLIGHT PERIOD *June–August.*
LARVAL FOODPLANT *Bramble (Rubus fruticosus) and violet (Viola).*
SIMILAR SPECIES *Twin-spot Fritillary (p.77), which lacks the lilac tinge on the hindwing underside, Lesser Marbled Fritillary (below).*
STATUS *Fairly common in southern areas.*

Lesser Marbled Fritillary

Brenthis ino (Nymphalidae)

ASSOCIATED *usually with damp meadows and grassy habitats at moderate altitudes, 500–1,500m.*

Although this species bears a strong resemblance to the Marbled Fritillary (above), it is smaller and typically has narrower and less rounded wings than its relative. The underside of the hindwing has a limited extent of purple marbling. However, a unique feature is the distinct pale yellow spot at the wing base, emphasized by the orange-brown ground colour bordering it.

orange ground colour

orange-brown forewing

yellow band

pale spot at wing base

twin row of black spots

up to 3.5cm long

WINGSPAN *4–4.5cm.*
FLIGHT PERIOD *June–August.*
LARVAL FOODPLANT *Meadowsweet (Filipendula ulmaria) and great burnet (Sanguisorba officinalis).*
SIMILAR SPECIES *Marbled Fritillary (above), which has no pale spot at the hindwing base.*
STATUS *Widespread but local.*

Titania's Fritillary

Boloria titania (Nymphalidae)

This butterfly has a distinctly upland distribution. The angular dark markings over its entire orange wing surface create a stained-glass effect. A pinkish purple tinge across the underside of the hindwing is a useful feature for identification. The race from the Alps is more strongly marked, the purple on the hindwing being particularly striking and intense.

INHABITS *open, sunny woodland as well as adjacent meadows, above altitudes of 1,500m.*

jagged black and brown markings

purple tinge

up to 2.5cm long

orange ground colour

numerous black spots

WINGSPAN *5cm.*
FLIGHT PERIOD *June–August.*
LARVAL FOODPLANT *Violet (Viola).*
SIMILAR SPECIES *Marbled Fritillary (left), which has a pale band within the purplish patch on the hindwing underside.*
STATUS *Locally common in suitable upland habitats.*

Provençal Fritillary

Melitaea deione (Nymphalidae)

In many ways, this species is very similar to the Heath Fritillary (p.71). Females are easier to identify than males, with alternating bands of orange and yellow-buff, separated by the black lines, on the upperwings. Both sexes typically lack the Heath Fritillary's striking dark inner margin along the pale marginal spots on the underside of the forewing.

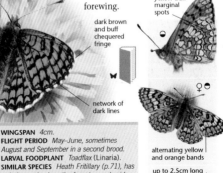

FAVOURS *flower-rich fields and meadows, often on hillsides, with a Mediterranean climate.*

orange ground colour

yellow-buff marginal spots

dark brown and buff chequered fringe

network of dark lines

♂

alternating yellow and orange bands

♀

up to 2.5cm long

WINGSPAN *4cm.*
FLIGHT PERIOD *May–June, sometimes August and September in a second brood.*
LARVAL FOODPLANT *Toadflax (Linaria).*
SIMILAR SPECIES *Heath Fritillary (p.71), has a dark margin along the forewing underside.*
STATUS *Locally common in the warm, sunny south.*

Cynthia's Fritillary

Euphydryas cynthia (Nymphalidae)

FOUND *in alpine heaths where juniper (Juniperus) and blueberry (Vaccinium) are dominant.*

Males of this species have a unique white pattern on the upperwings. Females are trickier to identify but the elongated wings rule out most other possibilities; its restricted range eliminate other contenders. Both sexes from slightly lower altitudes have an orange-brown ground colour compared to the dark brown upland form.

white markings

♀♂♂

orange- and yellow-buff bands

up to 2.5cm long

network of black markings

WINGSPAN *4.5–5cm.*
FLIGHT PERIOD *July–August.*
LARVAL FOODPLANT *Plantain (Plantago) and lady's mantles (Alchemilla).*
SIMILAR SPECIES *Scarce Fritillary (below) and Marsh Fritillary (right).*
STATUS *Local, but fairly common in suitable habitats.*

♂●

UPLAND FORM

dark brown ground colour

Scarce Fritillary

Euphydryas maturna (Nymphalidae)

CONFINED *to sunny, open woodland where both the summer and spring larval foodplants flourish.*

This attractively marked butterfly has upperwings adorned with bands of reddish orange and blackish brown, together with rows of pale spots. The underwings are orange, marked mainly with pale bands and spots. Like fellow members of the genus *Euphydryas*, it has rather narrow and elongated wings compared to other species of fritillary.

♂●

orange with pale spots and bands

reddish orange bands

up to 3.5cm long

pale spots

dark bands and lines

WINGSPAN *4.5–5cm.*
FLIGHT PERIOD *May–July.*
LARVAL FOODPLANT *Aspen (Populus) and ash (Fraxinus) in summer; plantain (Plantago) in spring.*
SIMILAR SPECIES *Cynthia's Fritillary female (above), Marsh Fritillary (right).*
STATUS *Local and generally rather scarce.*

Marsh Fritillary

Euphydryas aurinia (Nymphalidae)

Although this species is rather variable in appearance, its wings, which are comparatively narrow by fritillary standards, are characterized by a beautiful mosaic of reddish orange, yellow-buff, and brown. The underwings have similar markings, which are equally attractive but in subdued colours. The Marsh Fritillary is a rather sluggish butterfly that spends time sitting on low vegetation and basking in the sunshine with its wings open, a trait that aids close-up observation. Females are usually larger than males.

FAVOURS *grassy areas, often on marshy ground but also on dry slopes and moorland up to 2,000m.*

orange-buff ground colour

♂ ⚤

dark bands and lines

orange-buff ground colour

♀

pale bands and spots

black spots in orange band

up to 3cm long

NOTE

This is the most widespread *Euphydryas* fritillary species in the region and one of the most common members of this rather narrow-winged group you are likely to encounter in grassy areas. The Marsh Fritillary can be surprisingly hard to find on dull days since it tends to hide away in the deep cover of foliage.

WINGSPAN *4.5–5.2cm.*
FLIGHT PERIOD *May–July.*
LARVAL FOODPLANT *Devil's-bit scabious (Succisa pratensis), scabious (Scabiosa) and plantain (Plantago).*
SIMILAR SPECIES *Cynthia's Fritillary, female (left), Scarce Fritillary (left).*
STATUS *Widespread and locally common although populations fluctuate from year to year.*

Monarch

Danaus plexippus (Danaidae)

This large and unmistakable butterfly has orange wings with a network of black veins; a broad black band, studded with white spots, runs along the edges. A strongly migratory species within its North American range, in autumn, westerly gales divert a part of the southbound population across the Atlantic to Europe; some individuals also originate in the Canary Islands and the Azores.

FOUND *along west-facing coastlines that are open and grassy, only during the species' migration period.*

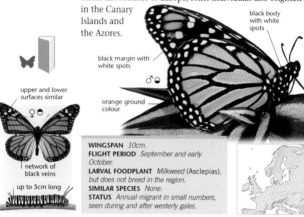

black body with white spots

black margin with white spots

♂♀

orange ground colour

upper and lower surfaces similar

♀♂

network of black veins

up to 5cm long

WINGSPAN *10cm.*
FLIGHT PERIOD *September and early October.*
LARVAL FOODPLANT *Milkweed (Asclepias), but does not breed in the region.*
SIMILAR SPECIES *None.*
STATUS *Annual migrant in small numbers, seen during and after westerly gales.*

Two-tailed Pasha

Charaxes jasius (Nymphalidae)

With its twin hindwing tail streamers and contrasting colours, the Two-tailed Pasha bears a passing resemblance to Swallowtails, a group to which it is entirely unrelated. The upperwings are orange and dark brown; the underwings are more striking, with an intricate chestnut and white pattern, and a row of blue spots along the hindwing margins.

RESTRICTED *to lush maquis in the Mediterranean, where the larval foodplant grows in abundance.*

♂♀

brown wing bases

broad orange margin

blue spots on hindwing

black bands

♂♀

twin tail streamers

up to 6cm long

WINGSPAN *7.5–8cm.*
FLIGHT PERIOD *May–June and August–September, in two broods.*
LARVAL FOODPLANT *Strawberry tree (Arbutus unedo).*
SIMILAR SPECIES *None.*
STATUS *Locally common within its distinctly southern range.*

Silver-washed Fritillary

Argynnis paphia (Nymphalidae)

Across much of its range an experienced observer can identify a Silver-washed Fritillary, with a reasonable degree of confidence, by its size and flight pattern alone. It is a relatively large butterfly with a fast, gliding flight. A close view of a resting individual reveals the forewings to be rather angular while the hindwings are relatively large and rounded. In most specimens, the upperwings have a rich orange ground colour. By contrast, the buffish yellow and greenish underwings are marked with metallic, silvery bands – a feature that gives this butterfly its common name.

ASSOCIATED *with wooded areas, favouring clearings, rides, and margins with brambles, which are a source of nectar for adult butterflies.*

silvery bands

♀⬤

NOTE

Females occur in two colour forms. Typically, they resemble a duller, more heavily spotted version of the male, but in the form A. p. valesina the upperwings are greenish buff, and superficially similar to a Cardinal (p.84).

orange-buff ground colour

♀⬤

prominent black spots

up to 4cm long

angular forewings

♂⬤

rich orange ground colour

rounded hindwings

WINGSPAN *6cm.*
FLIGHT PERIOD *June–August.*
LARVAL FOODPLANT *Violet (Viola).*
SIMILAR SPECIES *Cardinal (p.84), which, on the underside, has pink forewings and greenish hindwings.*
STATUS *Widespread and locally common in mature deciduous woodland.*

Cardinal

Argynnis pandora (Nymphalidae)

Although superficially similar to the Silver-washed Fritillary (p.83), the wing markings of the Cardinal are much more pronounced, especially in females. The ground colour of the upperwings is buffish orange, with an extensive greenish suffusion. On the underside, the forewing is mainly pink with dark spotting, while the hindwing is pale green with faint silver stripes.

FAVOURS grassy woodland rides, clearings, and flowery meadows.

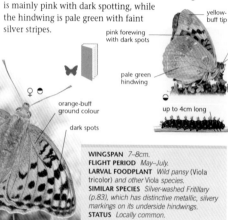

yellow-buff tip

pink forewing with dark spots

pale green hindwing

up to 4cm long

greenish suffusion

♀ ●

orange-buff ground colour

dark spots

WINGSPAN *7–8cm.*
FLIGHT PERIOD *May–July.*
LARVAL FOODPLANT *Wild pansy (Viola tricolor) and other Viola species.*
SIMILAR SPECIES *Silver-washed Fritillary (p.83), which has distinctive metallic, silvery markings on its underside hindwings.*
STATUS *Locally common.*

Dark Green Fritillary

Argynnis aglaja (Nymphalidae)

This butterfly of open habitats is unaffected by strong winds and has a fast and direct flight. Fortunately, it frequently feeds on the flowers of thistle and knapweed, allowing for close-up views. Like most other Fritillaries, it has orange upperwings with dark spots. The undersides of the hindwings, however, are a distinctive green colour, marked with white spots.

FOUND in grassy habitats from coastal dunes, to downland and open moors.

greenish ground colour

●

orange ground colour

♂ ●

crescent of 5 black spots on hindwing

striking white spots

up to 4cm long

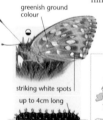

WINGSPAN *6–6.5cm.*
FLIGHT PERIOD *June–August.*
LARVAL FOODPLANT *Violet (Viola).*
SIMILAR SPECIES *High Brown Fritillary (right), which has buff rather than green underside hindwings that are marked with a crescent of chestnut spots.*
STATUS *Widespread and locally common.*

numerous black spots

High Brown Fritillary

Argynnis adippe (Nymphalidae)

This well-marked butterfly is capable of fast and vigorous flight and, in sunny weather, it seldom seems to pause, except to feed on bramble flowers. The upperwings are a rich orange-brown ground colour with striking black spots and streaks. On the underside, the forewings are orange-buff with dark spots while the hindwings are buff, often with a greenish tinge. Apart from bearing striking white spots, the hindwings also have a characteristic crescent of chestnut spots. The male High Brown Fritillary is typically smaller than the female. This is the most likely large and fast-flying Fritillary species to be encountered in upland grassland areas. In Britian and other areas on the margins of its range, this species has become decidedly scarce in recent decades.

FREQUENTS *sunny woodland and grassy scrub with plenty of open areas and sparse vegetation; occurs at altitudes up to 2,000m.*

orange-brown ground colour

black spots and markings

chequered fringe

crescent of chestnut spots

striking white spots

NOTE

Although the underwings vary in appearance, particularly in the extent of green suffusion, a crescent of chestnut dots on the hindwing is a constant feature and useful in identification; it is present in both the sexes.

up to 4cm long

WINGSPAN *6–6.5cm.*
FLIGHT PERIOD *July–August.*
LARVAL FOODPLANT *Violet (Viola).*
SIMILAR SPECIES *Dark Green Fritillary (left), which has green underside hindwings with white and no chestnut spots.*
STATUS *Widespread but distinctly local; rare in Britain.*

Large Tortoiseshell

Nymphalis polychloros (Nymphalidae)

FAVOURS *hedgerows, open woodland, and field margins up to 2,000m, mainly where elms are present.*

This butterfly is fast-flying and active. Although it occasionally basks on bare ground, or on the trunk of a tree, it typically favours tree canopies, which can make it rather difficult to observe closely. Its orange upperwings are marked with squarish black spots, while a close view of the hindwings reveals blue crescent-shaped spots along the black margins. The underwings are marbled sooty brown, providing camouflage when the butterfly is resting on tree bark with its wings closed. There is an indistinct blue band along the margin of both wings. Large Tortoiseshells are often found drinking oozing honeydew and sap from trees.

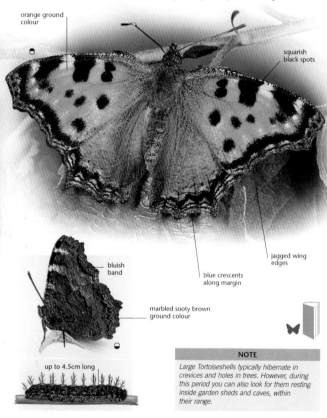

orange ground colour

squarish black spots

jagged wing edges

blue crescents along margin

bluish band

marbled sooty brown ground colour

up to 4.5cm long

NOTE

Large Tortoiseshells typically hibernate in crevices and holes in trees. However, during this period you can also look for them resting inside garden sheds and caves, within their range.

WINGSPAN *8cm.*
FLIGHT PERIOD *June–August, and again from March–April after hibernation.*
LARVAL FOODPLANT *Mainly elm (Ulmus), but also willow (Salix) and poplar (Populus).*
SIMILAR SPECIES *Comma (p.75).*
STATUS *Widespread and locally common; the species has been badly affected by the death of elms from Dutch elm disease.*

Southern Festoon

Zerynthia polyxena (Papilionidae)

This butterfly is the eastern counterpart of the Spanish Festoon (below), and there is very little overlap in their ranges. The black markings on its wings are variable and there is often a small red patch near the leading edge of the upper forewing, although sometimes it is absent. The limited extent of red, and overall paler ground colour, are useful features to distinguish it from the Spanish Festoon.

FLIES *over scrub-covered Mediterranean habitats; occasionally visits neighbouring flowery meadows.*

intricate pattern of black bands ♂●

cream ground colour

striking red spots on both wings

♂●

row of red spots on hindwings

Caterpillar not sufficiently known

WINGSPAN *4.5–5cm.*	
FLIGHT PERIOD *April–June.*	
LARVAL FOODPLANT *Birthwort* (Aristolochia).	
SIMILAR SPECIES *Spanish Festoon (below), which has more extensive red markings and a darker ground colour.*	
STATUS *Locally common.*	

Spanish Festoon

Zerynthia rumina (Papilionidae)

A mosaic of creamy yellow, black, and red creates a stained-glass effect on this butterfly's upperwings. As a result, it is almost unmistakable within its range, even though its appearance is rather variable. The Spanish Festoon is one of the first species to be observed on the wing in spring in its southern European range.

PREFERS *scrub-covered, open Mediterranean habitats: maquis, stony ground, and fallow fields, where the foodplant grows.*

intricate pattern of black bands

bright red spots

creamy yellow ground colour

dark grey bands

♂

WINGSPAN *4.5–5.5cm.*	
FLIGHT PERIOD *March–May.*	
LARVAL FOODPLANT *Birthwort* (Aristolochia).	
SIMILAR SPECIES *Southern Festoon (above), which has lighter markings.*	
STATUS *Locally common, although in decline due to changes in land use.*	

up to 3.5cm long

Painted Lady

Vanessa cardui (Nymphalidae)

With its distinctively patterned salmon-pink upperwings, the Painted Lady is one of the easiest European butterflies to recognize, even on the wing. Although duller in appearance, the underwing pattern is similar to that of the upperwings. The Painted Lady is resident in north Africa and southern Europe where adults may occur through much of the year. Further north, it is a summer visitor, often appearing in considerable numbers. Many of these visitors undoubtedly die with the onset of frosts in late autumn, but some make the return journey south to milder regions around the Mediterranean.

FOUND *in grassy places where flowers are in bloom, often visiting gardens on occasions. Its strong migratory habits mean that it can turn up anywhere in the region.*

forewing has dark tip with white spots

♂●

salmon-pink and black pattern

salmon-pink forewing

submarginal eyespots

hindwing marbled grey, buffish brown, and white

smoky brown wing base

up to 3cm long

NOTE

When feeding on nectar from flowers such as thistle (Carduus/Cirsium) and knapweed (Centaurea), the Painted Lady is usually oblivious to the approach of an observer. This is the best time to get a close and rewarding view of the species.

WINGSPAN *6cm.*
FLIGHT PERIOD *March–November in the far south; typically April–October further north.*
LARVAL FOODPLANT *Thistle (Carduus/Cirsium) and nettle (Urtica).*
SIMILAR SPECIES *None.*
STATUS *Migratory species; widespread and often abundant in the south; further north, numbers vary from year to year but it is usually common by late summer.*

Red Admiral

Vanessa atalanta (Nymphalidae)

The fact that it is a frequent visitor to gardens, along with its bright colours and distinctive markings, makes the Red Admiral one of the region's most familiar butterflies. Its jet-black upperwings are marked with bands of red and white spots, with a single blue spot at the base of each hindwing. The underside of the forewing has a similar pattern and colouring, along with a pinkish red patch. However, when resting, this is often concealed by the more cryptic undersurface of the hindwing, which is marbled smoky brown, bluish, and black.

OCCURS *in almost any flowery habitat, from grassy meadows, verges, and hedgerows to parks and gardens.*

pink patch on forewing

smoky brown hindwing

NOTE

Red Admirals are often found drinking fluid from rotting apples and other fallen fruit in autumn. At such times, they may even alight on the palm of a hand bearing fruit, in search of a meal.

up to 3.5cm long

white spots on wing tip

♂♀

red band on forewing

red hindwing margin

blue spot on hindwing base

WINGSPAN *6cm.*
FLIGHT PERIOD *May–October, and again in March and April after hibernation.*
LARVAL FOODPLANT *Nettle (Urtica).*
SIMILAR SPECIES *None.*
STATUS *Common resident in the south; further north, small numbers may survive winter hibernation, but the species is mainly a common migrant visitor.*

Peacock

Nymphalis io (Nymphalidae)

FREQUENTS *grassy and wayside habitats, from hedgerows and verges to meadows, gardens, and parks.*

Striking eyespots and gaudy colours make the Peacock an unmistakable butterfly. Like several of its colourful relatives, it is a frequent visitor to gardens, where it feeds on nectar; it is particularly fond of the flowers of buddleia and iceplant. When resting with its wings closed, the cryptic coloration of the undersides and the jagged wing margins make the species look like dead leaves or bark, affording it excellent camouflage. If startled, a resting Peacock will flash open its wings, the sudden revelation of the eyespots scaring off potential predators.

marbled brown ground colour

jagged edge

up to 4cm long

NOTE

Peacock larvae live communally, constructing conspicuous silken tents on their foodplants, which are members of the nettle family. Look for these wispy structures among the clumps of nettles during summer months.

reddish maroon ground colour

yellow, maroon, and bluish purple eyespot

blue and black eyespot on hindwing

WINGSPAN *6cm.*
FLIGHT PERIOD *July–September, and after hibernation, March–May.*
LARVAL FOODPLANT *Nettle (Urtica).*
SIMILAR SPECIES *None.*
STATUS *Widespread and common. One of the commonest butterflies found in the garden.*

Camberwell Beauty

Nymphalis antiopa (Nymphalidae)

Although the Camberwell Beauty may not be the most colourful of butterflies, the combination of rich maroon and a fringe of creamy white, separated by a lacy line of spots, on the upperwings, gives it undeniable appeal. This fast-flying species is often seen gliding around treetops, at a considerable height. Fortunately for observers, however, the Camberwell Beauty does descend to lower levels fairly frequently and can be seen basking on bare ground and tree trunks on sunny days.

FAVOURS *open woodland and scrub-covered slopes, from sea level to around 2,000m.*

rich maroon ground colour

small, bluish purple spots

creamy white border

sooty brown ground colour

jagged white margin

NOTE

The Camberwell Beauty is a strong migrant and can turn up almost anywhere within its given range; on occasions it even crosses open seas and reaches Britain. Most visitors turn up on the east coast of England, having crossed the North Sea during periods of easterly winds.

up to 5cm long

WINGSPAN *8cm.*
FLIGHT PERIOD *June–August, and March–April after hibernation.*
LARVAL FOODPLANT *Willow* (Salix), *birch* (Betula), *and elm* (Ulmus).
SIMILAR SPECIES *None; however, in old, worn specimens, the pale margin may be less apparent, creating some confusion.*
STATUS *Widespread but seldom particularly common; declining in parts of its range.*

Purple Hairstreak

Favonius quercus (Lycaenidae)

A familiar woodland species in many parts of Europe, the Purple Hairstreak is often seen flitting individually high among the treetops. Fortunately for observers, it often descends closer to ground level on dull days (particularly after rain) and at such times can be found resting on leaves at eye level. Unlike some of its Hairstreak relatives, it occasionally basks with its wings open, revealing the purple markings on its sooty brown upperwings. The Purple Hairstreak has small tail streamers at the tips of its hindwings. Its under surface is buffish grey with a white streak on both wings.

ASSOCIATED with mature oak woodland but colonies are sometimes found on isolated oak trees.

grey ground colour

black-edged white streak

♂●

small orange spots

NOTE

Consideration of habitat and distribution will help distinguish the Purple Hairstreak from the Spanish Purple Hairstreak. The former inhabits oak woodland and is found across most of Europe, while the latter is found near ash trees and is common in southwestern Europe.

♀●

less extensive purple sheen

small tail streamer

up to 2.5cm long

♂●

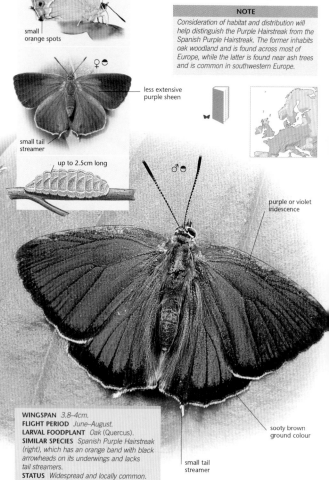

purple or violet iridescence

sooty brown ground colour

small tail streamer

WINGSPAN *3.8–4cm.*
FLIGHT PERIOD *June–August.*
LARVAL FOODPLANT *Oak (Quercus).*
SIMILAR SPECIES *Spanish Purple Hairstreak (right), which has an orange band with black arrowheads on its underwings and lacks tail streamers.*
STATUS *Widespread and locally common.*

Spanish Purple Hairstreak

Laeosopis roboris (Lycaenidae)

This species prefers to fly high in the treetops, fortunately viewers can get a close look as it often descends to feed on the nectar of wayside flowers. The sooty black upperwings have a bluish purple sheen, which is more extensive in males than females, while the undersides of both sexes are buffish grey with a striking orange margin.

FREQUENTS *open, sunny woodland, especially where ash trees are abundant; occurs from low levels up to altitudes of 1,500m.*

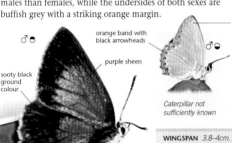

♂●

orange band with black arrowheads

purple sheen

sooty black ground colour

buffish grey ground colour

♂●

Caterpillar not sufficiently known

WINGSPAN *3.8–4cm.*
FLIGHT PERIOD *May–July.*
LARVAL FOODPLANT *Ash (Fraxinus).*
SIMILAR SPECIES *Purple Hairstreak (left), which has a white streak on its underwings, and small tail streamers.*
STATUS *Locally common in its distinctive southern range.*

Lesser Purple Emperor

Apatura ilia (Nymphalidae)

This fast-flying species is mainly a treetop-dweller but also descends to the ground to drink at the margins of muddy puddles. Only the male has an iridescent bluish tone on the brown upperwings; those of the female are a brown ground colour but with the same pattern of white markings as seen in the male.

FOUND *typically in damp woodland with plenty of tall, mature trees, often along watercourses.*

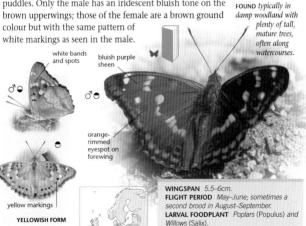

white bands and spots

bluish purple sheen

♂●

♂●

orange-rimmed eyespot on forewing

●

yellow markings

YELLOWISH FORM
up to 5cm long

WINGSPAN *5.5–6cm.*
FLIGHT PERIOD *May–June; sometimes a second brood in August–September.*
LARVAL FOODPLANT *Poplars (Populus) and Willows (Salix).*
SIMILAR SPECIES *Purple Emperor (p.94).*
STATUS *Local but fairly common in the south of its range.*

Purple Emperor

Apatura iris (Nymphalidae)

The large and impressive Purple Emperor is perhaps one of the most highly prized species for European butterfly-watchers. Not only is it beautifully marked, but it is also one of the region's most elusive butterflies and so finally spotting one is a definite achievement. Purple Emperors spend much of their adult lives flying around the tops of tall oak trees. The wing patterns are essentially similar in both sexes but the upperwings of the male reveal a glorious purple iridescence when seen at certain angles.

FOUND *in mature oak woodland with tall trees, which serve as territorial focal points for males.*

grey and brown wings

orange-ringed eyespot

up to 5.5cm long

NOTE

The Purple Emperor's rather unsavoury predilection for drinking fluids from carrion and fresh dung means that it occasionally visits the ground, rewarding observers with some excellent close-up views.

brown ground colour

white spots

bright purple sheen

white band

WINGSPAN *6–6.5cm.*
FLIGHT PERIOD *July–August.*
LARVAL FOODPLANT *Sallow, notably Goat Willow (Salix caprea).*
SIMILAR SPECIES *Lesser Purple Emperor (p.93), which has orange-ringed eyespots on both upperside wings, while the Purple Emperor has an indistinct eyespot on the upper hindwing only.*
STATUS *Widespread and locally common but easily overlooked because of its habit of keeping to the tops of trees.*

Gatekeeper

Maniola tithonius (Satyridae)

The emergence of this familiar wayside butterfly is perceived by many naturalists to be a sign that summer is at its height. The Gatekeeper is on the wing just as bramble flowers are at their best, and groups can be seen feeding on their nectar. Its upperwings are a rich orange colour with a brown margin and an eyespot bearing twin highlights on the forewing. The underwing coloration is rather similar, although the hindwing has a more marbled appearance. Male Gatekeepers are smaller than females, with more brightly coloured wings, and have a dark sex-brand on each forewing.

FREQUENTS *meadows, grassy hedgerows, and woodland margins, typically from sea level to around 750m.*

dark patch on forewing

highlights on twin eyespot

♂ ☙

buffish yellow ground colour

buff-brown margin

broad brown margin with pale fringe

up to 2cm long

NOTE

Throughout most of its range, this is the most common small- to medium-sized orange member of the Brown family, and is the species most likely to be seen feeding in groups on the flowers of bramble and other meadow and hedgerow plants.

WINGSPAN *4cm.*
FLIGHT PERIOD *July–August.*
LARVAL FOODPLANT *Various grasses (family Poaceae).*
SIMILAR SPECIES *Southern Gatekeeper (p.96), which has more rounded wings and larger twin highlights on the eyespots; Spanish Gatekeeper (p.96), which has a broad creamy-white band on the hindwing.*
STATUS *Widespread and common.*

Southern Gatekeeper

Maniola cecilia (Satyridae)

Although this butterfly is similar to the Gatekeeper (p.95), it has a number of distinct features. The wings are more rounded, and the twin highlights in the eyespots on the forewing are larger. With males, the dark sex-brand on the upper forewing is dissected by pale veins, while that of the Gatekeeper is unbroken.

FOUND *in sunny and grassy places, typically with a Mediterranean climate.*

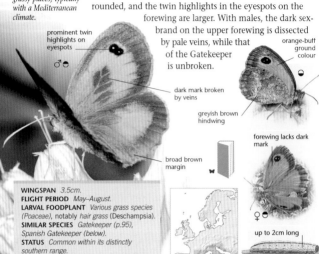

prominent twin highlights on eyespots

♂

orange-buff ground colour

dark mark broken by veins

greyish brown hindwing

forewing lacks dark mark

broad brown margin

♀

up to 2cm long

WINGSPAN *3.5cm.*
FLIGHT PERIOD *May–August.*
LARVAL FOODPLANT *Various grass species (Poaceae), notably hair grass (Deschampsia).*
SIMILAR SPECIES *Gatekeeper (p.95), Spanish Gatekeeper (below).*
STATUS *Common within its distinctly southern range.*

Spanish Gatekeeper

Maniola bathseba (Satyridae)

This well-marked, small butterfly can be distinguished easily by the presence of a single eyespot on the forewing and three black eyespots on the hindwing, all of which are visible on both surfaces. The broad, creamy white band on the underside of the hindwing is another good identifying feature of this sun-loving species.

FAVOURS *sunny, rough grassland and grassy margins of open woodland, typically below 1,000m.*

black eyespot

brown patch on forewing

buffish orange ground colour

♂

creamy white band

WINGSPAN *3.5–5cm.*
FLIGHT PERIOD *April–July.*
LARVAL FOODPLANT *Various grass species (Poaceae), notably false brome grass (Brachypodium).*
SIMILAR SPECIES *Gatekeeper (p.95), Southern Gatekeeper (above).*
STATUS *Locally fairly common.*

Caterpillar not sufficiently known

Small Heath

Coenonympha pamphilus (Satyridae)

Although small and not especially colourful, the Small Heath is easy to spot in the field. It can be extremely common in habitats that suit its needs, so observers should not find it difficult to get good views. On dull days, it can sometimes be found sitting on grass leaves and stems, allowing close inspection of the marbled grey undersurface of its hindwings and orange-brown underside of the forewings. The forewing is marked with a small, but striking black eyespot on both surfaces.

FREQUENTS *a range of grassy habitats, from meadows and verges, to heaths; from lower levels up to altitudes of 2,000m.*

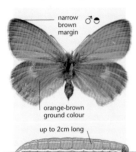

narrow brown margin ♂●

orange-brown ground colour

up to 2cm long

NOTE

The Small Heath always rests and feeds with its wings closed, making it almost impossible to obtain a view of the upperwings. Fortunately, its small size and underwing markings allow identification of most individuals.

orange-brown forewing

black eyespot

greyish margin

jagged, creamy white band

marbled grey and brown hindwing

WINGSPAN *3cm.*
FLIGHT PERIOD *May–September, in successive broods.*
LARVAL FOODPLANT *Various grasses (family Poaceae), notably fescue (Festuca).*
SIMILAR SPECIES *Dusky Heath (p.98), Pearly Heath (p.99), Large Heath (p.105).*
STATUS *One of the region's most common and widespread butterflies, although habitat degradation has caused local extinctions.*

Dusky Heath

Coenonympha dorus (Satyridae)

Resting individuals of this well-marked butterfly never reveal their upperwings. However, the Dusky Heath's underwings are distinctive enough to ensure identification: the orange-brown forewings bear a single eyespot while the hindwings show a jagged-edged, pale stripe marked with striking eyespots along its margin. The upperwings are dusky orange-brown and have several dark eyespots on both wings.

PREFERS *sunny, open, grassy slopes with a Mediterranean climate; occurs up to 2,000m.*

single eyespot on orange-buff forewings

pale-ringed dark spots

jagged edged pale stripe

dusky orange-brown ground colour

small eyespots

Caterpillar not sufficiently known

WINGSPAN *3.5cm.*
FLIGHT PERIOD *June–July.*
LARVAL FOODPLANT *Grasses (family Poaceae), notably fescue (Festuca).*
SIMILAR SPECIES *Small Heath (p.97), which has a jagged creamy white band on the hindwing underside; Pearly Heath (right).*
STATUS *Locally fairly common.*

False Ringlet

Coenonympha oedippus (Satyridae)

This butterfly's wings are rounded in shape; the upper surface, which is seen only occasionally, is uniformly sooty brown. The underwings, which have an orange-brown ground colour, have striking yellow-ringed dark eyespots that form a crescent on the hindwings, while the number and size of eyespots on the forewings is variable. Females are more strikingly marked than males.

FREQUENTS *damp meadows, grassy heaths, and woodland margins, below 750m.*

white line on hindwing

orange-brown ground colour

rounded wings

up to 2.5cm long

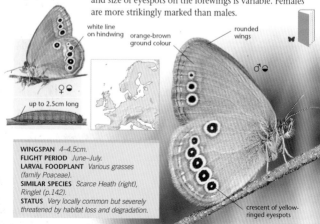

WINGSPAN *4–4.5cm.*
FLIGHT PERIOD *June–July.*
LARVAL FOODPLANT *Various grasses (family Poaceae).*
SIMILAR SPECIES *Scarce Heath (right), Ringlet (p.142).*
STATUS *Very locally common but severely threatened by habitat loss and degradation.*

crescent of yellow-ringed eyespots

Pearly Heath

Coenonympha arcania (Satyridae)

Since the Pearly Heath never reveals its upperwings at rest, the underwing details are best studied for identification; the orange-brown forewings are marked with a solitary eyespot, while the hindwings show a striking white stripe, along the outer margin of which are several small eyespots; some individuals have an additional eyespot near the middle of the hindwing leading edge.

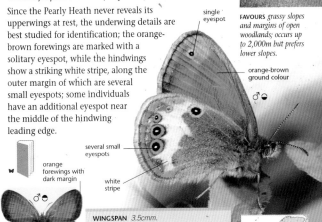

single eyespot

FAVOURS *grassy slopes and margins of open woodlands; occurs up to 2,000m but prefers lower slopes.*

orange-brown ground colour

♂♀

orange forewings with dark margin

several small eyespots

white stripe

up to 2.5cm long

♂♀

WINGSPAN *3.5cmm.*
FLIGHT PERIOD *June–July.*
LARVAL FOODPLANT *Various grasses (family Poaceae), notably brome (Bromus) and melick (Melica).*
SIMILAR SPECIES *Small Heath (p.97), Dusky Heath (left).*
STATUS *Widespread and locally common.*

Scarce Heath

Coenonympha hero (Satyridae)

A butterfly that is always seen with its under surface exposed at rest, the Scarce Heath has dark orange-brown underwings; the hindwings have a white jagged-edged line next to which lies a crescent of linked, orange-ringed dark eyespots. Both wings have an orange-buff margin and a submarginal pale line. The sooty brown upperwings have orange-ringed eyespots on the hindwings.

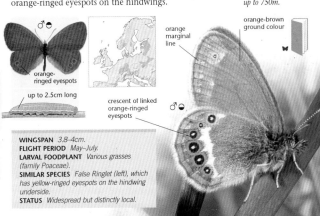

FOUND *in grassy meadows and open woodland margins, typically in damp locations at altitudes up to 750m.*

orange-brown ground colour

orange marginal line

♂♀

♂♀

orange-ringed eyespots

up to 2.5cm long

crescent of linked orange-ringed eyespots

WINGSPAN *3.8–4cm.*
FLIGHT PERIOD *May–July.*
LARVAL FOODPLANT *Various grasses (family Poaceae).*
SIMILAR SPECIES *False Ringlet (left), which has yellow-ringed eyespots on the hindwing underside.*
STATUS *Widespread but distinctly local.*

Alpine Heath

Coenonympha gardetta (Satyridae)

The Alpine Heath is a distinctive, small upland butterfly. Like many of its relatives, it does not reveal its upperwings at rest; these are brown with a variable extent of orange on the inner forewings. The underside forewing is orange-brown with a grey margin, while the underside hindwing is greyish brown with a striking white band towards the wing margin, inside of which is a row of small black eyespots.

RESTRICTED *to alpine meadows and grassy mountain slopes, at altitudes between 1,000m and 2,500m.*

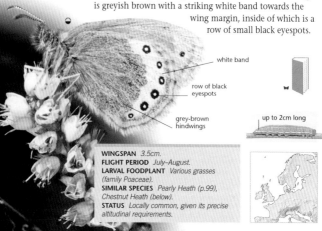

white band

row of black eyespots

grey-brown hindwings

up to 2cm long

WINGSPAN *3.5cm.*
FLIGHT PERIOD *July–August.*
LARVAL FOODPLANT *Various grasses (family Poaceae).*
SIMILAR SPECIES *Pearly Heath (p.99), Chestnut Heath (below).*
STATUS *Locally common, given its precise altitudinal requirements.*

Chestnut Heath

Coenonympha glycerion (Satyridae)

The rounded wings of this upland butterfly are coloured with rich tones. The underside of the forewing is a chestnut shade, while the hindwing underside is greyish brown, variably marked with eyespots. Resting individuals never reveal their upperwings, which have roughly similar patterns and colours to those on the underwings, but with less distinctive eyespots.

ASSOCIATED *with grassland areas in the hills, typically at altitudes between 500m and 1,500m.*

smoky brown ground colour

♂

up to 2cm long

rich chestnut-brown forewings

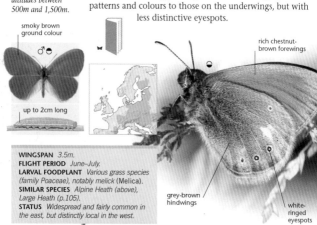

grey-brown hindwings

white-ringed eyespots

WINGSPAN *3.5m.*
FLIGHT PERIOD *June–July.*
LARVAL FOODPLANT *Various grass species (family Poaceae), notably melick (Melica).*
SIMILAR SPECIES *Alpine Heath (above), Large Heath (p.105).*
STATUS *Widespread and fairly common in the east, but distinctly local in the west.*

Chequered Skipper

Carterocephalus palaemon (Hesperiidae)

A well-defined upperwing pattern of dark brown with buffish orange spots, creating a chequerboard effect, makes this an easily identifiable species. The underwing pattern is broadly similar to that seen on the upperside although the colours are faded by comparison. The Chequered Skipper is an active species in sunshine, but it remains concealed on dull days and is easily overlooked.

FLIES *in grassy areas in scrub, open woodland, and clearings, from sea level to 1,500m.*

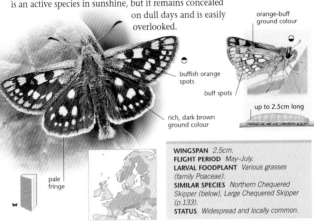

orange-buff ground colour

buffish orange spots

buff spots

rich, dark brown ground colour

up to 2.5cm long

pale fringe

WINGSPAN *2.5cm.*
FLIGHT PERIOD *May–July.*
LARVAL FOODPLANT *Various grasses (family Poaceae).*
SIMILAR SPECIES *Northern Chequered Skipper (below), Large Chequered Skipper (p.133).*
STATUS *Widespread and locally common.*

Northern Chequered Skipper

Carterocephalus silvicolus (Hesperiidae)

A distinctly northern species, this Skipper has pale buffish yellow wings variably marked with dark brown spots and patches. The hindwing undersides are brownish with large, dull yellow spots. Female butterflies tend to be smaller than males and show more extensive dark brown markings on their upperwings.

FAVOURS *clearings in open woodland and damp, grassy areas with scattered trees, below 500m.*

pale yellow spots

up to 2.5cm long

yellow-buff ground colour

brown patches

WINGSPAN *2.5–3cm.*
FLIGHT PERIOD *May–July.*
LARVAL FOODPLANT *Various grasses (family Poaceae), especially dog's-tail (Cynosurus).*
SIMILAR SPECIES *Chequered Skipper (above).*
STATUS *Widespread and locally fairly common in suitable habitats.*

Lulworth Skipper

Thymelicus acteon (Hesperiidae)

This active little grassland butterfly basks with its forewings slightly raised at an angle. The ground colour of the wings is typically olive-brown and males in particular show a suffusion of yellowish scales and a black line on the forewing. A "paw-print" shape of yellowish spots on the forewing upperside is more obvious in females than males.

FOUND *on rough, grassy slopes and in meadows from sea level to 1,500m.*

suffusion of yellow

yellow spots

olive-brown ground colour

up to 2.5cm long

♂●

WINGSPAN *2.5cm.*
FLIGHT PERIOD *May–July.*
LARVAL FOODPLANT *Grasses (Poaceae), notably false brome (Brachypodium).*
SIMILAR SPECIES *Essex Skipper (below), Small Skipper (right).*
STATUS *Widespread and fairly common, but local in the north of its range.*

Essex Skipper

Thymelicus lineola (Hesperiidae)

The bright orange-brown wings of the Essex Skipper catch the eye, both when it is resting and when in fast flight. The male has a small black line on its upper forewings. Very similar to the Small Skipper (right), it can be identified by its antennal club, which is black and not orange-brown as in its relative.

FAVOURS *inland meadows, roadside verges, and coastal grassland, from sea level to 2,000m.*

antennal club black below

♂●

♀●

wings lack dark line

dark margin

orange-brown wings

up to 2.5cm long

WINGSPAN *2.5cm.*
FLIGHT PERIOD *May–August.*
LARVAL FOODPLANT *Various grasses (family Poaceae).*
SIMILAR SPECIES *Lulworth Skipper (above), Small Skipper (right).*
STATUS *Widespread and generally common throughout most of its range.*

Small Skipper

Thymelicus sylvestris (Hesperiidae)

One of the most widespread and numerous butterflies in the region, the Small Skipper's colourful and rather uniform orange-brown wings are a useful clue to its identity. However, it is easily confused with the very similar Essex Skipper (left), although in this species the antennal club is black underneath, whereas in the Small Skipper it is orange-brown. It usually sunbathes with its forewings slightly elevated and angled, the manner adopted by many other Skippers.

INHABITS *all kinds of grassy places, from roadside verges and grassy lowland meadows, to lower mountain slopes up to 2,000m.*

NOTE

The male Small Skipper has a longer and more striking black line on the upperside of its forewing (sex-brand) than the male Essex Skipper. However, to distinguish females, look for the orange-brown, and not black, underside of the antennal club.

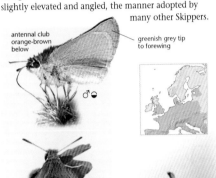

antennal club orange-brown below

greenish grey tip to forewing

♂

♀

lacks the dark male sex-brand

up to 2.5cm long

black line or sex-brand

narrow dark margin

♂

WINGSPAN 2.5cm.
FLIGHT PERIOD *May–September.*
LARVAL FOODPLANT *Various meadow species of grasses (family Poaceae).*
SIMILAR SPECIES *Lulworth Skipper (left), which has a "paw-print" of yellowish spots on its upper wings; Essex Skipper, females in particular (left).*
STATUS *Widespread and generally very common.*

Large Skipper

Ochlodes venata (Hesperiidae)

This familiar grassland butterfly has rich colours and markings on its upperwings. Like other members of the Skipper family, the male has a conspicuous sex-brand in the form of a dark line on the forewing. It generally has brighter colours than the otherwise similar female. The underwings of both sexes are yellowish with a variable suffusion of greenish scaling, and faint pale spots. Large Skippers visit flowers to feed on nectar and typically alight on them with their forewings swept back and elevated at an angle.

FAVOURS *a wide range of grassy habitats from meadows and open scrub to woodland and hedgerow margins; also hillsides up to 2,000m.*

rich ground colour

sex-brand on forewing

♂●

yellow-brown ground colour

●

dark veins

dark margin

pale yellow spots

dull ground colour

♀●

up to 3cm long

NOTE

This species has the buzzing, almost moth-like flight that is so characteristic of Skipper butterflies. At rest the wings are held open, and at an angle, in the manner of many other Skippers. This enables the observer to view both the upper and lower wing surfaces with ease.

WINGSPAN *2.8–3cm.*
FLIGHT PERIOD *May–September.*
LARVAL FOODPLANT *Various grasses (family Poaceae) including fescue (Festuca).*
SIMILAR SPECIES *Silver-spotted Skipper (right), which has silvery white spots on the underside hindwings.*
STATUS *Widespread and generally common throughout its extensive range in the region.*

Silver-spotted Skipper

Hesperia comma (Hesperiidae)

This species is easily recognized by the silvery white spots
that adorn the greenish yellow underside of the hindwings.
The orange-brown upperwings are also striking.
Active on sunny days, it spends much of its
time feeding on flowers or
sunbathing, so close-up
views are often possible.

RESTRICTED *to sparse
chalky grassland, from
sand dunes at sea level
to downland up to
2,000m.*

orange-brown
ground colour

yellow spots

dark
sex-brand

forewings
lack male
sex-brand

up to 3cm long

WINGSPAN 2.5–3cm.
FLIGHT PERIOD July–August.
LARVAL FOODPLANT A limited range of
grass species, notably fescue (Festuca) and
meadow grass (Poa).
SIMILAR SPECIES Large Skipper (left).
STATUS Widespread but extremely local
because of its precise habitat requirements.

Large Heath

Coenonympha tullia (Satyridae)

The Large Heath's upperwings are usually glimpsed only
momentarily, because they are never revealed by
individuals at rest. The underwings show orange-brown
on the forewing and are greyish on the hindwing. Active
in calm, sunny weather, at other times it hides among
grassy tussocks. This is an extremely variable species with
the forewing eyespots absent in some subspecies.

ASSOCIATED *with
moors, bogs, and
waterlogged grassland,
from sea level to
around 2,000m.*

grey margin

dark
eyespots

jagged
pale
band

orange-buff
ground colour

orange-brown
forewing

up to 2.5cm long

WINGSPAN 3.8–4cm.
FLIGHT PERIOD June–July.
LARVAL FOODPLANT Cotton grass
(Eriophorum) and white-beaked sedge
(Rhynchospora alba).
SIMILAR SPECIES Small Heath (p.97).
STATUS Widespread in upland areas but
typically rather local.

Wall Brown

Pararge megera (Satyridae)

The boldly patterned upperwings of the Wall Brown, with an orange ground colour, network of dark veins, and prominent eyespots, make it a comparatively easy species to identify. It sunbathes frequently, and so observers can usually obtain excellent close-up views with a little patience. The underside of the hindwings has a cryptic pattern that resembles tree bark or mottled stone. When the Wall Brown rests with its wings closed, the hindwings often cover the more colourful forewings and provide the butterfly with good camouflage.

FAVOURS *dry, grassy heaths, hillsides, and cliffs, typically with rocks and bare areas for sunbathing; occurs from sea level to around 2,000m.*

oblique dark band on forewing

large eyespot

orange ground colour

network of dark veins

♂

orange-buff forewing ♂

grey-brown marbled hindwing

row of eyespots on hindwings

orange ground colour

♀

up to 2.5cm long

NOTE

The Wall Brown could be confused with the southern form of the Speckled Wood (p.143). However, the latter has a brown ground colour with orange markings, and its forewings are more pointed, while its hindwings have a jagged edge.

WINGSPAN *4.5cm.*
FLIGHT PERIOD *May–September, in successive broods.*
LARVAL FOODPLANT *Grasses (Poaceae).*
SIMILAR SPECIES *Large Wall Brown (right), Northern Wall Brown (right), Speckled Wood (p.143).*
STATUS *Widespread but declining.*

Large Wall Brown

Pararge maera (Satyridae)

This species differs across its extensive range: the orange markings on its upperwings are darker in southern forms compared to those from the north. A single eyespot on the forewings, and two or three eyespots on the hindwings, remain constant features in all the forms. Underneath, the forewings of all individuals are orange, while the hindwings are marbled grey-brown.

FOUND *in rough grassland with plenty of bare, often rocky, areas; from sea level to around 2,000m.*

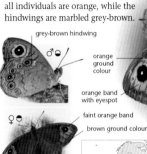

grey-brown hindwing

♂ ⬤▱

orange ground colour

orange band with eyespot

faint orange band

brown ground colour

♀ ⬤

brown wing base

♀ ⬤

SOUTHERN FORM

SCANDINAVIAN FORM

up to 3cm long

WINGSPAN *4.5–5cm.*
FLIGHT PERIOD *June–August.*
LARVAL FOODPLANT *Various grasses (family Poaceae).*
SIMILAR SPECIES *Wall Brown (left), Northern Wall Brown (below).*
STATUS *Widespread and locally fairly common.*

Northern Wall Brown

Pararge petropolitana (Satyridae)

This northern upland species is often found basking in the sun on bare ground. Both its brown upperwings have eyespots contained within orange bands, which are much more extensive in females than males. Underneath, the extent of orange on the forewing is greater in females, but both sexes have a striking forewing eyespot.

OCCURS *in rough grassland with areas of bare ground, up to 2,000m in southern mountains but at low levels in the north.*

large eyespot on forewing

♂ ⬤▱

brown ground colour

orange band with eyespot

♂ ⬤

up to 2.5cm long

6 yellow-ringed eyespots on hindwing

WINGSPAN *3.8–4.2cm.*
FLIGHT PERIOD *May–July.*
LARVAL FOODPLANT *Various grasses (family Poaceae), especially fescue (Festuca).*
SIMILAR SPECIES *Wall Brown (left), Large Wall Brown (above).*
STATUS *Widespread and fairly common in the north, but local in the south.*

Norse Grayling

Oeneis norna (Satyridae)

FLIES over rough, grassy moors and along clearings and margins of open woodland, typically at low altitudes.

At rest, the Norse Grayling closes its wings and seldom, if ever, reveals the upper surface. Consequently, it can be difficult to spot because the underside of the hindwing, which often cloaks the forewing, is marbled grey-brown, with cryptic markings that closely resemble the rocks on which it alights.

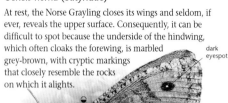

dark eyespot

pale band with eyespots

pale buff forewing

pale band

up to 3cm long

grey-brown hindwing

WINGSPAN 6cm.
FLIGHT PERIOD June–July.
LARVAL FOODPLANT Various grasses (family Poaceae).
SIMILAR SPECIES Alpine Grayling (below), and Baltic Grayling (right), both of which have different geographical ranges.
STATUS Locally common.

Alpine Grayling

Oeneis glacialis (Satyridae)

RESTRICTED to grassy, rocky mountain slopes, typically at altitudes of 1,500m but occasionally up to the tree line.

This hardy species is restricted to upland regions, mainly in the French and Italian Alps. In both sexes, the under surface of the hindwing is marbled grey-brown and resembles the texture of rock. By contrast, the remaining wing surfaces are mainly brownish in colour, paler in females than males.

brown ground colour

♂

broad, sandy buff band

sandy buff forewing

♀

dark eyespot

sandy-buff ground colour

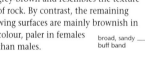

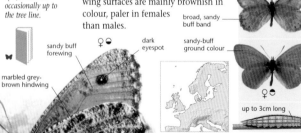

marbled grey-brown hindwing

♀

up to 3cm long

WINGSPAN 5cm.
FLIGHT PERIOD June–July.
LARVAL FOODPLANT Various grasses, notably Sheep's fescue (Festuca ovina).
SIMILAR SPECIES Norse Grayling (above), which has an entirely separate range.
STATUS Extremely local, but fairly common where it does occur.

Baltic Grayling

Oeneis jutta (Satyridae)

Although its precise colour is variable, the Baltic Grayling is typically dark brown. The underside of the hindwing has subtle, cryptic marbling, affording the butterfly excellent camouflage when resting with its wings closed. The upperwings have a buff band in which eyespots are located; however, they are seldom revealed in life.

RESTRICTED *to moors and open woodlands with rather sparse vegetation.*

buff-ringed eyespot

grey-brown marbling

♂⬤

dark sex-brand

variable buff band

♀⬤

up to 3cm long

WINGSPAN *5.5–6cm.*
FLIGHT PERIOD *June–August.*
LARVAL FOODPLANT *Various grasses (family Poaceae).*
SIMILAR SPECIES *Norse Grayling (left), which has a pale band on the hindwing underside.*
STATUS *Locally fairly common within its distinctly northern range.*

False Grayling

Hipparchia arethusa (Satyridae)

The False Grayling is difficult to spot until it flies, since its underside hindwings camouflage it on the rocks on which it rests. The buffish orange underside forewing has a single eyespot while the brown upperwings, which are seldom seen in life, show a broken orange-buff band. Females are more colourful than males.

FAVOURS *dry, free-draining grassy places, typically on chalky soils, from sea level to around 1,500m.*

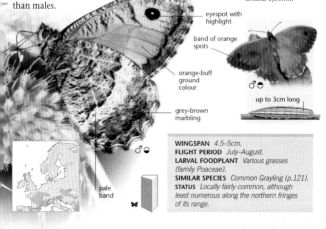

eyespot with highlight

band of orange spots

orange-buff ground colour

grey-brown marbling

♂⬤

up to 3cm long

pale band

WINGSPAN *4.5–5cm.*
FLIGHT PERIOD *July–August.*
LARVAL FOODPLANT *Various grasses (family Poaceae).*
SIMILAR SPECIES *Common Grayling (p.121).*
STATUS *Locally fairly common, although least numerous along the northern fringes of its range.*

Meadow Brown

Maniola jurtina (Satyridae)

FOUND *in a variety of grassy places, from meadows and roadside verges to woodland rides and hillsides up to 1,500m or more.*

This is probably the most numerous and widespread grassland butterfly species in the region. The underwings are most commonly seen: the forewing coloured orange and buff with a striking eyespot, and the brown hindwing with a paler band containing small black spots. Unlike many of its relatives, the Meadow Brown occasionally reveals its upperwings in the field. These are a rich brown colour with a patch of orange on the forewing, which contains an eyespot; the orange is more extensive in females than males.

orange forewings

♂ ⊖

buff band with black spots

eyespot on orange band

♀ ⊖

up to 2.5cm long

eyespot on faint orange-buff patch

♂ ⊖

brown ground colour

WINGSPAN *5cm.*
FLIGHT PERIOD *June–October.*
LARVAL FOODPLANT *Various grasses (family Poaceae).*
SIMILAR SPECIES *Dusky Meadow Brown (right).*
STATUS *Widespread and locally very common.*

Dusky Meadow Brown

Maniola lycaon (Satyridae)

Although superficially similar to the Meadow Brown (left), this species is identifiable with care. This is particularly so with females, where the mainly orange upper surface of the forewing is marked by two eyespots that are "blind" or have no highlights. In males, the dull orange forewings are marked by a sex-brand in the form of an oblique brown line.

FAVOURS *dry, grassy areas with rather sparse vegetation, from sea level to around 2,000m.*

single eyespot

dull orange forewings

♂●

oblique brown line

grey-brown hindwings

♂●

twin eyespots

♀●

up to 2.5cm long

WINGSPAN *4.5cm.*
FLIGHT PERIOD *July–October.*
LARVAL FOODPLANT *Various grasses (family Poaceae).*
SIMILAR SPECIES *Meadow Brown (left), both sexes of which have a single eyespot within an orange patch on the forewing.*
STATUS *Locally common.*

Woodland Brown

Pararge achine (Satyridae)

This butterfly's rich brown ground colour serves to emphasize the large, yellow-ringed black eyespots on both upper and lower surfaces of the wings. A white band runs along the row of eyespots on the hindwing under surface. This comparatively lethargic species often basks in woodland clearings.

FLIES *along grassy rides and clearings in woodland, from sea level to at least 1,000m.*

♂●

crescent of yellow-ringed black eyespots

rich brown ground colour

concentric yellow lines

pale line

♀●

WINGSPAN *5cm.*
FLIGHT PERIOD *June–July.*
LARVAL FOODPLANT *Various grasses (family Poaceae).*
SIMILAR SPECIES *None.*
STATUS *Locally fairly common, but populations tend to be isolated and rather widely separated from one another.*

up to 3cm long

Grizzled Skipper

Pyrgus malvae (Hesperiidae)

INHABITS *grassy heaths, woodland margins, and clearings; often found along tracks where foodplants flourish.*

Although it is a small butterfly, the Grizzled Skipper makes up for what it lacks in terms of size with the beautiful patterning on its wings. The upper surfaces are a rich brown colour, adorned with an intricate pattern of squarish pale spots. Fortunately, the butterfly frequently sunbathes with its wings open and spread out, giving observers plenty of opportunity to study them. The underwing ground colour is yellowish brown with a pattern of whitish spots similar to that seen on the upper surfaces of the wings.

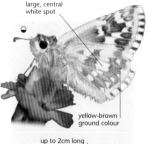

large, central white spot

yellow-brown ground colour

up to 2cm long

NOTE

The combination of its small size and the presence of squarish spots of rather uniform size and intensity across the upperwings are useful identification clues. Look also for the arc of pale spots on the upperside hindwing and the large central pale spot on the underside.

squarish pale spots

rich brown ground colour

crescent of pale spots

WINGSPAN *2cm.*
FLIGHT PERIOD *April–June, with a second brood in July–August in the south.*
LARVAL FOODPLANT *Wild strawberry (Fragaria vesca) and cinquefoil (Potentilla).*
SIMILAR SPECIES *Large Grizzled Skipper (right), Oberthür's Grizzled Skipper (right), Mother Shipton (p.189).*
STATUS *Locally common.*

Large Grizzled Skipper

Pyrgus alveus (Hesperiidae)

Compared to its superficially similar relatives, this species shows only a small number of small whitish spots on its upperwings and sometimes the hindwing is almost unmarked. Another useful identification feature can be found on the underside of the hindwing: a white band runs from the middle of the leading edge to the centre of the wing.

ASSOCIATED *with areas of flower-rich upland grassland, usually between 1,000m and 2,000m.*

grey-brown ground colour

♂

small white spots on forewing

faint white patches on hindwing

white band on hindwing

♀

up to 2.5cm long

WINGSPAN *3cm.*
FLIGHT PERIOD *June–August.*
LARVAL FOODPLANT *Rock-rose (Helianthemum), cinquefoil (Potentilla) and wild strawberry (Fragaria vesca).*
SIMILAR SPECIES *Grizzled Skipper (left), Oberthür's Grizzled Skipper (below).*
STATUS *Widespread and locally common.*

Oberthür's Grizzled Skipper

Pyrgus armoricanus (Hesperiidae)

This well-marked species is similar to, but larger than, the Grizzled Skipper (left). The white spots on the upperwing are bright but less intense and smaller than those of its relative. The spots are of similar intensity and density on both forewing and hindwing, which helps to distinguish it from the Large Grizzled Skipper (above).

FAVOURS *warm, dry, and flowery slopes and grassy meadows, usually below 1,500m.*

green-brown colour

grey-brown ground colour

small white spots

up to 2cm long

WINGSPAN *3cm.*
FLIGHT PERIOD *May–August, in two broods.*
LARVAL FOODPLANT *Rock-rose (Helianthemum), cinquefoil (Potentilla) and wild strawberry (Fragaria vesca).*
SIMILAR SPECIES *Grizzled Skipper (left), Large Grizzled Skipper (above).*
STATUS *Widespread and locally common.*

Olive Skipper

Pyrgus serratulae (Hesperiidae)

The Olive Skipper has a preference for upland areas. Although similar to many other Skippers, the limited extent of white spotting on the upperwings and greenish yellow colour to the underside of the hindwing are both useful pointers in identification. The sexes look alike although females typically have more of a yellowish tinge to the upperwings than males.

ASSOCIATED *with upland meadows and flowery slopes, around 1,500–2,000m, but sometimes higher.*

dark brown ground colour

small white spots on forewing

greenish yellow ground colour

chequered fringe

Caterpillar not sufficiently known

few pale spots on hindwing

WINGSPAN *2.5cm.*
FLIGHT PERIOD *May–August.*
LARVAL FOODPLANT *Lady's-mantle (Alchemilla), cinquefoil (Potentilla).*
SIMILAR SPECIES *Large Grizzled Skipper (p.113), Carline Skipper (below), Safflower Skipper (right), Sage Skipper (p.117).*
STATUS *Locally common.*

Carline Skipper

Pyrgus carlinae (Hesperiidae)

This active little upland butterfly is superficially similar to the Olive Skipper (above). However, the reddish brown, and not greenish yellow, ground colour of the hindwing underside is a good distinguishing feature of the two species. The sexes are broadly similar but females tend to have fewer pale spots on the upperwings than males, and a paler ground colour.

FAVOURS *flowery and grassy hill slopes; also alpine meadows up to 2,000m or more.*

additional white spots

small white spots

reddish brown ground colour

Caterpillar not sufficiently known

WINGSPAN *3cm.*
FLIGHT PERIOD *July–August.*
LARVAL FOODPLANT *Spring cinquefoil (Potentilla neumanniana).*
SIMILAR SPECIES *Olive Skipper (above), Rosy Grizzled Skipper (right), Safflower Skipper (right).*
STATUS *Widespread and locally common.*

Rosy Grizzled Skipper

Pyrgus onopordi (Hesperiidae)

This species is readily confused with other Grizzled Skippers, but close attention to the extent and shape of the white markings should ensure accurate identification. Well-defined white spots on the upperwings and the presence of a relatively large, "waisted" and jagged-edged white patch on the underside of the hindwing are both useful pointers.

FREQUENTS *warm, dry meadows and grassy slopes with plenty of flowers, below 1,000m.*

well-defined white spots

large white patch on hindwing

Caterpillar not sufficiently known

chequered edge

sooty brown ground colour

WINGSPAN *3cm.*
FLIGHT PERIOD *May–October, in two broods.*
LARVAL FOODPLANT *Cinquefoils (Potentilla) and similar plants.*
SIMILAR SPECIES *Carline Skipper (left).*
STATUS *Locally common within its distinctly southern range.*

Safflower Skipper

Pyrgus carthami (Hesperiidae)

Close attention to detail is needed to ensure accurate identification of this species. The white spots on the upper surface of the forewing are particularly noticeable but the most reliable features are found on the underside of the hindwing – typically, the white markings linked to form a pale marginal band, sometimes with two additional irregular bands across the middle of the wing.

FOUND *in a wide range of sunny, flower-rich grassy habitats from low levels to 2,000m.*

grey-brown ground colour

well-formed white spots

linked white spots

pale spots form indistinct band

Caterpillar not sufficiently known

WINGSPAN *3–3.2cm.*
FLIGHT PERIOD *July–September.*
LARVAL FOODPLANT *Cinquefoil (Potentilla), mallow (Malva), safflower (Carthamus tinctorius).*
SIMILAR SPECIES *Olive Skipper (left), Carline Skipper (left).*
STATUS *Widespread and locally common.*

Alpine Grizzled Skipper

Pyrgus andromedae (Hesperiidae)

This active species is restricted to alpine habitats. To identify it, observers should look for a line of three small white spots towards the trailing edge of each forewing upperside, in addition to other white spots present on this surface. There are several large pale spots on the hindwing underside, which are greenish brown; the forewing undersides are blackish brown.

RESTRICTED *to flowery mountain slopes, above 1,500m in the south, but at much lower altitudes in Scandinavia.*

sooty brown ground colour

well-defined white spots

chequered fringe

large pale spots

greenish brown hindwing

Caterpillar not sufficiently known

> **WINGSPAN** *3cm.*
> **FLIGHT PERIOD** *June–July.*
> **LARVAL FOODPLANT** *Cinquefoil (Potentilla) and lady's mantle (Alchemilla).*
> **SIMILAR SPECIES** *Northern Grizzled Skipper (below), Dusky Grizzled Skipper (right).*
> **STATUS** *Locally fairly common in its restricted habitat.*

Northern Grizzled Skipper

Pyrgus centaurae (Hesperiidae)

This butterfly's northerly range excludes it from being confused with other similar species. It has prominent white spots on the upper surfaces of both the forewing and the hindwing. However, observers should look closely at the under surface of the hindwing too: the ground colour is extremely dark with contrasting whitish veins and large white spots.

FLIES *over damp moorland, from sea level to lower mountain slopes, the altitude decreasing with greater latitude.*

sooty brown ground colour

white spots and veins

up to 2cm long

white spots

> **WINGSPAN** *3cm.*
> **FLIGHT PERIOD** *June–July.*
> **LARVAL FOODPLANT** *Cloudberry (Rubus chamaemorus).*
> **SIMILAR SPECIES** *Alpine Grizzled Skipper (above).*
> **STATUS** *Locally fairly common in its restricted northern range.*

Dusky Grizzled Skipper

Pyrgus cacaliae (Hesperiidae)

The upperwings of this alpine species are dusky grey-brown with only a few small white spots, which are confined to the forewings. On the underside, the ground colour is similarly dusky, the hindwings are marked with large white spots with indistinct margins. The wings have a pale chequered border.

LIMITED *to upland slopes with sparse vegetation, typically above 1,500m and mainly in the Alps.*

few, small
white spots

♂●

dusky grey-brown
ground colour

small white spots
on forewing

♀●

large, hazy white
spots on hindwing

*Caterpillar not
sufficiently known*

WINGSPAN *3cm.*
FLIGHT PERIOD *July–August.*
LARVAL FOODPLANT *Cinquefoil (Potentilla) and sibbaldia (Sibbaldia procumbens).*
SIMILAR SPECIES *Alpine Grizzled Skipper (left).*
STATUS *Extremely local due to its precise habitat requirements.*

Sage Skipper

Muschampia proto (Hesperiidae)

The grey-brown upperwings of the Sage Skipper have a few scattered white spots, which can be rather indistinct on the hindwing in some specimens. Below, the forewing is marked with white spots and white veins that are emphasized by an adjacent dark patch. The male upperwings are coated with subtle yellow scaling.

ASSOCIATED *with flowery Mediterranean habitats, typically on sunny hillsides and lower mountain slopes.*

grey-brown
ground colour

yellow scaling

♂●

white veins
and spots

♂●

few white spots

WINGSPAN *3cm.*
FLIGHT PERIOD *April–August in one brood.*
LARVAL FOODPLANT *Sage (Salvia) and Jerusalem sage (Phlomis).*
SIMILAR SPECIES *Olive Skipper (p.114), which does not have white veins on the hindwing underside.*
STATUS *Locally common.*

*Caterpillar not
sufficiently known*

Mallow Skipper

Carcharodus alceae (Hesperiidae)

FOUND *on waysides and flowery grassland, also on sunny hillside slopes between 1,000m and 1,500m.*

The upperwing pattern, marbled with buffish pink, grey, and sooty brown, gives this species an almost moth-like appearance. The grey-brown underwings are adorned with white spots that, on the hindwing, are typically arranged in the form of irregular crescents. However, the intensity of colour on both surfaces of the wings is variable.

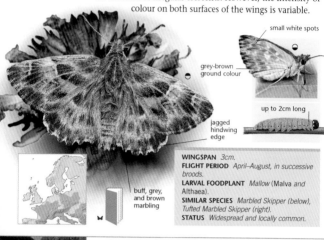

small white spots

grey-brown
ground colour

up to 2cm long

jagged
hindwing
edge

buff, grey,
and brown
marbling

WINGSPAN *3cm.*
FLIGHT PERIOD *April–August, in successive broods.*
LARVAL FOODPLANT *Mallow (Malva and Althaea).*
SIMILAR SPECIES *Marbled Skipper (below), Tufted Marbled Skipper (right).*
STATUS *Widespread and locally common.*

Marbled Skipper

Carcharodus lavatherae (Hesperiidae)

FAVOURS *sunny, dry slopes in upland limestone grassland, at altitudes between 1,000m and 1,500m.*

Although older, worn specimens of the Marbled Skipper can look distinctly pale, on newly emerged insects, the upperwings are patterned with a subtle yet beautiful marbling of brown, grey, and white. There is often a suffusion of yellowish scales, sometimes giving a pale and rather dusty look.

pale
greenish
grey

*Caterpillar not
sufficiently known*

marbled
grey, brown,
and white

yellow-olive
suffusion

white
spots

jagged
hindwing
edge

WINGSPAN *3.2cm.*
FLIGHT PERIOD *May–August, in successive broods.*
LARVAL FOODPLANT *Woundwort (Stachys) and related plants.*
SIMILAR SPECIES *Mallow Skipper (above).*
STATUS *Widespread but distinctly local, with a definitely southern distribution.*

Tufted Marbled Skipper

Carcharodus flocciferus (Hesperiidae)

This well-marked butterfly has darkish brown upperwings, adorned with a delicate marbling of grey and buff-brown and highlighted with small white spots. At rest, with its wings partly spread, it has a rather moth-like appearance. A close inspection of the underside of the male reveals a tuft of dark hairs on the forewing.

FREQUENTS *dry, flower-rich grassland; typically associated with hills and lower mountain slopes at around 1,500m or higher.*

greenish grey hindwing

Caterpillar not sufficiently known

marbled brown and grey

white spots

scalloped edge

WINGSPAN *3cm.*
FLIGHT PERIOD *May–August.*
LARVAL FOODPLANT *Woundwort (Stachys) and horehound (Marrubium).*
SIMILAR SPECIES *Mallow Skipper (left), which lacks white spots on its upperwings.*
STATUS *Widespread and locally common, given its preference for upland habitats.*

Red-underwing Skipper

Spialia sertorius (Hesperiidae)

As Skippers go, this tiny little butterfly is rather distinctive, although its size and the patterns on its wings vary across its geographical range. The most noticeable feature is the reddish underwings – the hindwings are particularly striking, with their rich red-brown ground colour offset by bold white spots.

INHABITS *a wide range of grassy and scrubby habitats, from sea level to 2,000m in the south.*

scattered white spots

reddish brown ground colour

dark brown ground colour

marginal white spots

♀♂

up to 2cm long

WINGSPAN *2–2.5cm.*
FLIGHT PERIOD *April–August.*
LARVAL FOODPLANT *Cinquefoil (Potentilla) and bramble (Rubus fruticosus) and related plants.*
SIMILAR SPECIES *None.*
STATUS *Widespread and locally common across S. and C. Europe.*

Dingy Skipper

Erynnis tages (Hesperiidae)

Although the Dingy Skipper may appear rather nondescript, its uniformly dark brown upperwings and pale brown underwings, when taken together, are unique and have diagnostic features: there are few butterflies with which it could be confused. However, observers should be aware that the buzzing flight and undeniably sombre appearance of this small butterfly do give it a distinctly moth-like appearance.

FOUND *in grasslands with plenty of flowers, often on chalky soils, from sea level to around 2,000m.*

indistinct, pale and dark bands

pale brown ground colour

faint pale spots

small, faint marginal spots

up to 2cm long

WINGSPAN *2.5cm.*
FLIGHT PERIOD *May–August.*
LARVAL FOODPLANT *Trefoil (Lotus), Crown vetch (Coronilla), and related plants in the pea family.*
SIMILAR SPECIES *None.*
STATUS *Widespread and locally common, although declining due to habitat loss.*

Tree Grayling

Hipparchia statilinus (Satyridae)

At rest among leaf litter or on tree bark, the Tree Grayling is hard to detect because the underside of its hindwings – often the only surface visible – so perfectly matches its surroundings. When disturbed, the butterfly may raise its forewings slightly to reveal the larger of two yellow-ringed eyespots. The upperwings are almost never revealed at rest.

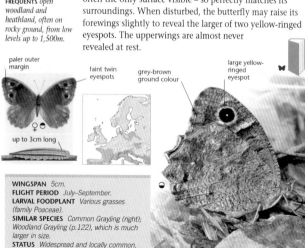

FREQUENTS *open woodland and heathland, often on rocky ground, from low levels up to 1,500m.*

paler outer margin

faint twin eyespots

grey-brown ground colour

large yellow-ringed eyespot

♀ ♂

up to 3cm long

WINGSPAN *5cm.*
FLIGHT PERIOD *July–September.*
LARVAL FOODPLANT *Various grasses (family Poaceae).*
SIMILAR SPECIES *Common Grayling (right); Woodland Grayling (p.122), which is much larger in size.*
STATUS *Widespread and locally common.*

Common Grayling

Hipparchia semele (Satyridae)

This sun-loving butterfly is usually found perched on bare patches of ground or on rocks. Although it is well marked with two prominent eyespots on the forewings, the Common Grayling can be difficult to spot since it rests with its wings angled so that they cast the least shadow. Furthermore, unless alarmed, the forewing undersides are often hidden by the hindwings, whose cryptic pattern affords the butterfly wonderful camouflage. The Common Grayling's upperwings are almost never revealed to observers.

FAVOURS *dry, sunny habitats including heaths, rocky slopes, and cliffs; occurs from sea level to lower mountain slopes.*

— two eyespots

♂●

marbled grey-brown ground colour

irregular whitish band

♂● — limited pale markings

— band of broad pale spots

♀● — variable buff-orange band

— up to 3cm long

NOTE

If you want to get a close-up view of a Common Grayling, crawl towards the butterfly at ground level to avoid casting a shadow over it, as this is almost guaranteed to make it fly off.

WINGSPAN *5cm.*
FLIGHT PERIOD *June–August.*
LARVAL FOODPLANT *Various grasses (family Poaceae).*
SIMILAR SPECIES *Tree Grayling (left), which has a large yellow-ringed eyespot on the forewing underside.*
STATUS *Widespread and locally common.*

The Hermit

Hipparchia briseis (Satyridae)

Keen eyesight is needed to catch a glimpse of this species' white-banded dark upperwing pattern in flight since this wing surface is never revealed when the butterfly is at rest. However, the marbled grey-brown underwings are also well marked, with a bold pattern of whitish buff and dark brown bands, and twin eyespots on the forewings.

ASSOCIATED *with dry, grassy and rocky areas with bare patches for sunbathing, from sea level to over 1,500m.*

pale buffish white central band

marbled grey-brown ground colour

sooty, dark brown ground colour

up to 3cm long

WINGSPAN *5–6cm.*
FLIGHT PERIOD *June–July.*
LARVAL FOODPLANT *Various grasses (family Poaceae).*
SIMILAR SPECIES *Striped Grayling (right), which has jagged, black and white stripes on the hindwing underside.*
STATUS *Widespread and locally common.*

Woodland Grayling

Hipparchia fagi (Satyridae)

Despite its large size, the Woodland Grayling can be difficult to spot at rest since the grey-brown marbling on its hindwing underside affords it excellent camouflage among leaf litter. Its upperwings are sooty brown with a broad pale band across both the wings. This band is indistinct with a single eyespot in males, and clear with twin eyespots on females.

LIVES *in open woodland and areas of dry, sunny scrub, typically at altitudes below 1,000m.*

white band

♂

up to 3.5cm long

sooty brown ground colour

♀

2 eyespots on forewing (1 in male)

WINGSPAN *7cm.*
FLIGHT PERIOD *July–August.*
LARVAL FOODPLANT *Various grasses (family Poaceae).*
SIMILAR SPECIES *Tree Grayling (p.120); Rock Grayling (right), which is smaller in size and is found at higher altitudes.*
STATUS *Widespread and locally common.*

Rock Grayling

Hipparchia alcyone (Satyridae)

At first glance, this butterfly appears very similar to the Woodland Grayling (left). However, it is smaller in size and occurs at higher altitudes than its relative. The bold upperwing pattern can be glimpsed in flight, but the only prolonged view that can be obtained is of the underwings: the hindwings are marbled grey-brown, while the forewings are sooty brown with grey tips.

FAVOURS *rocky ground and lower mountain slopes with scattered trees, between 1,000m and 2,000m.*

1 eyespot within pale band (2 in female)

♂♀

brown ground colour

♂♀

white band

up to 3.5cm long

irregular broad whitish band

WINGSPAN *6cm.*
FLIGHT PERIOD *June–July.*
LARVAL FOODPLANT *Various grasses (family Poaceae).*
SIMILAR SPECIES *Woodland Grayling (left), which has a darker ground colour and more prominent white bands on the upperwings.*
STATUS *Widespread and locally common.*

Striped Grayling

Hipparchia fidia (Satyridae)

The rather uniform dark brown upperwings of the Striped Grayling provide comparatively few clues to its identity, and are almost never revealed by resting individuals. However, the boldly striped underwings and twin yellow-ringed eyespots on the forewings are easier to observe in the field.

FOUND *on warm, rocky, and grassy slopes with a Mediterranean climate, typically between 1,000m and 2,000m.*

yellow-ringed eyespots

2 eyespots

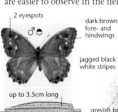

♂♀

dark brown fore- and hindwings

jagged black and white stripes

up to 3.5cm long

greyish brown hindwings

WINGSPAN *6cm.*
FLIGHT PERIOD *July–August.*
LARVAL FOODPLANT *Various grasses (family Poaceae).*
SIMILAR SPECIES *The Hermit (left), which has more subdued underwings, with small eyespots in a pale band on the forewing underside.*
STATUS *Locally common.*

Brown Argus

Aricia agestis (Lycaenidae)

FAVOURS free-draining, dry grassland areas, seeming equally at home on chalky or slightly acidic soils.

At first glance, the Brown Argus could be mistaken for a female Common Blue (p.30). However, the species is quite distinctive, the rich brown upperwings being adorned with bright orange crescent-shaped spots around the white-fringed margins. On the underwings, which are grey-brown, there are orange spots arranged in a pattern similar to that seen on the upperwings.

dark spots

white streak

up to 1.5cm long

rich brown ground colour

dark central spot

white fringe

submarginal row of orange spots

WINGSPAN *2.5cm.*
FLIGHT PERIOD *May–August, in successive broods.*
LARVAL FOODPLANT *Rock-rose (Helianthemum) and stork's bill (Erodium).*
SIMILAR SPECIES *Common Blue, female (p.30), Mountain Argus (below).*
STATUS *Widespread and locally common.*

Mountain Argus

Aricia artaxerxes (Lycaenidae)

ASSOCIATED with flower-rich, chalky grassland in upland areas between 1,000m and 2,000m.

To distinguish this species from the Brown Argus (above), look at the orange spots on the upperwings. Those of the Mountain (Northern Brown) Argus are small and are either absent or very faint on the forewing. Individuals from northern Britain often have a distinct white spot on the upper forewing.

dark spots

up to 1.5cm long

dark brown ground colour

submarginal row of small orange spots

WINGSPAN *2.5cm.*
FLIGHT PERIOD *June–July.*
LARVAL FOODPLANT *Rock-rose (Helianthemum).*
SIMILAR SPECIES *Common Blue, female (p.30), Brown Argus (above).*
STATUS *Locally common but widely scattered populations.*

Geranium Argus

Aricia eumedon (Lycaenidae)

This rather nondescript butterfly may be mistaken at first for females of several species of Blue butterflies, if the observer sees only the upperwings or the underwings, and not both. The Geranium Argus' upperwings are mainly brown, sometimes with a hint of blue at the wing base, and the underwings are pale grey, dotted with small dark spots.

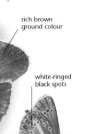

RESTRICTED *to grassy areas where the larval foodplant occurs, both at low levels and in mountains; prefers upland areas.*

rich brown ground colour

white-ringed black spots

hint of blue

pale fringe

up to 1.5cm long

WINGSPAN *3cm.*
FLIGHT PERIOD *June–August.*
LARVAL FOODPLANT *Wood cranesbill (Geranium sylvaticum) and other geranium species.*
SIMILAR SPECIES *Mountain Argus (left), Ripart's Anomalous Blue (below).*
STATUS *Fairly common, in east of range.*

Ripart's Anomalous Blue

Polyommatus ripartii (Lycaenidae)

The upperwings of this active little butterfly are a uniform dark brown and this gives the species a superficial resemblance to the females of several species of the Blue butterflies. Fortunately, there is a bold diagnostic white stripe on the grey-brown underside of the hindwing. This runs almost from the base of the wing to the margin.

dark brown ground colour

FOUND *on flower-rich, sunny slopes with a Mediterranean climate, usually below 1,000m.*

dark buff fringe

small black spots

white stripe

Caterpillar not sufficiently known

WINGSPAN *3.5cm.*
FLIGHT PERIOD *June–August.*
LARVAL FOODPLANT *Sainfoin (Onobrychis).*
SIMILAR SPECIES *Damon Blue, female (p.35), Geranium Argus (above).*
STATUS *Locally common, within its restricted southerly range.*

Brown Hairstreak

Thecla betulae (Lycaenidae)

The underwings of the Brown Hairstreak are its most outstanding feature with their rich orange-brown ground colour and fine black and white lines. While the male has uniform dark brown upperwings, the female has an orange patch on the forewings. Both sexes have hindwing tail streamers.

INHABITS areas of scrub, mature hedgerows, and woodland margins where larval foodplants grow.

fine black and white lines

orange-brown ground colour

tail streamer on hindwings

uniform dark brown wings

orange patch

dark brown ground colour

up to 2cm long

WINGSPAN *4–5cm.*
FLIGHT PERIOD *July–August.*
LARVAL FOODPLANT *Mainly blackthorn (Prunus spinosa) and related species, but also birch (Betula).*
SIMILAR SPECIES *None.*
STATUS *Widespread but distinctly local, forming discrete colonies.*

Sloe Hairstreak

Satyrium acaciae (Lycaenidae)

This rather small species is sometimes seen feeding on the flowers of bramble and other hedgerow plants. While doing so, it reveals only its underwings, which are grey-brown, marked with an irregular, wavy, black-edged white line. A row of black-bordered orange spots runs along the edge of the hindwing underside, on which a short tail streamer is also present.

FAVOURS hedgerows, scrub-covered slopes, and woodland margins where the larval foodplant grows in abundance.

irregular, black-edged white line

grey-brown ground colour

row of orange spots

up to 2cm long

WINGSPAN *2.5–3cm.*
FLIGHT PERIOD *June–July.*
LARVAL FOODPLANT *Blackthorn (Prunus spinosa).*
SIMILAR SPECIES *Ilex Hairstreak (right), which has rich brown underwings; False Ilex Hairstreak (right).*
STATUS *Widespread and locally common.*

Ilex Hairstreak

Satyrium ilicis (Lycaenidae)

This species rarely shows its upperwings. However, its relatively long tail streamers and the rich brown ground colour of the underwings are useful indicators to its identity. The underwings also bear an irregular, broken white line; and on the hindwing, a row of black-bordered, crescent-shaped orange spots near the margin.

FREQUENTS *areas of oak scrub and open wooded slopes, from sea level to around 1,500m.*

grey-brown ground colour

orange, crescent-shaped spots

dark brown ground colour

♂●

orange patch

♀●

up to 2cm long

WINGSPAN 3.5cm.
FLIGHT PERIOD *June–July.*
LARVAL FOODPLANT *Various oaks (Quercus).*
SIMILAR SPECIES *Sloe Hairstreak (left), False Ilex Hairstreak (below), which are both greyer brown.*
STATUS *Widespread and fairly common.*

False Ilex Hairstreak

Satyrium esculi (Lycaenidae)

This species is easy to confuse with the Ilex Hairstreak (above). However, its underside is paler grey-brown with smaller, redder submarginal spots on the hindwing that are distinctly separated. The dark brown upper surfaces of the wings are almost never revealed in resting individuals.

ASSOCIATED *with areas of Mediterranean scrubland, such as maquis, where low-growing oak species predominate.*

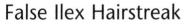

pale, grey-brown ground colour

up to 2cm long

discrete reddish spots

WINGSPAN 3.5cm.
FLIGHT PERIOD *June–July.*
LARVAL FOODPLANT *Low-growing species of oak (Quercus).*
SIMILAR SPECIES *Sloe Hairstreak (left), Ilex Hairstreak (above).*
STATUS *Fairly common in warm Mediterranean habitats.*

Blue-spot Hairstreak

Satyrium spini (Lycaenidae)

The upperwings of the Blue-spot Hairstreak are almost never revealed at rest. Fortunately, however, the diagnostic identification feature – a striking blue spot – is clearly visible on the underside of each hindwing when the insect is feeding on the flowers of low-growing plants. Like many of its relatives, this Hairstreak has small tail streamers on the hindwings.

PREFERS *extensive areas of hedgerows, scrub, and woodland margins where larval food-plants flourish.*

white stripe

tail streamer

striking blue spot

dark brown wings

orange spot

up to 1.5cm long

WINGSPAN *3.5cm.*
FLIGHT PERIOD *June–July.*
LARVAL FOODPLANT *Buckthorn (Rhamnus) and blackthorn (Prunus spinosa).*
SIMILAR SPECIES *None.*
STATUS *Widespread and locally common, often forming comparatively small and discrete colonies.*

Black Hairstreak

Satyrium pruni (Lycaenidae)

A close view reveals the Black Hairstreak to be a most attractive and well-marked species, particularly when it displays its underwings. The rich brown ground colour is adorned with a white streak, and the orange submarginal band is studded with white-edged black spots. This rather sluggish species can sometimes be found crawling slowly over the leaves of hedgerow shrubs.

FAVOURS *blackthorn scrub, mature hedgerows, woodland margins and clearings, to around 1,000m.*

dark brown ground colour

up to 1.5cm long

white stripe

tail streamer

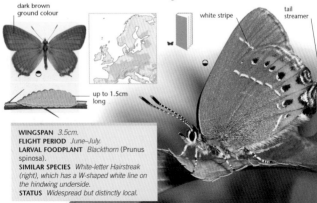

WINGSPAN *3.5cm.*
FLIGHT PERIOD *June–July.*
LARVAL FOODPLANT *Blackthorn (Prunus spinosa).*
SIMILAR SPECIES *White-letter Hairstreak (right), which has a W-shaped white line on the hindwing underside.*
STATUS *Widespread but distinctly local.*

White-letter Hairstreak

Satyrium w-album (Lycaenidae)

As Hairstreak butterflies go, this is a rather distinctive species. Its best diagnostic feature is the white streak on the underside of the hindwing, shaped like the letter 'W'. The underwing ground colour is a rich brown and the hindwing is also marked with a fused row of submarginal, crescent-shaped orange spots. In addition to the hindwing's obvious tail streamer, a second, smaller projection can be seen on the margin. The uniform brown upperwings are seldom seen when at rest.

FOUND *invariably in the vicinity of elm trees and so occurs in mature hedgerows and along woodland margins and rides.*

W-shaped white streak

tail streamer

crescent-shaped orange marking

dark brown ground colour

faint orange spot

up to 1.5cm long

NOTE

Although adult White-letter Hairstreaks spend much of their brief lives flying around the tops of elm trees, they are partial to the nectar of bramble flowers where they can often be very closely observed.

WINGSPAN *3.5cm.*
FLIGHT PERIOD *July.*
LARVAL FOODPLANT *Elm (Ulmus).*
SIMILAR SPECIES *Black Hairstreak (left), which has black spots along the orange band on the hindwing underside.*
STATUS *Widespread but local; affected by the impact of Dutch Elm disease on elms.*

Poplar Admiral

Limenitis populi (Nymphalidae)

This large butterfly is invariably associated with woodland habitats. Although it spends much of its time in treetops, it descends occasionally to the ground to drink fluids from fresh dung and liquefying carrion. Both the grey-brown upperwings and orange underwings are boldly patterned with white spots and bluish margins.

FLIES *in mature woodland, typically in damp valleys where the larval foodplants flourish.*

dirty white spots

grey-brown ground colour

bluish margin

black-bordered orange spots

orange ground colour

row of white spots ♀

up to 5cm long

WINGSPAN *7–8cm.*
FLIGHT PERIOD *June–July.*
LARVAL FOODPLANT *Poplars, notably aspen (Populus tremula).*
SIMILAR SPECIES *None.*
STATUS *Widespread and locally common, but hard to detect as it tends to fly among the treetops.*

Mountain Ringlet

Erebia epiphron (Satyridae)

Each upland region in which the Mountain Ringlet occurs may appear to have its own distinct form. However, in all cases, the ground colour of the wings is dark brown. Each wing has an orange band, varying in size and intensity, and it contains a variable number of small black spots. The upper and lower surfaces of the wings are rather similar.

FOUND *in upland areas, notably grassy moorland, usually at altitudes from 500m to 2,500m.*

black spots

brown ground colour

dark brown ground colour

orange band

up to 2cm long

variable number of black spots

WINGSPAN *3.2cm.*
FLIGHT PERIOD *July–August.*
LARVAL FOODPLANT *Various grasses (family Poaceae).*
SIMILAR SPECIES *Lesser Mountain Ringlet (right), which has smaller black spots within the orange band that runs across the wings.*
STATUS *Widespread and locally common.*

Blind Ringlet

Erebia pharte (Satyridae)

This sluggish, high altitude butterfly can be recognized by the complete absence of dark spots within the orange bands on the wings. The intensity and size of the bands themselves may vary according to the geographical location, but the ground colour of both surfaces of the wings is always dark brown.

RESTRICTED *to mountain grassland in the Alps and Tatra mountains, from 1,500m to 2,500m.*

dark brown ground colour

orange band with no eyespots

variable orange band

less distinct orange band on hindwing

WINGSPAN *3.5–4cm.*
FLIGHT PERIOD *July–August.*
LARVAL FOODPLANT *Various grasses (family Poaceae).*
SIMILAR SPECIES *None – it is the only butterfly of this group that does not have eyespots on the orange bands.*
STATUS *Distinctly local within its range.*

up to 2cm long

Lesser Mountain Ringlet

Erebia melampus (Satyridae)

Subtle differences in the wing markings distinguish this species from other similar butterflies. The orange bands on the wings contain black spots that are tiny in comparison with those of the Mountain Ringlet (left), and there are usually fewer than four such spots on the hindwing. The upper and lower surfaces of the wings are very similar.

INHABITS *grassy, alpine moorland between 1,000m and 2,000m.*

typically 4 eyespots on forewings

dull orange band

dark brown ground colour

up to 2cm long

WINGSPAN *3.5–4cm.*
FLIGHT PERIOD *July–August.*
LARVAL FOODPLANT *Various grasses (family Poaceae).*
SIMILAR SPECIES *Mountain Ringlet (left), Sudetan Ringlet (p.132).*
STATUS *Extremely local within its limited alpine range.*

Sudetan Ringlet

Erebia sudetica (Satyridae)

FOUND *in areas of upland grassland, in open country and light woodland, between 1,000m and 2,000m.*

Like several of its close relatives, this species' dark brown upperwings are marked with orange bands, which are often of similar intensity on both the forewing and hindwing. Within these bands can be seen small black spots; typically there are four or five on both the forewing and hindwing. The upper and lower surfaces of the wings are rather similar.

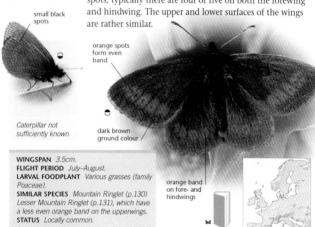

small black spots

orange spots form even band

Caterpillar not sufficiently known

dark brown ground colour

orange band on fore- and hindwings

WINGSPAN *3.5cm.*
FLIGHT PERIOD *July–August.*
LARVAL FOODPLANT *Various grasses (family Poaceae).*
SIMILAR SPECIES *Mountain Ringlet (p.130) Lesser Mountain Ringlet (p.131), which have a less even orange band on the upperwings.*
STATUS *Locally common.*

Silky Ringlet

Erebia gorge (Satyridae)

RESTRICTED *to stony, mountain slopes with scattered grassy areas, at 2,000–3,000m.*

This variable species typically has a rich brown ground colour to the upperwings. There is a broad reddish orange band on the forewing and its width is useful in identification. The band is present but variably less intense on the hindwing. The number and size of the eyespots within the band varies across the species' range; confusingly, in some populations eyespots are absent altogether.

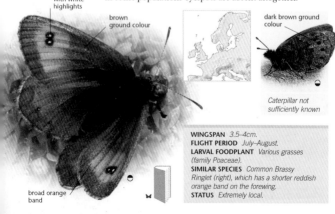

two spots with white highlights

brown ground colour

dark brown ground colour

Caterpillar not sufficiently known

broad orange band

WINGSPAN *3.5–4cm.*
FLIGHT PERIOD *July–August.*
LARVAL FOODPLANT *Various grasses (family Poaceae).*
SIMILAR SPECIES *Common Brassy Ringlet (right), which has a shorter reddish orange band on the forewing.*
STATUS *Extremely local.*

Common Brassy Ringlet

Erebia cassiodes (Satyridae)

At certain angles, the dark brown upperwings of the male show a greenish, brassy sheen. The forewing has a broad orange patch with two eyespots; the hindwing a less distinct band with three or four eyespots. The underside of the forewing resembles the upperside, while the hindwing is marbled grey and brown.

CONFINED to mountain grassland, invariably above altitudes of 1,500m and often above 2,000m.

orange ground colour

brassy greenish tinge

marbled grey and brown hindwing

up to 2.5cm long

orange patch

orange patch with 3–4 eyespots

WINGSPAN *3.5–4cm.*
FLIGHT PERIOD *July–August.*
LARVAL FOODPLANT *Various grasses (family Poaceae), notably mat grass (Nardus stricta) and fescues (Festuca).*
SIMILAR SPECIES *Silky Ringlet (p.132), which lacks the greenish tinge.*
STATUS *Locally fairly common.*

Large Chequered Skipper

Heteropterus morpheus (Hesperiidae)

This boldly marked butterfly is unmistakable when its underside can be clearly seen. The uniformly dark upperwings have a scattering of faint pale marks on the forewing. The markings on the hindwing underside are a diagnostic network of black-ringed, white oval spots.

FLIES *in open woodland, grassy heaths, and damp meadows, typically at altitudes below 1,000m.*

black-ringed white oval spots

few pale spots on forewing

up to 2.5cm long

uniform, dark brown wings

WINGSPAN *3cm.*
FLIGHT PERIOD *June–August.*
LARVAL FOODPLANT *Various grasses (family Poaceae), notably purple moor-grass (Molinia caerulea).*
SIMILAR SPECIES *None.*
STATUS *Locally common in its range but declining due to habitat loss.*

Black Satyr

Hipparchia actaea (Satyridae)

PREFERS *rocky slopes with scattered grassy patches, at altitudes between 1,000m and 2,000m.*

Only rarely does the Black Satyr reveal its sooty brown upperwings at rest; at such times, keen-eyed observers may glimpse the forewing eyespots – two in females but one in males. It is more usual to see the underwings on display. These are marbled grey-brown, marked by a large eyespot on the forewing, and two pale concentric bands on the hindwing.

whitish bands

striking eyespot

dark brown ground colour

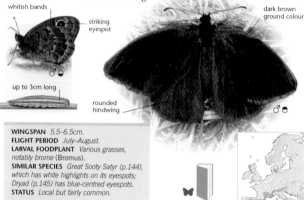

♂

up to 3cm long

rounded hindwing

♂ ●

WINGSPAN *5.5–6.5cm.*
FLIGHT PERIOD *July–August.*
LARVAL FOODPLANT *Various grasses, notably brome (Bromus).*
SIMILAR SPECIES *Great Sooty Satyr (p.144), which has white highlights on its eyespots; Dryad (p.145) has blue-centred eyespots.*
STATUS *Local but fairly common.*

Sooty Ringlet

Erebia pluto (Satyridae)

ASSOCIATED *with stony and grassy slopes, at altitudes from 2,000m to 3,000m.*

In some races of this confusingly variable alpine species, all wing surfaces in males are almost black. Most females, however, and the males of many races, have sooty brown wings marked with variable forewing patches of dull orange-red. Forewing eyespots are found in some races, but the underside of the hindwing is unmarked in all individuals.

reddish patch on forewings

♂ ●

blackish brown ground colour

♂ ●

unmarked hindwings

up to 2.5cm long

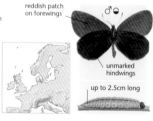

WINGSPAN *5cm.*
FLIGHT PERIOD *July–August.*
LARVAL FOODPLANT *Various grasses (family Poaceae).*
SIMILAR SPECIES *None, given the species' restricted habitat and altitudinal range.*
STATUS *Locally fairly common, but with an extremely restricted range.*

Arran Brown

Erebia ligea (Satyridae)

This species' appearance is surprisingly constant across its extensive range. The dark brown upperwings show an orange band containing eyespots with white highlights. This pattern is reflected on the underside of the forewing although the orange is more diffused. On the hindwing, the orange is confined to rings around the eyespots; an

irregular white line marks the inner margin of the band of eyespots.

FOUND *in grassy places in open woodland and on rough slopes and heaths, usually at 500–1,500m.*

white line

dark brown ground colour

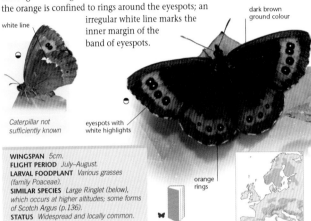

Caterpillar not sufficiently known

eyespots with white highlights

orange rings

WINGSPAN *5cm.*
FLIGHT PERIOD *July–August.*
LARVAL FOODPLANT *Various grasses (family Poaceae).*
SIMILAR SPECIES *Large Ringlet (below), which occurs at higher altitudes; some forms of Scotch Argus (p.136).*
STATUS *Widespread and locally common.*

Large Ringlet

Erebia euryale (Satyridae)

The Large Ringlet is a well-marked upland butterfly, the dark brown upperwings bearing an orange band with dark eyespots. It is similar to the Arran Brown (above) but typically occurs at higher altitudes. The Large Ringlet male lacks the bold white line seen on the underside of the

Arran Brown's hindwing. However, the female hindwing underside often displays a greyish white band.

INHABITS *grassy clearings in open woodland (often coniferous), typically at altitudes between 1,000m and 2,000m.*

black eyespots on orange band

grey band

♀

up to 3cm long

chequered fringe

dark brown ground colour

WINGSPAN *4–4.5cm.*
FLIGHT PERIOD *July–September.*
LARVAL FOODPLANT *Various grasses (family Poaceae).*
SIMILAR SPECIES *Arran Brown (above); Scotch Argus (p.136), which has more striking white highlights on the eyespots.*
STATUS *Widespread but local.*

Yellow-spotted Ringlet

Erebia manto (Satyridae)

The Yellow-spotted Ringlet is extremely variable in terms of the extent of orange markings on its brown upperwings. In fact, in some races, the butterfly is uniformly dark brown. The females of the species are relatively easy to identify because they have bold yellowish spots on the underside of the hindwing; unfortunately, these are not present in males.

RESTRICTED *to high alpine meadows and mountain grassland, usually between 1,500m and 2,500m.*

orange band with eyespots

orange patches
♂

yellow spots on hindwing
♀

up to 2.5cm long

♂

dark brown ground colour

WINGSPAN *4cm.*
FLIGHT PERIOD *July–August.*
LARVAL FOODPLANT *Various grasses (family Poaceae).*
SIMILAR SPECIES *Various Erebia species, although the typical female is unmistakable.*
STATUS *Locally fairly common within its restricted range.*

Scotch Argus

Erebia aethiops (Satyridae)

This upland butterfly is easy to observe since it is slow-flying and often basks on vegetation. Its upperwing ground colour is rich dark brown and both wings are patterned with reddish orange bands containing eyespots with white highlights. The underside of the forewing resembles the upperside, but the hindwing is sooty brown with a lilac-grey submarginal band.

FOUND *in grassy places in open woodland and on moors, usually between 500m and 1,500m.*

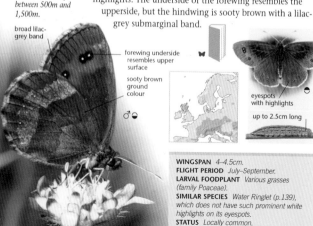

broad lilac-grey band

forewing underside resembles upper surface

sooty brown ground colour

♂

eyespots with highlights
♂

up to 2.5cm long

WINGSPAN *4–4.5cm.*
FLIGHT PERIOD *July–September.*
LARVAL FOODPLANT *Various grasses (family Poaceae).*
SIMILAR SPECIES *Water Ringlet (p.139), which does not have such prominent white highlights on its eyespots.*
STATUS *Locally common.*

Lapland Ringlet

Erebia embla (Satyridae)

The striking markings of the Lapland Ringlet make it a comparatively easy species to identify within its Arctic and sub-Arctic range. The dark brown upperwings are marked with yellow-ringed black eyespots, usually four on each wing; the two nearest the forewing tip are joined together and may have white highlights. On the underside, only the forewings have yellow-ringed eyespots, while the hindwing is unmarked.

FAVOURS *grassy, and often damp, areas with scattered conifers, usually below 500m.*

yellow-ringed eyespots

♂

four eyespots on upperwings

dark brown ground colour

Caterpillar not sufficiently known

WINGSPAN *5cm.*
FLIGHT PERIOD *June–July.*
LARVAL FOODPLANT *Various grasses (family Poaceae).*
SIMILAR SPECIES *Arctic Ringlet (p.138), which has four or five linked, orange-ringed eyespots on the forewing.*
STATUS *Locally common.*

De Prunner's Ringlet

Erebia triaria (Satyridae)

Like many of its relatives, this ringlet has predominantly dark brown wings. On the upper surface of both wings there is an orange band containing several black eyespots with white highlights; the front three forewing spots are typically linked and arranged in a line. Underneath, the forewing pattern is a dull version of that seen above, while the hindwing is dark overall.

ASSOCIATED *with mountain grassland, often with scattered conifers; typically between 1,000m and 2,000m.*

plain brown hindwing

linked eyespots near front of forewing

forewing underside pattern reflects upperside

broad orange band

WINGSPAN *4.5–5cm.*
FLIGHT PERIOD *May–July.*
LARVAL FOODPLANT *Various grasses (family Poaceae).*
SIMILAR SPECIES *Piedmont Ringlet (p.141), which has a well-defined, reddish orange band on the forewing underside.*
STATUS *Distinctly local and seldom common.*

up to 2.5cm long

Arctic Ringlet

Erebia disa (Satyridae)

OCCURS *in open woodland in damp valleys and on grassy moors, often at moderate altitudes.*

The Arctic Ringlet is one of the very few *Erebia* species with such a northerly range. Given its distinctive and constant appearance, it is easy to identify. All the wing surfaces are dark brown. The hindwings are unmarked while on the forewings there are four or five linked, orange-ringed dark eyespots with no white highlights. The underside pattern is similar to that on the upper surface.

linked, orange-ringed eyespots

dull chequered fringe

dark brown ground colour

unmarked hindwing

Caterpillar not sufficiently known

WINGSPAN *4.5–5cm.*
FLIGHT PERIOD *June–July.*
LARVAL FOODPLANT *Various grasses (family Poaceae).*
SIMILAR SPECIES *Lapland Ringlet (p.137), which has white highlights in the two anterior eyespots on the upper forewing.*
STATUS *Local and fairly common.*

Woodland Ringlet

Erebia medusa (Satyridae)

FOUND *in grassy woodland rides and clearings, meadows, and moors, at low levels in the north, and on lower mountain slopes in the south.*

The dark brown wings of the Woodland Ringlet have an orange-yellow band on the forewing, with two linked and striking eyespots near the tip, and one or more smaller eyespots behind. Occasionally, a tiny spot occurs below the front pair. On the hindwing there are four or more orange-ringed eyespots. The upper and lower surfaces are similar; females are usually paler than males.

two large, linked eyespots

smaller eyespots

orange-yellow band

dark brown ground colour

up to 2.5cm long

WINGSPAN *4–4.5cm.*
FLIGHT PERIOD *May–June.*
LARVAL FOODPLANT *Various grasses (family Poaceae).*
SIMILAR SPECIES *Water Ringlet (right), which has a lilac-grey band on the hindwing underside; Bright-eyed Ringlet (p.140).*
STATUS *Widespread and fairly common.*

Almond-eyed Ringlet

Erebia alberganus (Satyridae)

Although this species can be quite variable, a typical specimen is distinctive. Its dark brown wings are patterned with a band of oval- or almond-shaped eyespots, enhanced by the dark centre spots, most of which have white highlights. Upper and lower surfaces of the wings are similar.

FAVOURS *alpine meadows and upland grassland, between 1,200m and 1,500m.*

dark brown ground colour

dark spots with white highlights

oval- or almond-shaped orange spots

♂

♀

up to 2.5cm long

WINGSPAN *4cm.*
FLIGHT PERIOD *June–July.*
LARVAL FOODPLANT *Various grasses (family Poaceae).*
SIMILAR SPECIES *Bright-eyed Ringlet (p.140).*
STATUS *Fairly common but local within its restricted alpine range.*

Water Ringlet

Erebia pronoe (Satyridae)

Both wings of the Water Ringlet have orange bands; on the forewings there are two linked eyespots, with one or two others further down, while on the hindwings there are three or four eyespots. The upper forewing pattern is reflected on the underside. However, the hindwing is marbled brown with a broad grey band that is tinged lilac.

ASSOCIATED *with grassy slopes and clearings in upland woodlands, between 1,000m and 3,000m.*

lilac-grey band on hindwing

greyish tip

twin eyespots

dark brown ground colour

♂

♂

Caterpillar not sufficiently known

WINGSPAN *4.5–5cm.*
FLIGHT PERIOD *July–September.*
LARVAL FOODPLANT *Various grasses (family Poaceae).*
SIMILAR SPECIES *Scotch Argus (p.136), Woodland Ringler (left), Stygian Ringlet (p.140), Autumn Ringlet (p.142).*
STATUS *Fairly common in its upland habitat.*

Stygian Ringlet

Erebia styx (Satyridae)

Two linked eyespots mark the orange band on the dark brown upper forewings of this butterfly; sometimes there are smaller additional spots. Three or four eyespots adorn the hindwing. Below, the dull orange forewing has eyespots similar to the upperwings; the hindwing is marbled grey-brown, with three or four faint eyespots. Overall, the female is paler than the male.

ASSOCIATED *with rocky places and broken ground on mountain slopes, usually at 1,000–2,000m.*

grey-brown marbling

dark brown ground colour

twin eyespots on orange band

up to 2.5cm long

WINGSPAN *4.5–5cm.*
FLIGHT PERIOD *July–August.*
LARVAL FOODPLANT *Various grasses (family Poaceae).*
SIMILAR SPECIES *Water Ringlet (p.139), Bright-eyed Ringlet (below), Marbled Ringlet (right).*
STATUS *Locally common.*

Bright-eyed Ringlet

Erebia oeme (Satyridae)

Well-marked individuals of this species are relatively easy to identify. Their jet-black eyespots have relatively large highlights that are bright white and well defined. However, in some subspecies the spots are smaller and less distinct; in this case the tips of the antennae must serve as an identifying feature: they are black in this species but brown in similar relatives.

FAVOURS *damp ground in mountain meadows and upland woodland at 1,000–2,000m.*

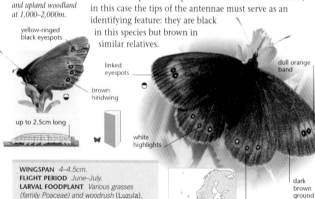

yellow-ringed black eyespots

linked eyespots

brown hindwing

up to 2.5cm long

dull orange band

white highlights

dark brown ground colour

5 or 6 eyespots on hindwing

WINGSPAN *4–4.5cm.*
FLIGHT PERIOD *June–July.*
LARVAL FOODPLANT *Various grasses (family Poaceae) and woodrush (Luzula).*
SIMILAR SPECIES *Woodland Ringlet (p.138), Piedmont Ringlet (right).*
STATUS *Fairly common but local within its upland range.*

Piedmont Ringlet

Erebia meolans (Satyridae)

One of this species' key characteristics is the presence of a particularly well-defined reddish orange band on the underside of the otherwise dark brown forewing; within the band are two linked eyespots with white highlights and smaller, solitary ones too. The underside of the hindwing is typically dark with small, faint eyespots.

INHABITS *mountain slopes and high alpine meadows, typically at 1,000–2,000m.*

dark brown ground colour

twin eyespots on orange band

smaller eyespots

reddish orange band

up to 2cm long

WINGSPAN *5cm.*
FLIGHT PERIOD *June–July.*
LARVAL FOODPLANT *Various grasses (family Poaceae).*
SIMILAR SPECIES *De Prunner's Ringlet (p.137), Bright-eyed Ringlet (left).*
STATUS *Locally common within its restricted, upland range.*

Marbled Ringlet

Erebia montana (Satyridae)

Both upper and lower wing surfaces will need to be seen before this species can be identified. The dark brown upperwings have well-defined reddish orange bands in which there are linked eyespots, with occasional smaller eyespots. The underside forewing pattern resembles that on the upperside, while the hindwing is marbled grey-brown, typically with an irregular, white central line. Female butterflies are usually paler than males but otherwise are similar.

FOUND *on stony mountain slopes and other rocky upland areas, usually at 1,000–2,000m.*

grey-brown marbling

twin, linked eyespots

well-defined orange band

up to 2.5cm long

WINGSPAN *4.5–5cm.*
FLIGHT PERIOD *July–August.*
LARVAL FOODPLANT *Various grasses (family Poaceae).*
SIMILAR SPECIES *Stygian Ringlet (left), Autumn Ringlet (p.142).*
STATUS *Locally common within its limited upland range.*

Autumn Ringlet

Erebia neoridas (Satyridae)

FOUND *in upland grassland on mountain slopes and open woodland, usually at 1,000–2,000m.*

The shape of the reddish orange patch on the forewing upperside is probably the single best identification feature for this species. It tapers almost to a point and looks triangular; in related species, the patch tapers more gradually and is blunt-ended. In other respects the Autumn Ringlet is similar to many other species of *Erebia*.

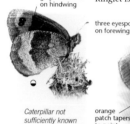

grey-buff band on hindwing

three eyespots on forewing

brown ground colour

Caterpillar not sufficiently known

orange patch tapers to point

WINGSPAN *4.5–5cm.*
FLIGHT PERIOD *August–September.*
LARVAL FOODPLANT *Various grasses (family Poaceae).*
SIMILAR SPECIES *Marbled Ringlet (p.141), which has a central white line on the hindwing.*
STATUS *Locally fairly common.*

Ringlet

Aphantopus hyperantus (Satyridae)

INHABITS *grassy places from meadows, hedgerows, and verges to woodland clearings; common at low levels.*

This is a widespread and familiar butterfly. The upper surfaces of the wings are sooty brown; they are darkest in males, and sometimes appear almost black. Small black eyespots may or may not be visible on the upper surfaces of the wings, but the brown undersurfaces are adorned with yellow-ringed black eyespots that have white highlights.

brown ground colour

white highlights

yellow-ringed black eyespots

up to 3cm long

♂

two faint eyespots on each wing

dark, sooty brown ground colour

WINGSPAN *4.5–5cm.*
FLIGHT PERIOD *June–July.*
LARVAL FOODPLANT *Various grasses (family Poaceae).*
SIMILAR SPECIES *False Ringlet (p.98), which has an orange-brown rather than brown underside.*
STATUS *Widespread and common.*

Speckled Wood

Pararge aegeria (Satyridae)

Rather confusingly, the Speckled Wood occurs in two very distinct forms across two geographical regions. In much of its range as covered by this book, the upperwings are dark brown with an extensive pattern of yellow-buff spots; eyespots are present in some of the pale areas. South of a line drawn between Brittany and northern Italy, individuals have the pale buff replaced by orange and bear a passing resemblance to the Wall Brown (p.106). The underwing pattern and colour of both forms reflects those on the upperwings.

ASSOCIATED *with woodland and typically found on the margins of sunny clearings and rides.*

eyespot on forewing

marbled hindwing with pale spots

NOTE

The male Speckled Wood defends its territory by launching aerial assaults on intruding males, and on butterflies of other species too. After a battle, the victor returns to one of a handful of favoured vantage points, typically on a sunlit spray of leaves.

orange and brown ground colour

SOUTHERN FORM

up to 2.5cm long

single eyespot on forewing

yellow-buff spots

several eyespots on hindwing

dark brown ground colour

WINGSPAN *4.5cm.*
FLIGHT PERIOD *March–October, in successive broods.*
LARVAL FOODPLANT *Various woodland species of grasses (family Poaceae).*
SIMILAR SPECIES *Southern form reminiscent of Wall Brown (p.106), which has a row of eyespots on the hindwings.*
STATUS *Widespread and locally common – a familiar butterfly across much of its range.*

Dewy Ringlet

Erebia pandrose (Satyridae)

Although the ground colour of the Dewy Ringlet's upper forewing is dark brown, it bears a large reddish orange patch typically dissected by a dark line, with a row of four black eyespots. There are usually four indistinct, orange-ringed eyespots on the upper surface of the hindwing.

RESTRICTED *to low-lying tundra in Scandinavia, and alpine meadows, at 2,000–3,000m in the south of its range.*

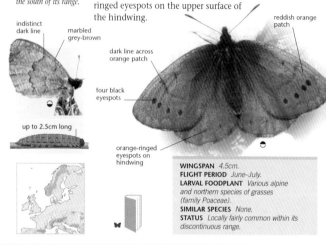

indistinct dark line

marbled grey-brown

reddish orange patch

dark line across orange patch

four black eyespots

up to 2.5cm long

orange-ringed eyespots on hindwing

WINGSPAN *4.5cm.*
FLIGHT PERIOD *June–July.*
LARVAL FOODPLANT *Various alpine and northern species of grasses (family Poaceae).*
SIMILAR SPECIES *None.*
STATUS *Locally fairly common within its discontinuous range.*

Great Sooty Satyr

Hipparchia ferula (Satyridae)

There are striking differences between the sexes of this species. Male upperwings are often so dark that only the white highlights of the two to four eyespots are visible. In females, the upperwings are dark brown, with two large eyespots on a dull orange band on the forewing. On the underside, both sexes show two large eyespots on the forewing.

FOUND *on dry, rocky hills and lower mountain slopes, usually between 500m and 1,500m.*

white highlights

♂

dark sooty brown upperwings

marbled dark brown

♂

pale band on hindwing

two eyespots on orange band

♀

faint orange band

up to 3cm long

WINGSPAN *5.5–6.5cm.*
FLIGHT PERIOD *July–August.*
LARVAL FOODPLANT *Various grasses (family Poaceae).*
SIMILAR SPECIES *Dryad (right), which has large blue-centred eyespots on forewings that are diagnostic.*
STATUS *Locally common.*

Dryad

Hipparchia dryas (Satyridae)

This is a large and rather distinctive butterfly. A characteristic feature in both sexes is two large blue-centred eyespots on the upper and lower surfaces of the forewings. These are most noticeable in females, whose wings are brown; in males they tend not to show up so well because their upperwings are extremely dark.

ASSOCIATED with dry grassland and open country with scattered trees, below 1,000m.

blue-centred eyespots

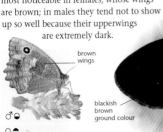

brown wings

blackish brown ground colour

♂●

♂●

♀●

brown ground colour

up to 3cm long

WINGSPAN 5–6cm.
FLIGHT PERIOD July–August.
LARVAL FOODPLANT Various grasses (family Poaceae).
SIMILAR SPECIES None, so long as the blue-centred eyespots are seen, otherwise it may be confused with Great Sooty Satyr (left).
STATUS Widespread and locally common.

Southern White Admiral

Limenitis reducta (Nymphalidae)

Although this species is similar to the White Admiral (p.146), it is possible to distinguish between the two with care. The Southern White Admiral's upperwings have a darker ground colour with broader white markings and usually an isolated white spot towards the base of the forewing. Below, there is a single submarginal row of black spots on the hindwing.

orange-brown colour

FAVOURS woodland and scrubby Mediterranean habitat such as maquis, usually at low levels.

up to 2.5cm long

single white spot towards forewing base

blackish ground colour

broad band of white patches

WINGSPAN 5cm.
FLIGHT PERIOD May–July.
LARVAL FOODPLANT Honeysuckle (Lonicera).
SIMILAR SPECIES White Admiral (p.146), which has two rows of submarginal black spots on the hindwing.
STATUS Widespread and locally common.

White Admiral

Limenitis camilla (Nymphalidae)

A widespread and familiar woodland butterfly, the White Admiral is fast-flying and alert to danger. However, it also feeds on the flowers of brambles and typically is reluctant to leave a good source of nectar. Consequently, it can often be observed at close range for extended periods if you approach it without making any sudden movements. The blackish brown upperwings are marked with distinctive white bands; the pattern of white is similar, but more extensive, on the underwings, which have a rich orange-brown ground colour.

FOUND *in mature woodland with sunny clearings and rides, and an abundance of larval foodplants, usually below 1,000m.*

bold white markings

blackish brown ground colour

white markings

orange-brown ground colour

double row of black spots

scalloped white edging

up to 3cm long

NOTE

You can use flight patterns to distinguish this species from the superficially similar Hungarian Glider (p.150). Although both glide well, the White Admiral's direct flight is strong and powerful, whereas that of the Hungarian Glider is slower and more flitting.

WINGSPAN *5cm.*
FLIGHT PERIOD *June–August.*
LARVAL FOODPLANT Honeysuckle (Lonicera), *typically plants growing in gloomy, shady settings.*
SIMILAR SPECIES Southern White Admiral (p.145); Hungarian Glider (p.150); second generation Map Butterflies (right), *which have similar upperwings but strikingly different underwings.*
STATUS *Widespread and locally common.*

Map Butterfly

Araschnia levana (Nymphalidae)

This butterfly produces two generations of adults each year. In itself this is not unusual, but the upperwing colours and markings are so different in each brood that you could be forgiven for assuming you were dealing with two separate species. The first generation is Fritillary-like with orange and black markings. By contrast, the second generation has blackish upperwings that are adorned with white markings. Fortunately, the wing shape and intricate, map-like pattern on the underwing, created by the complex white veins, are similar in all individuals.

FAVOURS *woodland margins and rough, disturbed ground – usually at low altitudes.*

maroon and lilac ground colour

white band

intricate pattern of white veins

orange-brown ground colour

NOTE

There is potential for confusing the first brood with a Fritillary and the second with a White Admiral (left). However, the Map Butterfly's relatively small size, angular wing outline, and underwing markings should dispel any doubts as to its identity.

FIRST BROOD

up to 2cm long

black ground colour

angular wing shape

broken white fringe

SECOND BROOD

WINGSPAN *4–4.5cm.*
FLIGHT PERIOD *April–June, and August–September, in two distinct broods.*
LARVAL FOODPLANT *Nettle (Urtica).*
SIMILAR SPECIES *None, although the first brood could be confused with a Fritillary, and the second with a White Admiral (left).*
STATUS *Widespread and fairly common.*

Marbled White

Melanargia galathea (Satyridae)

An attractive and well-marked butterfly, the Marbled White exhibits some variation in its appearance. However, typically the upperwings are pale creamy white, with an extensive pattern of linked black veins and patches. Compared to other *Melanargia* species, the proportion of black to white is evenly balanced and distributed across the wings. The pattern on the underwings is similar but many of the black markings are replaced by grey, making the wings look much paler overall. While males and females are usually alike, females often have a yellowish suffusion on the underside of the hindwing.

FAVOURS *flower-rich, grassy places such as meadows and verges; most common below 1,500m.*

pale, creamy white ground colour

grey band with eyespots

grey patches

extensive black patches and veins

white scalloped margin

up to 2cm long

WINGSPAN *5cm.*
FLIGHT PERIOD *June–August.*
LARVAL FOODPLANT *Various grasses (family Poaceae).*
SIMILAR SPECIES *Esper's Marbled White (right), Western Marbled White (right).*
STATUS *Widespread and locally common, typically forming discrete colonies.*

NOTE

The Marbled White is by far the most common and widespread of the three Melanargia *species in this book. It is generally much darker than its relatives and lacks the jagged black wing markings that are specific to the other two species.*

Esper's Marbled White

Melanargia russiae (Satyridae)

The black markings of this butterfly's upperwings are concentrated on the outer half and make the basal half look pale. A jagged black line dissects the forewing cell (the white basal area near the leading edge). The eyespots on the underside hindwing are not enclosed in a grey band as in the Marbled White (left).

ASSOCIATED *with areas of flower-rich, upland grassland, between 1,000m and 2,000m.*

jagged black line

five eyespots on hindwing

up to 3cm long

black markings on outer side

white ground colour

WINGSPAN *5–5.5cm.*
FLIGHT PERIOD *June–July.*
LARVAL FOODPLANT *Various grasses (family Poaceae).*
SIMILAR SPECIES *Marbled White (left) has blacker markings, Western Marbled White (below) has blue-centred eyespots.*
STATUS *Locally common.*

Western Marbled White

Melanargia occitanica (Satyridae)

Compared to the Marbled White (left), this species' white wings have fewer black markings; apart from the dark veins, these are confined mainly to the outer margins. In common with Esper's Marbled White (above), a jagged black line dissects the forewing cell. However, the most distinctive feature is the five blue-centred eyespots on the upper and lower surfaces of the hindwings.

FREQUENTS *grassy hillsides and meadows on lower mountain slopes, from 1,000m to 1,500m.*

black patches denser on margin

network of black veins

brown veins on hindwing

jagged black line

five blue-centred eyespots

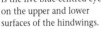

up to 3cm long

WINGSPAN *5–5.5cm.*
FLIGHT PERIOD *May–July.*
LARVAL FOODPLANT *Various grasses (family Poaceae).*
SIMILAR SPECIES *Marbled White (left), which has more black markings, Esper's Marbled White (above).*
STATUS *Locally common.*

Hungarian Glider

Neptis rivularis (Nymphalidae)

With its rather broad and rounded wings, the Hungarian Glider can undertake prolonged bouts of gliding flight. Its upperwings are mainly blackish but are adorned with white markings. Underneath, the ground colour is a rich orange-brown with a pattern of white markings similar to that seen on the upper wing surfaces.

OCCURS *in open, often damp, woodland, particularly along rides and in clearings, below 1,000m.*

blackish ground colour

rounded wing outline

orange-brown ground colour

♂●

white band

up to 4cm long

WINGSPAN *5cm.*
FLIGHT PERIOD *July–September.*
LARVAL FOODPLANT *Spiraea (Spiraea).*
SIMILAR SPECIES *Southern White Admiral (p.145); White Admiral (p.146), which has two rows of black spots on its hindwings.*
STATUS *Distinctly local, and possibly declining in the west.*

Great Banded Grayling

Hipparchia circe (Satyridae)

This large and impressive butterfly is capable of powerful flight. Fortunately, however, it is also spends time sunbathing and so the well-marked upperwings – blackish with white bands – can sometimes be closely observed. The underwings, which are the more usual wing surface to be seen, are marbled brown but with the same pattern of white as on the upperwings.

FOUND *in grassy areas with scattered trees and scrub, from sea level to 1,500m.*

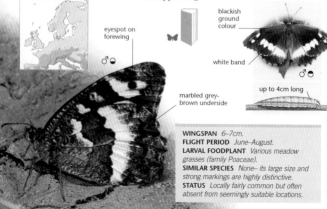

eyespot on forewing

blackish ground colour

♂●

white band

marbled grey-brown underside

♂●

up to 4cm long

WINGSPAN *6–7cm.*
FLIGHT PERIOD *June–August.*
LARVAL FOODPLANT *Various meadow grasses (family Poaceae).*
SIMILAR SPECIES *None– its large size and strong markings are highly distinctive.*
STATUS *Locally fairly common but often absent from seemingly suitable locations.*

Moths

Over 8,000 species of moths, nearly 95% of the continent's
Lepidoptera, occur in Europe, yet they are generally less well
known than butterflies. Although most fly at night, there are
many day-flying species, and almost any moth may be seen by
day if disturbed from its resting place. Moths range in size from
tiny 'micro-moths' with wingspans of just a few millimetres,
to the large hawk-moths, such as the Elephant Hawk-moth
shown below. Moths are often unfairly thought of as rather
dull; while some are indeed mainly brown or grey to provide
camouflage, many are just as brightly coloured as butterflies.

MOTHER
SHIPTON

CHINESE CHARACTER

THE CINNABAR

OAK EGGAR

Diamond-back Moth

Plutella xylostella (Yponomeutidae)

This tiny moth occurs throughout the world and migrates long distances, sometimes moving northwards in such large numbers that the caterpillars become pests in cabbage fields. The adult Diamond-back Moth has a distinctive row of buff-coloured diamond-shaped marks along the edges of its folded wings. It flies by day and night and is attracted to light.

BREEDS *mainly in fields of cabbages and other brassicas, but as a migrant the adults may be found in almost any habitat.*

forward-pointing antennae

buff diamond-shaped marks

long, thin wings

up to 0.5cm long

WINGSPAN *1.2–1.7cm.*
TIME OF FLIGHT *Day and night.*
FLIGHT PERIOD *May–September.*
LARVAL FOODPLANT *Cultivated and wild species of brassicas (Brassicaceae).*
SIMILAR SPECIES *None.*
STATUS *Widespread and common; often regarded as a pest.*

White-shouldered House-moth

Endrosis sarcitrella (Oecophoridae)

The upperwings of this House-moth are grey-brown and heavily mottled, while its head and thorax are white. This is a common and distinctive species, often found in birds' nests, houses, and outbuildings where grain or other produce is stored. Adult moths may be seen indoors at any time of the year, and frequently come to light sources.

LIVES *in houses, barns, and outhouses; sometimes also found in old birds' nests.*

dark mottling

up to 1cm long

white head and thorax

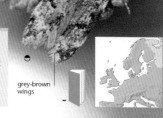

grey-brown wings

WINGSPAN *1.3–2cm.*
TIME OF FLIGHT *Night.*
FLIGHT PERIOD *Throughout the year.*
LARVAL FOOD *Almost any vegetable matter, stored grain, wood, and birds' droppings and feathers.*
SIMILAR SPECIES *None.*
STATUS *Widespread and common.*

Green Oak Tortrix

Tortrix viridana (Tortricidae)

This moth is a member of the large family of Micro-moths known as Leaf-rollers, from the larva's habit of rolling a leaf of the foodplant into a tube in which it lives. Entirely green forewings and greyish hindwings, make this Tortrix one of the more easily recognized species. It can be abundant in oak woods, and the caterpillars sometimes defoliate entire trees.

FEEDS *on the leaves of oak trees, and is common in any deciduous wood where the foodplant grows.*

reddish-brown limbs and body

wing colour blends with oak leaves

green forewings

up to 1cm long

WINGSPAN *1.6–2.4cm.*
TIME OF FLIGHT *Mainly at night.*
FLIGHT PERIOD *June–August.*
LARVAL FOODPLANT *Oak (Quercus).*
SIMILAR SPECIES *Cream-bordered Green Pea (Earias clorana), which has white hindwings.*
STATUS *Widespread and common.*

Codling Moth

Cydia pomonella (Tortricidae)

The grey-brown wings of the Codling Moth are marked with black and gold on the tips. The larvae are sometimes found inside apples and other fruit, and can be a major pest in orchards. In commercial orchards, however, they are controlled either by pesticides or by pheromone traps, which catch the males in large numbers by attracting them to a synthetic version of the female's scent.

FOUND *wherever wild or cultivated fruit trees grow, especially in orchards and gardens.*

mottled grey and brown wings

brown patch on forewing

black and gold markings

up to 1.5cm long

WINGSPAN *1.4–2.2cm.*
TIME OF FLIGHT *Night.*
FLIGHT PERIOD *May–August, sometimes in two broods.*
LARVAL FOODPLANT *Fruit of various trees, including apple (Malus) and pear (Pyrus).*
SIMILAR SPECIES *None.*
STATUS *Widespread and common.*

Twenty-plume Moth

Alucita hexadactyla (Alucitidae)

This moth gets its name from the six linked feather-like "plumes" that make up each of its wings. At rest it often adopts a triangular posture, with the plumes held tightly together, and can look like an ordinary moth until its wings are spread, revealing the individual plumes. The adult hibernates, but may fly on mild nights in the winter.

FOUND *in gardens, woodland, and commons – wherever its larval foodplant, honeysuckle, grows.*

dark double band on forewing

plumes spread out

up to 0.5cm long

feathery plumes

WINGSPAN *1.4–1.6cm.*
TIME OF FLIGHT *Night.*
FLIGHT PERIOD *Adults occur at any time of the year.*
LARVAL FOODPLANT *Honeysuckle (Lonicera).*
SIMILAR SPECIES *None.*
STATUS *Common.*

Small Magpie

Eurrhypara hortulata (Pyralidae)

One of the most attractive and familiar of the Micro-moths, the Small Magpie is easily recognized by its black and white wings, and yellow and black body. The caterpillar feeds on nettles, and the adult moth is easily disturbed from vegetation during the day. The moth's natural time of flight is from early evening onwards, and it is attracted to light.

FREQUENTS *any habitat where nettles grow, favouring damper areas of woodland, commons, and gardens.*

yellow and black body

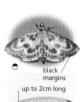

black margins

up to 2cm long

white wings with black spots

WINGSPAN *3.3–3.5cm.*
TIME OF FLIGHT *Night.*
FLIGHT PERIOD *May–August.*
LARVAL FOODPLANT *Nettle (Urtica) and other plants.*
SIMILAR SPECIES *Magpie Moth (p.173), which is much larger.*
STATUS *Widespread and common.*

Mother of Pearl

Pleuroptya ruralis (Pyralidae)

The Mother of Pearl is one of the larger Micro-moths, larger, in fact, than some of the Macro-moths. Its wings have an attractive pinkish pearly sheen, which resembles the inside of an oyster shell. Although it flies mainly at night, when it is attracted to light, it can be disturbed from nettles during the day.

FAVOURS *areas where nettles grow, including gardens, wasteland, and damper woodland.*

pearly sheen

pale buff forewings

pointed wing tips

brownish markings

up to 2cm long

WINGSPAN *3.3–3.7cm.*
TIME OF FLIGHT *Night; but can be disturbed easily during the day.*
FLIGHT PERIOD *June–August.*
LARVAL FOODPLANT *Common nettle (Urtica dioica).*
SIMILAR SPECIES *None.*
STATUS *Widespread and common.*

Bee Moth

Aphomia sociella (Pyralidae)

The adult Bee Moth rolls, rather than folds, its pinkish brown wings when at rest. Its larvae live in the nests of bees and wasps, where they feed on honeycomb and bee or wasp larvae. An infested nest may contain hundreds of Bee Moth caterpillars, which make silk-lined tunnels, and later pupate in tough, papery cocoons.

OCCURS *in all habitats where bees or wasps nest, including woodland, gardens, and scrub.*

pinkish brown forewings

dark spot

wings rolled at rest

♂

up to 2cm long

♀

WINGSPAN *2.5–3.8cm.*
TIME OF FLIGHT *Night.*
FLIGHT PERIOD *June–August.*
LARVAL FOOD *Honeycomb and larvae of bees and wasps; does not feed on plant matter.*
SIMILAR SPECIES *None.*
STATUS *Widespread and common.*

White Plume-moth

Pterophorus pentadactyla (Pterophoridae)

FOUND *in grassy places, gardens, commons, hedgerows, and wherever the foodplant grows.*

This is the only completely white Plume moth. Although its wings are made up of feather-like plumes similar to those of the Twenty-plume Moth (p.154), the two are not closely related. Its forewings are divided into two plumes, and the hindwings into three. At rest it holds its wings outstretched. The moth flies mainly at dawn and dusk, and is often found sitting at lighted windows at night.

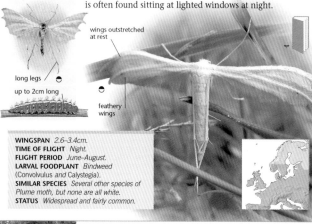

wings outstretched at rest

long legs

up to 2cm long

feathery wings

WINGSPAN *2.6–3.4cm.*
TIME OF FLIGHT *Night.*
FLIGHT PERIOD *June–August.*
LARVAL FOODPLANT *Bindweed* (Convolvulus *and* Calystegia).
SIMILAR SPECIES *Several other species of Plume moth, but none are all white.*
STATUS *Widespread and fairly common.*

Chinese Character

Cilix glaucata (Drepanidae)

INHABITS *hedgerows, gardens, commons, bushy places, waste ground, and open woodland.*

At rest, with its antennae, body, and legs all hidden under its folded wings, this moth bears a striking resemblance to a bird dropping. Its camouflage is obviously highly effective, as it may be found resting on the outside of a moth trap or on nearby foliage, when other more conspicuous species have been taken by birds.

white ground colour

black and grey markings

smooth appearance

PALER FORM

up to 2cm long

WINGSPAN *2.2–2.7cm.*
TIME OF FLIGHT *Night.*
FLIGHT PERIOD *May–August, in two broods.*
LARVAL FOODPLANT *Hawthorn* (Crataegus), *blackthorn* (Prunus spinosa), *and occasionally other trees and plants.*
SIMILAR SPECIES *None.*
STATUS *Widespread and common.*

Pebble Hook-tip

Drepana falcataria (Drepanidae)

One of several species of moths known as Hook-tips, from the distinctive shape of their wing tips, the Pebble Hook-tip has an intricate mottled pattern on its wings, making it look like a dead leaf or a piece of bark as it rests during the day. It has a distinctive resting posture, with the forewings partly concealing the hindwings, giving the moth an almost oval outline.

FEEDS *on birch, and is found wherever the tree grows, in woodland, heathland, commons, and gardens.*

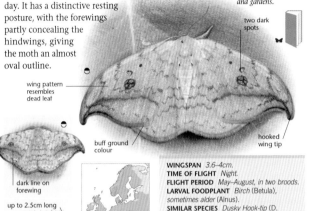

two dark spots

wing pattern resembles dead leaf

buff ground colour

hooked wing tip

dark line on forewing

up to 2.5cm long

WINGSPAN *3.6–4cm.*
TIME OF FLIGHT *Night.*
FLIGHT PERIOD *May–August, in two broods.*
LARVAL FOODPLANT *Birch (Betula), sometimes alder (Alnus).*
SIMILAR SPECIES *Dusky Hook-tip (D. curvatula), has a smaller spot on hindwing.*
STATUS *Locally common.*

Peach Blossom

Thyatira batis (Thyatiridae)

A beautiful and unmistakable moth, the Peach Blossom has an unusual wing pattern made up of large pink, buff, and white spots on a brown background. The young caterpillar resembles a bird dropping, and rests exposed on the upperside of a bramble leaf during the day. As it grows, it becomes browner, and hides among leaf litter, coming out to feed only at night.

OCCURS *in woodland with bramble, but also in gardens, commons, and waste ground.*

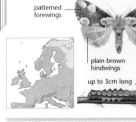

patterned forewings

plain brown hindwings

up to 3cm long

white spots with pinkish buff centres

dark brown ground colour

WINGSPAN *3.9–4.4cm.*
TIME OF FLIGHT *Night.*
FLIGHT PERIOD *May–August, sometimes in two broods.*
LARVAL FOODPLANT *Bramble/Blackberry (Rubus fruticosus).*
SIMILAR SPECIES *None.*
STATUS *Widespread and fairly common.*

Six-spot Burnet

Zygaena filipendulae (Zygaenidae)

INHABITS *downland, meadows, woodland rides, and other flower-rich places; also cliff tops and sand hills.*

This attractive day-flying species can be told apart from the similar Five-spot Burnet by the presence of three pairs of red spots on an iridescent greenish black or bluish green background. The hindwings, revealed in flight, are the same bright crimson-red as the forewing spots. All species of burnet moth contain cyanide, and have bright colours warning predators they are toxic. However, despite this fact, they are occasionally eaten by birds.

A rare colour variant of this moth has the red areas of the wings replaced by yellow instead. The papery cocoon may be found on the foodplant after the moth has emerged.

black head and body

papery cocoon

MOTH ON COCOON

NOTE
The extra red spot which separates this species from the Five-spot Burnet is at the tip of the forewing, making up three distinct pairs of spots.

up to 2.5cm long

thick, clubbed antennae

3 pairs of red spots on forewing

iridescent blue-green ground colour

WINGSPAN *2.5–4cm.*
FLIGHT PERIOD *June–August.*
LARVAL FOODPLANT *Bird's-foot trefoil (Lotus corniculatus).*
SIMILAR SPECIES *Five-spot Burnet (Z. trifolii), which has fewer red spots on its forewing; Cinnabar (p.180).*
STATUS *Widespread and fairly common.*

Hornet Moth

Sesia apiformis (Sesiidae)

With its transparent wings, yellow and black striped abdomen, and thickened antennae, the Hornet Moth bears a striking resemblance to a hornet or large wasp. All the Clearwing moths, of which this is one of the larger representatives, fly during the day, especially in sunshine, but are very rarely seen. The larva spends at least two years, sometimes three, in this stage before emerging as an adult. This is probably because of the low nutritional value of wood, on which it feeds.

FAVOURS *areas where mature poplar trees grow, often near water or in damp habitats such as marshes and river valleys.*

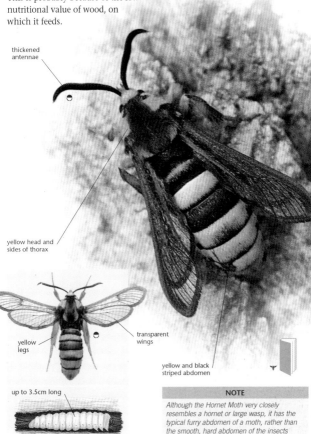

thickened antennae

yellow head and sides of thorax

yellow legs

transparent wings

yellow and black striped abdomen

up to 3.5cm long

NOTE

Although the Hornet Moth very closely resembles a hornet or large wasp, it has the typical furry abdomen of a moth, rather than the smooth, hard abdomen of the insects that it mimics.

WINGSPAN *3.4–5cm.*
FLIGHT PERIOD *July–August.*
LARVAL FOODPLANT *Feeds on the trunks and roots of black poplar (Populus nigra); occasionally on other poplar (Populus) species.*
SIMILAR SPECIES *Lunar Hornet Moth has no yellow on the sides of the thorax.*
STATUS *Widely distributed throughout Europe, but local; commoner in the south of the region.*

Double-striped Pug

Gymnoscelis rufifasciata (Geometridae)

The Pugs are a notoriously difficult group of moths to identify, being mostly small and dull brown, with few distinguishing features. The Double-striped Pug is one of the more distinctive species, however, with rather pointed wing tips and two dark wavy lines across the forewings. The adults feed at flowers, and are attracted to light.

FREQUENTS *many habitats, including open woodland, gardens, commons, waste ground, and hedgerows.*

reddish buff ground colour

two squarish dark marks near wing tip

up to 1.5cm long

wavy dark lines

WINGSPAN *1.5–1.9cm.*
TIME OF FLIGHT *Night; easily disturbed during the day.*
FLIGHT PERIOD *April–August, in two broods.*
LARVAL FOODPLANT *Flowers of holly (Ilex), gorse (Ulex), and heather (Erica/Calluna).*
SIMILAR SPECIES *Many other Pug species.*
STATUS *Widespread and fairly common.*

Foxglove Pug

Eupithecia pulchellata (Geometridae)

One of the more distinctive Pugs, the Foxglove Pug usually has a strong reddish buff ground colour on its forewings, crossed by alternating dark and light brown bands. Some individuals are a paler buff, but even these have the light and dark bands. Like most of the Pugs, the Foxglove Pug is attracted to light.

FOUND *wherever foxgloves grow, in gardens, woodland, and on downland, moors, and shingle beaches.*

dark central band

buff ground colour

darker edge

up to 2cm long

WINGSPAN *1.8–2.2cm.*
TIME OF FLIGHT *Night.*
FLIGHT PERIOD *May–June.*
LARVAL FOODPLANT *Foxglove (Digitalis purpurea).*
SIMILAR SPECIES *Toadflax Pug (E. linariata), which has a darker band on forewings.*
STATUS *Locally common.*

Green Pug

Pasiphila rectangulata (Geometridae)

When freshly emerged, the Green Pug usually lives up to its name, with a distinctly green coloration on its wings. However, this colour quickly fades. Some specimens may also be darker, occasionally almost black. The Green Pug is strongly attracted to light, and is often found at windows or in moth traps after dark.

INHABITS *orchards and other places where fruit trees grow, such as gardens, woodland, and commons.*

wavy lines on forewing

greenish ground colour

DARKER FORM

dark line at centre of forewing

up to 1.5cm long

WINGSPAN *1.7–2.1cm.*
TIME OF FLIGHT *Night.*
FLIGHT PERIOD *June–July.*
LARVAL FOODPLANT *Flowers of fruit trees.*
SIMILAR SPECIES *V-Pug (Chloroclystis v-ata), which has a black "V" on forewings; Sloe Pug (P. chloerata), which is less green.*
STATUS *Widespread and common.*

Lime-speck Pug

Eupithecia centaureata (Geometridae)

This unmistakable Pug bears some resemblance to a bird dropping, being largely white with dark markings, which may help to reduce predation by birds. The moth rests with its slender wings stretched out at right angles to the body, the hindwings mostly concealed beneath the forewings.

OCCURS *in a variety of habitats including parks, gardens, waste ground, commons, and open woodland.*

white thorax

black spot on forewing

grey-brown band near outer edge

white ground colour

up to 2cm long

blackish abdomen

WINGSPAN *2–2.4cm.*
TIME OF FLIGHT *Night.*
FLIGHT PERIOD *April–September, usually in two broods.*
LARVAL FOODPLANT *Various flowers, including ragwort (Senecio).*
SIMILAR SPECIES *None.*
STATUS *Widespread and generally common.*

Latticed Heath

Chiasmia clathrata (Geometridae)

FAVOURS *a wide variety of habitats, including flowery meadows, downland, heathland, commons, and open woodland.*

On first sight, the Latticed Heath could be mistaken for a Skipper butterfly, particularly the Grizzled Skipper (p.112), which occurs in similar habitats. However, a close view will show that the moth is usually browner, while the Grizzled Skipper is more black and white. A rather variable moth – some specimens are darker or lighter than the typical form; the ground colour also varies from yellow-buff to whitish. The Latticed Heath flies by day in sunshine. However, it also flies at night, when it is attracted to light. The females are usually slightly smaller.

wings often held closed

network of dark lines

buff or whitish background

pattern similar on upper- and lower surfaces

NOTE

Although the Latticed Heath resembles the Grizzled Skipper (p.112), a close look will reveal that its wings are pale with a network of dark lines, whereas the butterfly's wings are black with small white rectangles.

up to 2.5cm long

WINGSPAN *2.6–3.2cm.*
FLIGHT PERIOD *May–September, in two broods.*
LARVAL FOODPLANT *Various clovers and trefoils (Trifolium/Lotus); also lucerne (Medicago sativa).*
SIMILAR SPECIES *Grizzled Skipper (p.112), Dingy Skipper (p.120), Common Heath (Ematurga atomaria), which has a less sharply defined pattern of dark brown and buff on its wings.*
STATUS *Widespread and locally common.*

Barred Yellow

Cidaria fulvata (Geometridae)

A small, brightly-coloured, and striking geometrid moth, the Barred Yellow rests with its wings swept back and its abdomen raised. Its natural flight time is at dusk, when it can be seen fluttering around vegetation, but some continue to fly throughout the night, when they are sometimes attracted to light.

FREQUENTS *gardens, hedges, and other bushy places; also found in commons and open woodland.*

buff hindwing

up to 2cm long

bright yellow ground colour

brown "V"-shaped band on forewing

WINGSPAN *2.5–3cm.*
FLIGHT PERIOD *June–August.*
LARVAL FOODPLANT *Wild and cultivated roses (Rosa).*
SIMILAR SPECIES *Yellow Shell (p.166), The Spinach (p. 167), Brimstone Moth (p.167).*
STATUS *Locally common.*

Green Carpet

Colostygia pectinataria (Geometridae)

A freshly emerged Green Carpet is moss green, but fades to yellowish in a few days, older moths being almost white. Wavy lines extend across the wings from three dark triangles along the forewing leading edge. The moth rests with its forewings swept back, concealing the hindwings.

FOUND *in hedgerows, gardens, commons, heathland, downland, and open woodland.*

dark triangles on leading edge

dark wavy lines

FRESHLY EMERGED MOTH

OLDER MOTH

up to 2cm long

WINGSPAN *2.5–2.9cm.*
FLIGHT PERIOD *May–July.*
LARVAL FOODPLANT *Bedstraws (Galium).*
SIMILAR SPECIES *None – this moth is unique in the region.*
STATUS *Widespread and common throughout the region.*

Garden Carpet

Xanthorhoe fluctuata (Geometridae)

The Garden Carpet may be distinguished from other small geometrid moths by the dark patch across the forewings, which extends only halfway across the wing. A common moth, even in suburban areas, it may be found during the day resting on walls, trees, or fences. It flies at dusk, and is attracted to light.

APPEARS *in various habitats with flowers, including gardens, commons, waste ground, and hedgerows.*

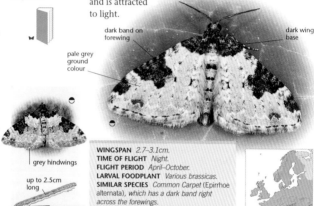

dark band on forewing

dark wing base

pale grey ground colour

grey hindwings

up to 2.5cm long

WINGSPAN *2.7–3.1cm.*
TIME OF FLIGHT *Night.*
FLIGHT PERIOD *April–October.*
LARVAL FOODPLANT *Various brassicas.*
SIMILAR SPECIES *Common Carpet* (Epirrhoe alterna)*, which has a dark band right across the forewings.*
STATUS *Widespread and common.*

Argent and Sable

Rheumaptera hastata (Geometridae)

This day-flying moth has a striking white and black wing pattern, giving rise to its common name Argent and Sable. It is generally a northern species that is found most commonly on moorland habitats, where it feeds on plants such as bilberry. Like most other day-flying species, this moth is more active in warm and sunny weather.

INHABITS *open birchwoods and northern moorland where the larval foodplants grow.*

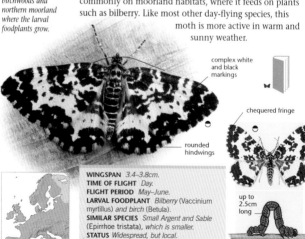

complex white and black markings

chequered fringe

rounded hindwings

up to 2.5cm long

WINGSPAN *3.4–3.8cm.*
TIME OF FLIGHT *Day.*
FLIGHT PERIOD *May–June.*
LARVAL FOODPLANT *Bilberry* (Vaccinium myrtillus) *and birch* (Betula)*.*
SIMILAR SPECIES *Small Argent and Sable* (Epirrhoe tristata)*, which is smaller.*
STATUS *Widespread, but local.*

Winter Moth

Operophtera brumata (Geometridae)

The Winter Moth, as its common name suggests, flies only during the winter months. As is the case with several other geometrids, only the male moth flies; the female is almost wingless, and rather spider-like in appearance. Both sexes may be found after dark sitting on tree trunks, and the male is often seen at lighted windows on mild nights.

FOUND *wherever there are deciduous trees and shrubs. This species can be a serious pest in orchards.*

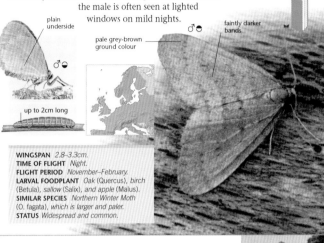

plain underside

♂●

up to 2cm long

pale grey-brown ground colour

♂●

faintly darker bands

WINGSPAN *2.8–3.3cm.*
TIME OF FLIGHT *Night.*
FLIGHT PERIOD *November–February.*
LARVAL FOODPLANT *Oak (Quercus), birch (Betula), sallow (Salix), and apple (Malus).*
SIMILAR SPECIES *Northern Winter Moth (O. fagata), which is larger and paler.*
STATUS *Widespread and common.*

Chimney Sweeper

Odezia atrata (Geometridae)

At first glance the Chimney Sweeper's wings appear entirely sooty black, but a closer view reveals the narrow white borders to the tips of the forewings. Older specimens may fade to a dull brown. This day-flying moth is most active in sunny weather. It can sometimes be seen in large numbers in damp meadows.

OCCURS *in damp meadows, on chalk downland, and along woodland edges, where the foodplant grows.*

sooty black ground colour

●

dull brown wings

●

white border on wing tip

up to 2.5cm long

WINGSPAN *2.7–3cm.*
TIME OF FLIGHT *Day.*
FLIGHT PERIOD *June–July.*
LARVAL FOODPLANT *Flowers and seeds of pignut (Conopodium majus), and other members of the carrot family.*
SIMILAR SPECIES *None.*
STATUS *Locally common.*

Yellow Shell

Camptogramma bilineata (Geometridae)

The Yellow Shell is rather variable in appearance. The typical form is mainly yellow, but darker varieties occur, particularly in the more northerly parts of its range. Its natural time of flight is from dusk onwards, however, it is easily disturbed from its resting place, and may be seen flying during the day.

INHABITS *a variety of habitats, including woodland, gardens, hedgerows, heathland, and commons.*

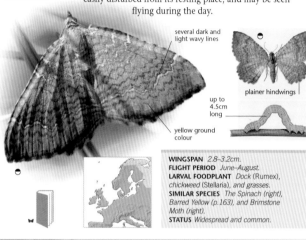

several dark and light wavy lines

plainer hindwings

up to 4.5cm long

yellow ground colour

WINGSPAN *2.8–3.2cm.*
FLIGHT PERIOD *June–August.*
LARVAL FOODPLANT *Dock (Rumex), chickweed (Stellaria), and grasses.*
SIMILAR SPECIES *The Spinach (right), Barred Yellow (p.163), and Brimstone Moth (right).*
STATUS *Widespread and common.*

Speckled Yellow

Pseudopanthera macularia (Geometridae)

An attractive, day-flying species, the Speckled Yellow typically lives up to its common name, although the ground colour is variable, and some individuals may be cream or almost white. It prefers warmer climates, and is commoner in the south of its range, but may be found in mountainous areas.

OCCURS *in open woodland and scrubland, both in lowland and mountainous regions.*

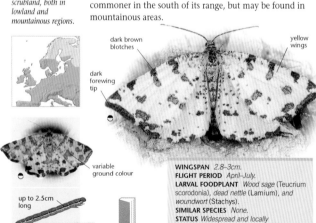

dark brown blotches

yellow wings

dark forewing tip

variable ground colour

up to 2.5cm long

WINGSPAN *2.8–3cm.*
FLIGHT PERIOD *April–July.*
LARVAL FOODPLANT *Wood sage (Teucrium scorodonia), dead nettle (Lamium), and woundwort (Stachys).*
SIMILAR SPECIES *None.*
STATUS *Widespread and locally fairly common.*

The Spinach

Eulithis mellinata (Geometridae)

This geometrid moth has an unusual resting posture, sitting with its wings held at right angles to its body, and the hindwings almost completely concealed beneath the forewings. Both the Barred Straw (*Eulithis pyraliata*) and the Northern Spinach (*Eulithis populata*) resemble this species and have a similar resting position, but both lack the chequered wing fringes of The Spinach.

FREQUENTS any habitat where currants grow, in gardens, allotments, or open woodland.

2 brown wavy lines across forewings

diagonal markings at tips

chequered fringes

up to 2.5cm long

WINGSPAN *3.3–3.8cm.*
FLIGHT PERIOD *June–August.*
LARVAL FOODPLANT *Blackcurrant (Ribes nigrum) and redcurrant (Ribes rubrum).*
SIMILAR SPECIES *Yellow Shell (left); Barred Yellow (p.163); Barred Straw and Northern Spinach, which lack the chequered fringe.*
STATUS *Widespread and common.*

Brimstone Moth

Opisthograptis luteolata (Geometridae)

This bright yellow geometrid moth sometimes flies by day, when it may be mistaken for a butterfly. More usually, it flies from dusk onwards, and is a common visitor to moth traps and lighted windows. This moth usually has several reddish brown marks along the leading edge of the wing, but occasional plain yellow specimens may also be found.

FOUND in hedgerows, gardens, covered bushy places, as well as open woodland.

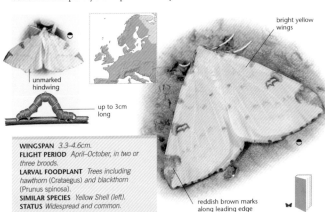

bright yellow wings

unmarked hindwing

up to 3cm long

WINGSPAN *3.3–4.6cm.*
FLIGHT PERIOD *April–October, in two or three broods.*
LARVAL FOODPLANT *Trees including hawthorn (Crataegus) and blackthorn (Prunus spinosa).*
SIMILAR SPECIES *Yellow Shell (left).*
STATUS *Widespread and common.*

reddish brown marks along leading edge

Blood-vein

Timandra comai (Geometridae)

The Blood-vein is a rather delicate moth with pointed tips to both the forewings and hindwings. At rest, the reddish lines on each wing join up to form a continuous stripe. The sexes are similar, but the male can be distinguished by its feathered antennae.

FREQUENTS *a wide range of habitats, including wasteland, commons, gardens, field margins, and meadows.*

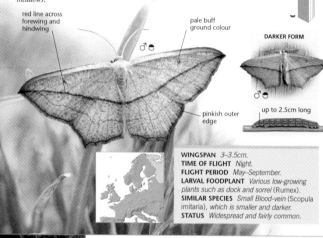

red line across forewing and hindwing

pale buff ground colour

DARKER FORM

♂●

♂●

pinkish outer edge

up to 2.5cm long

WINGSPAN *3–3.5cm.*
TIME OF FLIGHT *Night.*
FLIGHT PERIOD *May–September.*
LARVAL FOODPLANT *Various low-growing plants such as dock and sorrel (Rumex).*
SIMILAR SPECIES *Small Blood-vein (Scopula imitaria), which is smaller and darker.*
STATUS *Widespread and fairly common.*

Riband Wave

Idaea aversata (Geometridae)

This moth occurs in two forms – one with a dark band across the wings and another non-banded form. Both are equally common. The Riband Wave is easily disturbed from its resting place during the day. However, the natural time of flight is at night, when it is attracted to light.

OCCURS *in gardens, commons, and wasteland with low-growing weeds.*

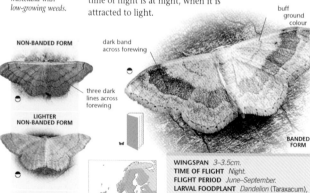

buff ground colour

NON-BANDED FORM

●

dark band across forewing

three dark lines across forewing

●

LIGHTER NON-BANDED FORM

●

BANDED FORM

up to 2.5cm long

WINGSPAN *3–3.5cm.*
TIME OF FLIGHT *Night.*
FLIGHT PERIOD *June–September.*
LARVAL FOODPLANT *Dandelion (Taraxacum), knotgrass (Polygonum), chickweed (Stellaria).*
SIMILAR SPECIES *Plain Wave (I. straminata), which is smaller and glossier.*
STATUS *Widespread and common.*

Scallop Shell

Rheumaptera undulata (Geometridae)

One of the most attractive geometrid moths, the Scallop Shell's wings are covered with an intricate pattern of light and dark zig-zag lines. Like many members of its family, it rests with its wings swept back, the forewings concealing the hindwings. Attracted to light, it flies at night, but rarely in large numbers.

FOUND *often in open woodland, especially with an undergrowth of bilberry. Also found in very damp places such as marshes.*

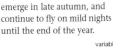

rounded wing

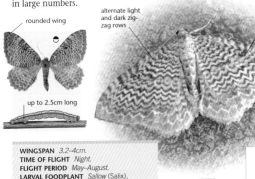

alternate light and dark zig-zag rows

forewings cover hindwings

up to 2.5cm long

WINGSPAN *3.2–4cm.*
TIME OF FLIGHT *Night.*
FLIGHT PERIOD *May–August.*
LARVAL FOODPLANT *Sallow (Salix), aspen (Populus tremula), and bilberry (Vaccinium myrtillus).*
SIMILAR SPECIES *None.*
STATUS *Locally fairly common.*

Mottled Umber

Erannis defoliaria (Geometridae)

This very variable species ranges from light buff with brown bands to wholly dark brown. The female, light brown with black spots on the abdomen, is completely wingless, and may be found sitting on tree trunks after dark. Adults emerge in late autumn, and continue to fly on mild nights until the end of the year.

INHABITS *deciduous woodland, hedgerows, and orchards, where the caterpillar may be a pest.*

DARK BROWN FORM

brown band across wing

variable buff to brown colour

wingless female

up to 3.5cm long

WINGSPAN *4–4.5cm.*
TIME OF FLIGHT *Night.*
FLIGHT PERIOD *September–December.*
LARVAL FOODPLANT *Oak (Quercus), birch (Betula), and hawthorn (Crataegus).*
SIMILAR SPECIES *Dotted Border (Agriopis marginaria) has dots along forewing edge.*
STATUS *Widespread and common.*

Orange Underwing

Archiearis parthenias (Geometridae)

FOUND *in areas where birch grows, such as heathland and open woodland.*

An attractive day-flying species, the Orange Underwing can be found flying around birch trees on sunny days in early spring. It is a difficult moth to see well, as it spends most of its time high up around the treetops. However, it does occasionally descend to drink at patches of wet ground. At rest, the bright orange hindwings are concealed below the mottled brown forewings. It should not be confused with any of the Yellow Underwings, as they are nocturnal, and fly much later in the year.

hindwings concealed at rest

NOTE

The Orange Underwing usually flies high up around the tops of birch trees. However, since it flies by day, it can be identified even at that height by its bright orange hindwings, which are visible in flight.

dark markings on upperwing

up to 2.5cm long

light patches on dark brown forewing

orange hindwing

dark border

WINGSPAN *3.5–4cm.*
TIME OF FLIGHT *Day.*
FLIGHT PERIOD *March–April.*
LARVAL FOODPLANT *Birch (Betula).*
SIMILAR SPECIES *Light Orange Underwing (A. notha), which is slightly smaller and has less orange on its hindwings.*
STATUS *Widespread and locally common.*

March Moth

Alsophila aescularia (Geometridae)

At rest, the March Moth does not look like a typical geometrid, as it holds its pointed wings tightly together, with one forewing overlapping the other. The wings have a subtle pattern of grey and brown, with a jagged whitish line across the centre of the forewings. The female is wingless and crawls around on tree trunks.

FEEDS *on many species of trees and shrubs, in woodland, hedgerows, gardens, and orchards, where the larvae may be a pest.*

white stripe

subtle grey and brown pattern

pointed wings

♂⊝

plain hindwings

♂⊝

up to 3cm long

WINGSPAN	*3.4–4cm.*
TIME OF FLIGHT	*Night.*
FLIGHT PERIOD	*March–April.*
LARVAL FOODPLANT	*Oak (Quercus), birch (Betula), hawthorn (Crataegus), and other deciduous trees.*
SIMILAR SPECIES	*None.*
STATUS	*Widespread and common.*

Scorched Wing

Plagodis dolabraria (Geometridae)

This attractive moth's wings look as if they have been charred by fire. The pattern on the wings, in subtle shades of brown, provides very effective camouflage as the moth rests on a tree trunk or branch during the day. The Scorched Wing flies at night, and the male is attracted to light.

INHABITS *deciduous or mixed woodland, preferring open woods, rides, and clearings.*

dark forewing base

dark brown lines on forewing

pale buff ground colour

up to 4cm long

scorched look

WINGSPAN	*3.4–4cm.*
TIME OF FLIGHT	*Night.*
FLIGHT PERIOD	*May–June.*
LARVAL FOODPLANT	*Various deciduous trees including oak (Quercus), birch (Betula), and sallow (Salix).*
SIMILAR SPECIES	*None.*
STATUS	*Fairly common.*

Bordered White

Bupalus piniaria (Geometridae)

Also known as the Pine Looper, this moth is often seeing flying by day in conifer plantations. At rest, it holds its wings closed over its back, in butterfly-like fashion, which makes it difficult to identify when comparing it to pinned specimens. However, there are no similar species, and it can be confidently identified from the underwing pattern alone. The ground colour of the males' forewings varies from yellowish in the south to white in the north, and the females are darker in the north. The larvae can cause damage in conifer plantations.

INHABITS *both natural and planted conifer woods, usually pine, but may also be found on other conifers.*

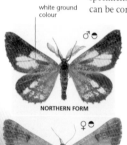

white ground colour

♂●

NORTHERN FORM

♀●

dark outer edge

up to 3.5cm long

NOTE

No other day-flying species that holds its wings over its back has this pattern of white or yellowish blotches on the underside of the hindwings.

whitish patches

wings held back at rest

♂●

WINGSPAN *3.5–4cm.*
TIME OF FLIGHT *Day and night.*
FLIGHT PERIOD *May–June.*
LARVAL FOODPLANT *Pine (Pinus).*
SIMILAR SPECIES *None – the pale patches on its underwings make it unique.*
STATUS *Widespread and common; often considered a pest in pine plantations.*

Magpie Moth

Abraxas grossulariata (Geometridae)

This strikingly marked species is highly variable, with some forms showing very few black spots, and others being almost entirely black. However, these aberrations are usually the result of captive breeding, and are very rarely seen in the wild. The bold patterning suggests that the moth is distasteful, and serves as a warning to predators. Interestingly, the caterpillar has a similar pattern of black spots on a whitish body, and a reddish stripe along the sides. It may be a pest on currant and gooseberry bushes.

FOUND *in gardens and allotments where currant and gooseberry are grown; also in hedgerows and open deciduous woodland.*

yellow and black thorax and abdomen

yellow S-shaped line

DARKER FORM

large black patches

white ground colour

black spots

LIGHTER FORM

fewer black spots

up to 3.5cm long

NOTE

The caterpillar of the Magpie Moth is just as variable in its coloration as the adult moth. While most caterpillars are whitish with black spots, some are darker, or even completely black as in the case of the adult.

WINGSPAN *4.2–4.8cm.*
TIME OF FLIGHT *Night (occasionally day).*
FLIGHT PERIOD *July–August.*
LARVAL FOODPLANT *Currant (Ribes), gooseberry (Ribes uva-crispa), blackthorn (Prunus spinosa), and hazel (Corylus avellana).*
SIMILAR SPECIES *Small Magpie (p.154), which is much smaller and belongs to the Micro-moth group.*
STATUS *Widespread and common.*

Brindled Beauty

Lycia hirtaria (Geometridae)

FEEDS *on almost any deciduous tree, so may be found in a variety of habitats, including orchards, woods, parks, and gardens.*

The Brindled Beauty is a rather variable species, with a furry thorax and abdomen, and subtle coloration of buffs, browns, and greys. These patterns of colours provide excellent camouflage when the moth is at rest on a tree trunk during the day. The male is typically yellowish buff with blackish lines and mottling, while the female is usually plainer and darker, with dark grey-brown wings. However, some males, which can be told by their feathered antennae, may be almost black. The caterpillar, which feeds on the foliage of broad-leaved trees, is occasionally a pest in orchards.

furry thorax and abdomen

feathered antennae

LIGHTER FORM

♂●

mottled buff, grey, and brown wings

brown and white pattern

up to 5.5cm long

NOTE

The Brindled Beauty can be found during the day by careful examination of tree trunks, but you need sharp vision to spot them against the bark, as they are highly camouflaged. They may also be found on walls and fences.

WINGSPAN *4.2–5.2cm.*
TIME OF FLIGHT *Night.*
FLIGHT PERIOD *March–May.*
LARVAL FOODPLANT *Various trees and shrubs including sallow (Salix), birch (Betula), lime (Tilia), hawthorn (Crataegus), and alder (Alnus).*
SIMILAR SPECIES *Peppered Moth (p.176), Pale Brindled Beauty (Apocheima pilosaria), which is lighter in colour; flies earlier in the year.*
STATUS *Widespread and common.*

Purple Thorn

Selenia tetralunaria (Geometridae)

The group of geometrid moths known as Thorns rest with their wings raised. The Purple Thorn can be told from similar species by its habit of holding its wings half open over its back. The moth has two, sometimes three broods each year,

OCCURS *in deciduous woodland; also in parks, gardens, and commons.*

the later generations usually being smaller and darker than the spring brood.

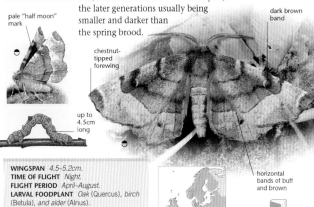

pale "half moon" mark

dark brown band

chestnut-tipped forewing

up to 4.5cm long

horizontal bands of buff and brown

WINGSPAN *4.5–5.2cm.*
TIME OF FLIGHT *Night.*
FLIGHT PERIOD *April–August.*
LARVAL FOODPLANT *Oak (Quercus), birch (Betula), and alder (Alnus).*
SIMILAR SPECIES *Early Thorn (Selenia dentaria), which is paler.*
STATUS *Widespread and fairly common.*

Light Emerald

Campaea margaritata (Geometridae)

The Light Emerald's green coloration quickly fades almost to white. However, the pattern of two greenish brown lines bordered by white is usually visible, making this moth easy to identify, while a newly-emerged moth has small red-brown wing-tips. The females are larger than the males.

FOUND *in gardens, parks, woodland, hedgerows, and commons.*

faded colours

OLDER SPECIMEN

greenish white ground colour

up to 4cm long

WINGSPAN *4–5.5cm.*
TIME OF FLIGHT *Night.*
FLIGHT PERIOD *July–September.*
LARVAL FOOD PLANT *Oak (Quercus), birch (Betula), beech (Fagus), and hawthorn (Crataegus).*
SIMILAR SPECIES *Large Emerald (p.177).*
STATUS *Widespread and common.*

Peppered Moth

Biston betularia (Geometridae)

The Peppered Moth has three distinct forms – light, intermediate, and dark – and is often cited as an example of natural selection. In industrial areas, where tree trunks are blackened with soot, the lighter moths are highly visible to birds, and therefore more often eaten. The darker forms, however, are camouflaged, resulting in less predation; thus more dark moths survive to pass on their genes to their offspring. On the other hand, recent studies have shown how the darker form has become less common in areas formerly blighted by pollution, but where the situation has improved once clean air laws have taken effect. Both sexes fly at night and are strongly attracted to light.

FREQUENTS *woodland, gardens, parks, hedgerows, and commons, where there are trees for the caterpillar to feed on.*

DARK FORM

plain blackish wings

evenly mottled light and dark wings

INTERMEDIATE FORM

LIGHTER FORM

lightly mottled wings

up to 6cm long

whitish background

dark mottling

NOTE

The three forms are genetically distinct from each other. The intermediate form cannot be reproduced by crossing the light form with the dark form. All three forms may occur in the same area, but one will usually predominate over the other two. The intermediate form is generally the least common.

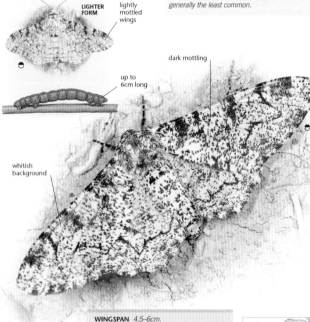

WINGSPAN *4.5–6cm.*
FLIGHT PERIOD *May–August.*
LARVAL FOODPLANT *Trees, including sallow (Salix), birch (Betula), lime (Tilia), and hawthorn (Crataegus).*
SIMILAR SPECIES *Brindled Beauty (p.174), which is more buff and brown.*
STATUS *Widespread and common.*

Swallow-tailed Moth

Ourapteryx sambucaria (Geometridae)

This large, pale yellow moth has a very distinctive shape, and should not be confused with any other European species. The hindwings have projecting "tails" reminiscent of the Swallowtail Butterfly (p.53), and the forewings are also sharply pointed. This moth is strongly attracted to light, and is frequently found resting on lighted windows after dark.

OCCURS *in woodland, gardens, parks, hedgerows, and commons.*

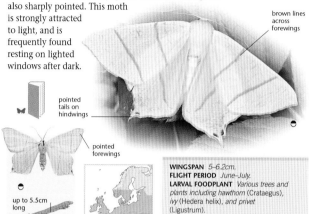

brown lines across forewings

pointed tails on hindwings

pointed forewings

up to 5.5cm long

WINGSPAN	*5–6.2cm.*
FLIGHT PERIOD	*June–July.*
LARVAL FOODPLANT	*Various trees and plants including hawthorn (Crataegus), ivy (Hedera helix), and privet (Ligustrum).*
SIMILAR SPECIES	*None.*
STATUS	*Fairly common.*

Large Emerald

Geometra papilionaria (Geometridae)

One of the larger and more robust members of its family, the Large Emerald's wings and body are a beautiful bright green when fresh, with delicate white markings. Like all green moths, this colour quickly fades especially in museum specimens. This moth typically flies late at night, and is attracted to light.

FOUND *in areas where birch grows, such as heathland and open woodland.*

white scalloped line across forewing

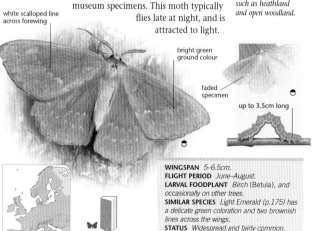

bright green ground colour

faded specimen

up to 3.5cm long

WINGSPAN	*5–6.5cm.*
FLIGHT PERIOD	*June–August.*
LARVAL FOODPLANT	*Birch (Betula), and occasionally on other trees.*
SIMILAR SPECIES	*Light Emerald (p.175) has a delicate green coloration and two brownish lines across the wings.*
STATUS	*Widespread and fairly common.*

Yellow-tail

Euproctis similis (Lymantriidae)

The Yellow-tail, and the closely-related Brown-tail moth, contains irritating chemicals at all stages of its life cycle, which can cause a severe allergic reaction in some people if they are touched. The hairy black, white, and red caterpillars in particular should not be handled. The adult moth has an unusual defensive posture: if disturbed, it lies on its side, with its yellow-tipped abdomen projecting beyond the trailing edge of the wings. The males have small dark marks on the forewings, while the females' wings are pure white.

INHABITS *hedgerows, scrub, and other areas with bushy vegetation, where there is plenty of larval foodplant available.*

furry body

display of yellow-tipped abdomen

up to 4.5cm long

NOTE

In common with several other members of the Lymantriidae family, the female Yellow-tail protects her eggs by covering them with the irritant yellow hairs from her abdomen tip.

white ground colour

small dark marks

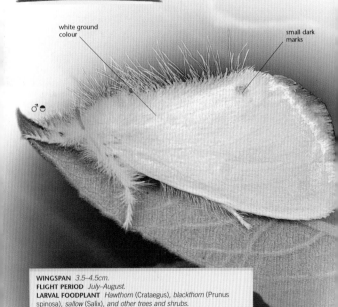

WINGSPAN *3.5–4.5cm.*
FLIGHT PERIOD *July–August.*
LARVAL FOODPLANT *Hawthorn (Crataegus), blackthorn (Prunus spinosa), sallow (Salix), and other trees and shrubs.*
SIMILAR SPECIES *Brown-tail (Euproctis chrysorrhoea) has a dark brown tip to the abdomen, White Satin (Leucoma salicis), which has pure white wings, but lacks the yellow abdomen tip.*
STATUS *Widespread and generally common.*

Common Footman

Eilema lurideola (Arctiidae)

This moth rests with its long thin forewings folded flat over its back. However, if seen in flight, it appears much larger, owing to its broad yellowish hindwings. Flying from dusk onwards, it may be found feeding at thistle flowers (*Cirsium* and *Carduus*) or Traveller's Joy (*Clematis vitalba*). Like most members of the "Footman" family, the larvae feed on lichens.

FOUND *in hedgerows, gardens, and open woodland, wherever there are lichen-covered trees for the larvae to feed on.*

long, thin forewings

pale yellow leading edge

yellow-grey ground colour

broad yellowish hindwings

up to 2.5cm long

WINGSPAN *3.1–3.8cm.*
FLIGHT PERIOD *July–August.*
LARVAL FOODPLANT *Lichens growing on trees, walls, fences, or rocks.*
SIMILAR SPECIES *Scarce Footman (Eilema complana), which rests with its wings rolled around its body.*
STATUS *Widespread and common.*

Ruby Tiger

Phragmatobia fuliginosa (Arctiidae)

One of the smaller members of its family, the Ruby Tiger has plain reddish brown forewings with two small blackish dots. The hindwings vary from orange-red with dark markings to plain black. This moth flies mainly at night, when it often comes to light, but may sometimes be found flying on sunny days.

OCCURS *in waste ground, gardens, commons, heathland, and moorland.*

red-brown ground colour

furry head and thorax

red and black hindwings

blackish spots

plain forewings

up to 3.5cm long

WINGSPAN *2.8–3.8cm.*
FLIGHT PERIOD *April–September, in two broods.*
LARVAL FOODPLANT *Various plants including dock (Rumex) and dandelion (Taraxacum).*
SIMILAR SPECIES *None.*
STATUS *Widespread and common.*

White Ermine

Spilosoma lubricipeda (Arctiidae)

This attractive species is very variable – typical specimens have small black spots evenly scattered over the white forewings, but some may have larger or smaller spots. Occasionally, individuals may be seen with much more black, the spots being joined up to form bars. The ground colour also varies, some moths being more buff-coloured.

FOUND *in a wide variety of habitats, as the caterpillar is not at all fussy about what foodplants it feeds on.*

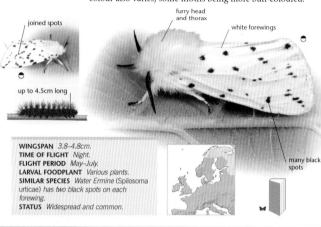

joined spots

up to 4.5cm long

furry head and thorax

white forewings

many black spots

WINGSPAN *3.8–4.8cm.*
TIME OF FLIGHT *Night.*
FLIGHT PERIOD *May–July.*
LARVAL FOODPLANT *Various plants.*
SIMILAR SPECIES *Water Ermine (Spilosoma urticae) has two black spots on each forewing.*
STATUS *Widespread and common.*

The Cinnabar

Tyria jacobaeae (Arctiidae)

This distinctive and familiar species is sometimes seen flying by day, when the bright crimson hindwings draw attention to it. At rest, the crimson hindwings are concealed beneath the forewings, which are glossy dark grey, with red lines and spots. Unlike most members of its family, the caterpillars are gregarious, and can be found in large numbers on ragwort (*Senecio*) plants.

OCCURS *wherever ragwort and groundsel grow; on waste ground, commons, and meadows.*

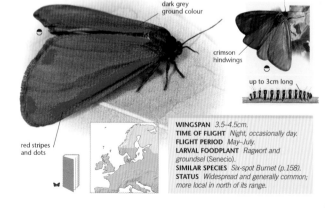

dark grey ground colour

crimson hindwings

up to 3cm long

red stripes and dots

WINGSPAN *3.5–4.5cm.*
TIME OF FLIGHT *Night, occasionally day.*
FLIGHT PERIOD *May–July.*
LARVAL FOODPLANT *Ragwort and groundsel (Senecio).*
SIMILAR SPECIES *Six-spot Burnet (p.158).*
STATUS *Widespread and generally common; more local in north of its range.*

Garden Tiger

Arctia caja (Arctiidae)

The large and strikingly-marked Garden Tiger has declined dramatically in many parts of its range in recent years, possibly due to climatic change. The complex pattern of dark brown and cream on the forewings varies from moth to moth. The contrasting hindwings are a bright orange ground colour with prominent black spots. Also orange, the abdomen is marked with black bars. The caterpillar of the Garden Tiger is sometimes known as the "woolly bear" since it is covered with many long brown hairs. These contain an irritant poison and should never be handled.

INHABITS *gardens, parks, commons, waste ground, and any habitat where low plants grow.*

NOTE

The Garden Tiger is a very variable species, and individuals may sometimes be found with almost entirely brown forewings or, in contrast, with the brown markings much reduced. The hindwing colour also varies from the usual orange to yellow or dark brown.

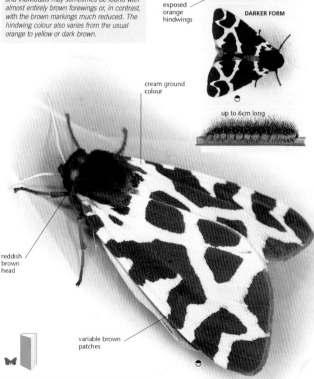

exposed orange hindwings

DARKER FORM

cream ground colour

up to 6cm long

reddish brown head

variable brown patches

WINGSPAN *5–7.8cm.*
TIME OF FLIGHT *Night.*
FLIGHT PERIOD *July–August.*
LARVAL FOODPLANT *Various wild and cultivated plants.*
SIMILAR SPECIES *None.*
STATUS *Widespread, but not as common as it once was.*

Chocolate-tip

Clostera curtula (Notodontidae)

This attractive moth has an unusual resting position, sitting with its wings wrapped around its body and the tip of its abdomen raised. Its head and thorax are furry, with a well-defined dark brown stripe contrasting with the greyish background. It is often abundant in habitats where its larval foodplants grow.

FOUND *mainly in woodland, but also along rivers and in open country with scattered trees.*

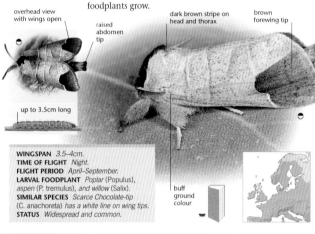

overhead view with wings open

raised abdomen tip

dark brown stripe on head and thorax

brown forewing tip

up to 3.5cm long

buff ground colour

WINGSPAN *3.5–4cm.*
TIME OF FLIGHT *Night.*
FLIGHT PERIOD *April–September.*
LARVAL FOODPLANT *Poplar (Populus), aspen (P. tremula), and willow (Salix).*
SIMILAR SPECIES *Scarce Chocolate-tip (C. anachoreta) has a white line on wing tips.*
STATUS *Widespread and common.*

The Vapourer

Orgyia antiqua (Lymantriidae)

The red-brown male Vapourers are often seen flying rapidly in sunshine, but the females are wingless and rarely move far from the cocoon after hatching. Males also fly at night, and are attracted to light. The larvae have red and yellow tufts, and black and brown hairs, which can cause irritation if handled.

FREQUENTS *a wide variety of habitats, including gardens, woodland, commons, and urban areas.*

♂ plain hindwings

WINGLESS FEMALE

white spots on forewing

fat, furry body

♀ ●

up to 4cm long

red-brown ground colour

WINGSPAN *3.5–4cm.*
TIME OF FLIGHT *Day and night.*
FLIGHT PERIOD *July–October, in two broods.*
LARVAL FOODPLANT *Many deciduous trees and shrubs.*
SIMILAR SPECIES *Scarce Vapourer (O. recens) has a white mark at the forewing tip.*
STATUS *Widespread and common.*

Sallow Kitten

Furcula furcula (Notodontidae)

This is the commonest of three closely related species which differ in the shape of the central band on the strongly marked forewings. One of the smaller Prominent moths, it shares the family habit of resting with its wings raised over its body. Its head, thorax, and legs are furry.

OCCURS *in damp woodland, waterside habitats, and wherever sallows grow; also found in gardens, parks, and on commons.*

grey band across forewings

furry black thorax

black dots on wing margin

up to 3.5cm long

WINGSPAN *3.5–4.2cm.*
TIME OF FLIGHT *Night.*
FLIGHT PERIOD *May–August, in two broods.*
LARVAL FOODPLANT *Sallow (Salix).*
SIMILAR SPECIES *Alder Kitten (F. bicuspis) has a darker, strongly indented forewing band; Poplar Kitten (F. bifida) has a straighter band.*
STATUS *Widespread and common.*

Pale Prominent

Pterostoma palpina (Notodontidae)

At rest during the day, the Pale Prominent relies on its excellent camouflage to avoid detection by predators, closely resembling a broken piece of wood. As with many highly camouflaged species, the moth contributes to the deception by remaining absolutely still; even if disturbed, it will often fall onto its side rather than fly off in alarm.

INHABITS *deciduous woodland, preferring damper areas; also occurs in gardens, parks, and on commons.*

very long mouth-parts

protruding abdomen tip

serrated forewing margin

up to 4cm long

WINGSPAN *4–6cm.*
TIME OF FLIGHT *Night.*
FLIGHT PERIOD *May–August, in two broods.*
LARVAL FOODPLANT *Poplar (Populus) and sallow (Salix).*
SIMILAR SPECIES *None.*
STATUS *Widespread and common.*

Buff-tip

Phalera bucephala (Notodontidae)

FOUND *in hedgerows, gardens, and open woodland, wherever there are trees for the caterpillars to feed on.*

A superbly camouflaged species, the Buff-tip almost perfectly resembles a broken-off birch twig. At rest, the moth's wings are rolled around its body in a tubular shape, with the pale hindwings concealed. Most of the forewing is an intricately mottled silvery grey, with delicate black and brown lines running across it; the wing tips are a contrasting pale buff, as are the fluffy head and thorax. Like all the members of this family, the adult moths have no proboscis, and so do not feed. The Buff-tip tends to fly late at night, when it is attracted to light.

scalloped forewing margins

furry buff head and thorax

up to 7.5cm long

NOTE

The yellow and black Buff-tip caterpillars are gregarious at first, later becoming solitary before pupation. They often cause severe damage to trees by stripping the leaves off branches.

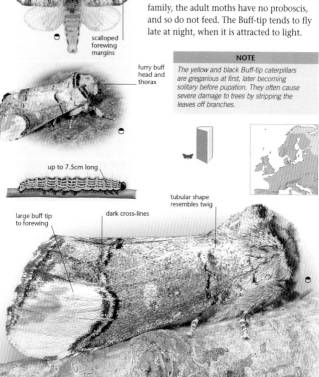

large buff tip to forewing

dark cross-lines

tubular shape resembles twig

WINGSPAN *5.5–7cm.*
TIME OF FLIGHT *Night.*
FLIGHT PERIOD *May–July.*
LARVAL FOODPLANT *Many deciduous trees and shrubs.*
SIMILAR SPECIES *None.*
STATUS *Widespread and common.*

Puss Moth

Cerura vinula (Notodontidae)

This large and attractive member of the Prominent family is tinged with a delicate green when freshly emerged. However, this colour quickly fades to a lighter shade. The white forewings of the adult moth are patterned with black lines. It does not seem to be strongly attracted to light, and is consequently not often seen. The caterpillar is one of the most extraordinary of the moth world. It has a large head, and two red-tipped "tails", which are actually modified hindlegs. If threatened, it waves these in the air, while rearing up its head to make itself look bigger.

INHABITS *hedgerows, open woodland, parks, and gardens; also found at watersides, where poplar and sallow, the larval foodplants, grow.*

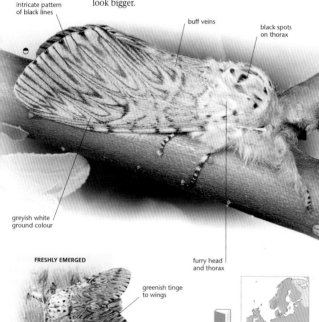

intricate pattern of black lines

buff veins

black spots on thorax

greyish white ground colour

furry head and thorax

FRESHLY EMERGED

greenish tinge to wings

zig-zag markings

up to 6.5cm long

red-tipped hindlegs

NOTE

The bright green and brown caterpillar can squirt formic acid from special glands in the throat to deter predators. The young larvae are very similar to those of the Sallow Kitten (p.183) and can be found feeding in pairs.

WINGSPAN *6–8cm.*
TIME OF FLIGHT *Night.*
FLIGHT PERIOD *May–July.*
LARVAL FOODPLANT *Poplar (Populus) and sallow (Salix).*
SIMILAR SPECIES *None.*
STATUS *Widespread and fairly common.*

Marbled Beauty

Cryphia domestica (Noctuidae)

One of the smaller noctuids, the Marbled Beauty is attractively marked with black and grey on a cream background. As its scientific name implies, it is often found around houses and other buildings since the larvae feed particularly on lichens that grow on walls. Some individuals are greenish, and can be confused with the Marbled Green.

FOUND *mainly in urban areas, but also on cliffs in open countryside, and other places with lichen.*

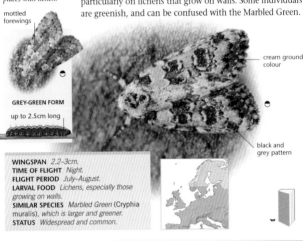

mottled forewings

GREY-GREEN FORM

up to 2.5cm long

cream ground colour

black and grey pattern

WINGSPAN *2.2–3cm.*
TIME OF FLIGHT *Night.*
FLIGHT PERIOD *July–August.*
LARVAL FOOD *Lichens, especially those growing on walls.*
SIMILAR SPECIES *Marbled Green (Cryphia muralis), which is larger and greener.*
STATUS *Widespread and common.*

Antler Moth

Cerapteryx graminis (Noctuidae)

This moth varies greatly in size, with females generally being larger than males. The wing pattern is also rather variable – in some individuals the white "antler" marks are much reduced or even lacking altogether. Adults may be seen flying and feeding at flowers during the day, but also fly at night, when they are attracted to light.

INHABITS *grassy areas such as meadows, moorland, downland, and commons.*

REDDISH BROWN FORM

GREYISH FORM

up to 3.5cm long

dark band on forewing

white "antler" pattern

WINGSPAN *2.5–4cm.*
TIME OF FLIGHT *Day and night.*
FLIGHT PERIOD *July–September.*
LARVAL FOODPLANT *Various grasses (family Poaceae), notably sheep's fescue (Festuca ovina) and mat-grass (Nardus stricta).*
SIMILAR SPECIES *None.*
STATUS *Locally common.*

Centre-barred Sallow

Atethmia centrago (Noctuidae)

The dark orange bar across the forewings, from which this species gets its common name, varies in intensity; on some specimens it hardly contrasts with the yellowish ground colour. The hindwings are whitish with an orange border. This moth flies at night and is attracted to light in small numbers.

FREQUENTS *woodland, parks, hedgerows, meadows, commons, and gardens; found wherever ash grows, the availability of the larval foodplant being the common factor.*

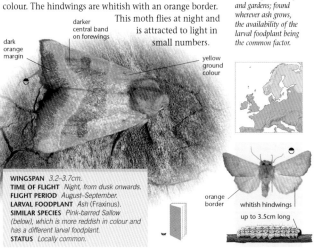

darker central band on forewings

dark orange margin

yellow ground colour

WINGSPAN *3.2–3.7cm.*
TIME OF FLIGHT *Night, from dusk onwards.*
FLIGHT PERIOD *August–September.*
LARVAL FOODPLANT *Ash (Fraxinus).*
SIMILAR SPECIES *Pink-barred Sallow (below), which is more reddish in colour and has a different larval foodplant.*
STATUS *Locally common.*

orange border

whitish hindwings

up to 3.5cm long

Pink-barred Sallow

Xanthia togata (Noctuidae)

This moth's coloration, typical of many species that fly in autumn, is a camouflage against fallen leaves. The Pink-barred Sallow is attracted to light, and also feeds at flowers and ripe blackberries, rich in energy-providing sugar. The caterpillar, which feeds inside sallow or poplar catkins, is a rather dull brown colour.

OCCURS *in damp woodland, marshland, and riverbanks where sallows and poplars grow.*

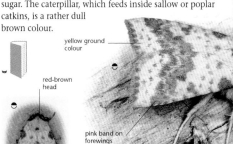

yellow ground colour

red-brown head

pink band on forewings

brown blotches on forewings

up to 3.5cm long

WINGSPAN *2.8–3.7cm.*
TIME OF FLIGHT *Night.*
FLIGHT PERIOD *September–October.*
LARVAL FOODPLANT *Catkins of sallow (Salix) and poplar (Populus).*
SIMILAR SPECIES *Centre-barred Sallow (above); several other Sallow species.*
STATUS *Widespread and common.*

Common Rustic

Mesapamea secalis (Noctuidae)

Until recently, it was thought that there was just one species of Common Rustic in Europe. However, studies have shown that there are actually three very closely related species. These are the Common Rustic, the Lesser Common Rustic, and the very rare Remm's Rustic. All three species are so similar that they cannot be identified on wing pattern, but only on the structure of the genitalia, which requires dissection by experts. As a general rule, however, the Lesser Common Rustic is smaller and darker than the other two.

OCCURS *in a wide range of grassy habitats, such as meadows, commons, gardens, heathland, and moorland.*

DARKER FORM

dark brown ground colour

whitish spot on forewing

PLAIN BROWN FORM

NOTE

The Common Rustic is a variable moth, with many different forms; some are plain brown, while others are mottled light and dark brown. However, the same basic pattern can be found on most individuals.

up to 3cm long

mottled ground colour

lacks white spot on forewing

MOTTLED LIGHT AND DARK BROWN FORM

WINGSPAN *2.8–3.6cm.*
TIME OF FLIGHT *Night.*
FLIGHT PERIOD *July–August.*
LARVAL FOODPLANT *Various grasses (family Poaceae).*
SIMILAR SPECIES *Lesser Common Rustic (M. didyma) and Remm's Rustic (M. remmi), which have different internal characteristics; several other brownish members of the noctuid family.*
STATUS *Widespread and often abundant.*

The Spectacle

Abrostola tripartita (Noctuidae)

This moth has two distinctive, blackish circles on the front of the thorax, which resemble a pair of spectacles. In some urban industrial areas, a very dark form occurs, which has almost black wings. The Spectacle flies at night, and is a common visitor to moth traps. It may also be found feeding at flowers after dark.

FOUND *in damp woodland, gardens, river valleys, and wasteland, even in urban areas.*

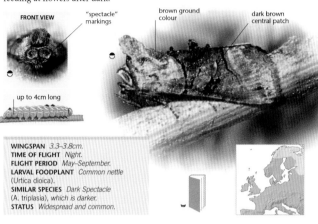

FRONT VIEW

"spectacle" markings

brown ground colour

dark brown central patch

up to 4cm long

WINGSPAN *3.3–3.8cm.*
TIME OF FLIGHT *Night.*
FLIGHT PERIOD *May–September.*
LARVAL FOODPLANT *Common nettle* (Urtica dioica).
SIMILAR SPECIES *Dark Spectacle* (A. triplasia), *which is darker.*
STATUS *Widespread and common.*

Mother Shipton

Callistege mi (Noctuidae)

This day-flying species is often found in the same habitats as Dingy and Grizzled Skipper butterflies, and may be mistaken for them in flight. At rest, however, its wing patterns are quite different. The moth gets its common name, Mother Shipton, from a legendary witch whose profile, with its long, hooked nose and pointed chin, is said to be reflected in the markings.

INHABITS *grassy places such as downland, meadows and heaths; also open woodland and marshes.*

complex light and dark pattern

"chin of witch's profile"

white-spotted hindwings

up to 4cm long

WINGSPAN *3–3.5cm.*
TIME OF FLIGHT *Day.*
FLIGHT PERIOD *May–June.*
LARVAL FOODPLANT *Clover* (Trifolium).
SIMILAR SPECIES *Grizzled Skipper* (p.112) *and Dingy Skipper* (p.120), *butterflies often mistaken for moths.*
STATUS *Locally common.*

Pine Beauty

Panolis flammea (Noctuidae)

FOUND *in coniferous woodland and other places where pine trees grow.*

This orange and brown moth is extremely unpopular with foresters, as the caterpillars can be serious pests in conifer plantations, defoliating huge areas in the years when they are common. As with many spring-flying species, the adults feed at sallow blossom at night, and are drawn to light. The Pine Beauty is a variable moth, with three main colour forms: the mainly orange typical form, a darker, browner one, and a more heavily marked orange form; however all forms have two pale spots on the forewings.

BROWNER FORM

ORANGE FORM

NOTE

The green and white striped caterpillars are very well camouflaged among pine needles, and difficult to find. They assist this resemblance by remaining rigid if disturbed or dislodged from the pine needles.

heavily marked forewings

up to 4cm long

mottled orange and brown forewings

2 pale spots on forewing

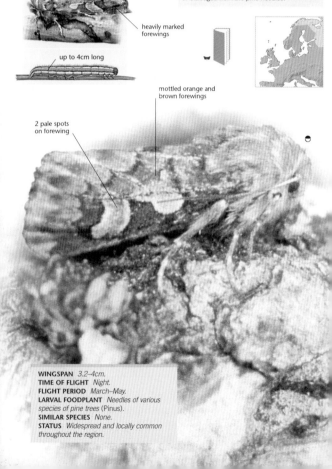

WINGSPAN *3.2–4cm.*
TIME OF FLIGHT *Night.*
FLIGHT PERIOD *March–May.*
LARVAL FOODPLANT *Needles of various species of pine trees (Pinus).*
SIMILAR SPECIES *None.*
STATUS *Widespread and locally common throughout the region.*

Hebrew Character

Orthosia gothica (Noctuidae)

A very common moth, the Hebrew Character occurs in
almost all habitats, including mountainous regions and
within the Arctic Circle. Although it emerges to feed on
sallow blossom after dark, it is also attracted to light. The
black C-shaped mark is absent in some specimens, and the
colour of the wings ranges from grey to red-brown.

FREQUENTS *almost
every possible habitat;
particularly common
in gardens.*

C-shaped mark on
both wings

grey-brown
ground colour

brown
margin

PALER FORM

up to 4.5cm long

WINGSPAN *3–4cm.*
TIME OF FLIGHT *Night.*
FLIGHT PERIOD *March–May.*
LARVAL FOODPLANT *Trees and shrubs.*
SIMILAR SPECIES *Setaceous Hebrew
Character (Xestia c-nigrum), which is larger,
darker, and flies later in the year.*
STATUS *Widespread and common.*

Common Wainscot

Mythimna pallens (Noctuidae)

This is a rather plain species, with few distinguishing
marks. The colour of the forewings varies from pale yellow
to a darker orange-buff, on which the pale veins stand out
more clearly. The hindwings are always white. It may be
found resting on grass stems after dark, or feeding at
flowers, and is strongly attracted to light.

LIVES *in grassy
habitats, such as
meadows, commons,
heaths, marshes,
and gardens.*

DARKER FORM

pale veins

pale yellow
ground colour

orange-buff wings

up to 4.5cm long

WINGSPAN *3–4cm.*
TIME OF FLIGHT *Night.*
FLIGHT PERIOD *June–October.*
LARVAL FOODPLANT *Various grasses
(family Poaceae).*
SIMILAR SPECIES *Smoky Wainscot
(M. impura), which has grey hindwings.*
STATUS *Widespread and common.*

Green Silver-lines

Pseudoips prasinana (Noctuidae)

LIVES *mainly in deciduous woodland; also hedgerows, parks, and gardens.*

This beautiful moth is aptly named, marked with silvery-white lines on a delicate green background. When freshly emerged, the wing fringes, legs, and antennae are tinged red. The slightly larger female is paler, with white hindwings, whereas those of the male are tinged with yellow.

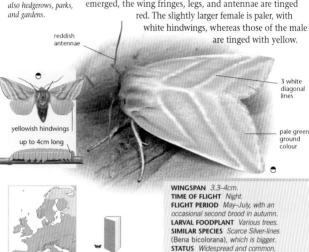

reddish antennae

3 white diagonal lines

pale green ground colour

yellowish hindwings

up to 4cm long

WINGSPAN *3.3–4cm.*
TIME OF FLIGHT *Night.*
FLIGHT PERIOD *May–July, with an occasional second brood in autumn.*
LARVAL FOODPLANT *Various trees.*
SIMILAR SPECIES *Scarce Silver-lines (Bena bicolorana), which is bigger.*
STATUS *Widespread and common.*

Common Quaker

Orthosia cerasi (Noctuidae)

PREFERS *deciduous woodland, but also found in gardens, parks, and hedgerows.*

One of the commonest of the spring-flying species, this moth can be abundant in deciduous woodland. Like many species that emerge early in the year, it feeds at sallow blossom after dark, and is drawn to light. The colour of the forewings varies from light brown to dark reddish brown.

PALER FORM

DARKER FORM

up to 4cm long

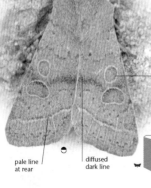

2 pale rings on brown forewings

pale line at rear

diffused dark line

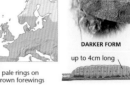

WINGSPAN *3.5–4cm.*
TIME OF FLIGHT *Night.*
FLIGHT PERIOD *March–April.*
LARVAL FOODPLANT *Trees, including oak (Quercus) and sallow (Salix).*
SIMILAR SPECIES *Powdered Quaker (O. gracilis), Small Quaker (O. cruda).*
STATUS *Widespread and common.*

Bird's Wing

Dypterygia scabriuscula (Noctuidae)

This species gets its common name from the pattern on the forewings, which resembles a stylized bird's wing. These pale marks and the pale thorax break up the outline of the moth at rest, making it difficult for predators to spot. There is very little variation, enabling easy identification.

FOUND *in deciduous woodland and open habitats such as meadows, parkland, and gardens.*

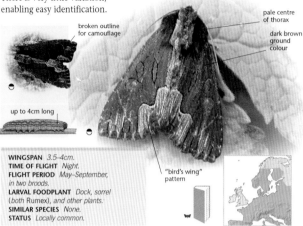

broken outline for camouflage

up to 4cm long

pale centre of thorax

dark brown ground colour

"bird's wing" pattern

WINGSPAN *3.5–4cm.*
TIME OF FLIGHT *Night.*
FLIGHT PERIOD *May–September, in two broods.*
LARVAL FOODPLANT *Dock, sorrel (both Rumex), and other plants.*
SIMILAR SPECIES *None.*
STATUS *Locally common.*

Frosted Orange

Gortyna flavago (Noctuidae)

The mottled orange and brown forewings of this moth provide good camouflage against decaying autumn leaves. There is little variation, but northern specimens may be darker. At night it is attracted to light, but does not appear to feed at flowers. The rather maggot-like caterpillars live inside the stems and roots of the foodplants.

OCCURS *in fields, open countryside, commons, marshes, wasteland, and gardens.*

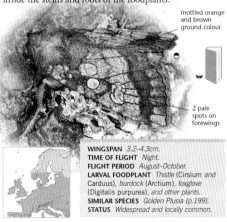

mottled orange and brown ground colour

2 pale spots on forewings

brown band

pale grey markings

up to 4cm long

WINGSPAN *3.2–4.3cm.*
TIME OF FLIGHT *Night.*
FLIGHT PERIOD *August–October.*
LARVAL FOODPLANT *Thistle (Cirsium and Carduus), burdock (Arctium), foxglove (Digitalis purpurea), and other plants.*
SIMILAR SPECIES *Golden Plusia (p.199).*
STATUS *Widespread and locally common.*

The Snout

Hypena proboscidalis (Noctuidae)

At rest, the Snout has a triangular outline, with long palps projecting from the front of its head like a snout. The forewings are dull brown, with two darker bands and a row of faint, pale dots. The Snout flies around nettles at dusk, and is also attracted to light later in the night.

FREQUENTS *gardens and waste ground, but also found in open woodland, and on marshland and commons.*

row of pale dots

up to 3cm long

projecting palps

dull brown ground colour

dark bands on forewings

triangular outline

WINGSPAN *3.4–4cm.*
TIME OF FLIGHT *Night.*
FLIGHT PERIOD *June–October, in two broods.*
LARVAL FOODPLANT *Common nettle (Urtica dioica).*
SIMILAR SPECIES *None.*
STATUS *Widespread and common.*

Heart and Dart

Agrotis exclamationis (Noctuidae)

One of the commonest European moths, the Heart and Dart is found in a wide range of habitats. The ground colour of the forewings ranges from light brown to dark brown, but the markings, a blackish "heart" and "dart" on each wing are fairly constant. The hindwings are pure white in colour. It feeds at flowers after dark, and is a very frequent visitor to moth traps.

FOUND *in almost every possible habitat as the larvae feed on a wide variety of plants; a particularly common garden species.*

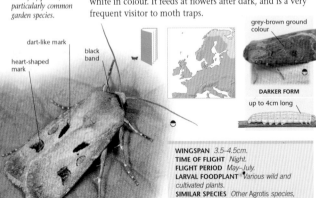

dart-like mark

heart-shaped mark

black band

grey-brown ground colour

DARKER FORM

up to 4cm long

WINGSPAN *3.5–4.5cm.*
TIME OF FLIGHT *Night.*
FLIGHT PERIOD *May–July.*
LARVAL FOODPLANT *Various wild and cultivated plants.*
SIMILAR SPECIES *Other Agrotis species, which lack the "heart and dart" markings.*
STATUS *Widespread and often abundant.*

Bright-line Brown-eye

Lacanobia oleracea (Noctuidae)

This species is also known as the Tomato Moth because of the caterpillar's fondness for feeding inside tomatoes, a habit that makes it unpopular with gardeners. The adult Bright-line Brown-eye has two main identifying features on the plain brown forewings, from which it gets its common name: a wavy white line along the trailing edge, and an orange-brown spot or "eye". The hindwings are light greyish brown.

FAVOURS *gardens and allotments where tomatoes are grown; also found in open countryside and in salt marshes.*

wavy white line

brown forewings

orange-brown spot

lighter hindwings

up to 4.5cm long

WINGSPAN	*3.5–4.5cm.*
TIME OF FLIGHT	*Night.*
FLIGHT PERIOD	*May–July; occasionally a second brood in autumn.*
LARVAL FOODPLANT	*Various plants, including tomato (Lycopersicon esculentum).*
SIMILAR SPECIES	*None.*
STATUS	*Widespread and common.*

Burnished Brass

Diachrysia chrysitis (Noctuidae)

The forewings of this moth have brassy scales that may form two patches, or may be joined into a larger patch. It is found after dark feeding at red valerian and honeysuckle flowers, and is also attracted to light. The Slender Burnished Brass is a southern European species with slimmer wings, and a single crescent-shaped, metallic patch.

INHABITS *gardens, waste ground, open woodland, marshland, and commons; or anywhere that nettles are found growing.*

brassy scales

reddish brown head

brown ground colour

single brassy patch

up to 4cm long

WINGSPAN	*3.5–4.5cm.*
TIME OF FLIGHT	*Night.*
FLIGHT PERIOD	*June–September, in two broods.*
LARVAL FOODPLANT	*Nettle (Urtica).*
SIMILAR SPECIES	*Slender Burnished Brass (D. orichalcea).*
STATUS	*Widespread and common.*

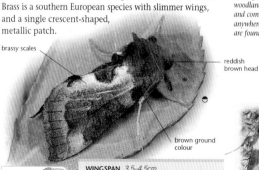

Grey Dagger

Acronicta psi (Noctuidae)

APPEARS *mainly in deciduous woodland; also hedgerows, parks, and gardens, and wherever there are trees for larvae to feed on.*

The Grey Dagger forms a species pair with the almost identical Dark Dagger. The two are so similar as adults that they can reliably be told apart only by examining the genitalia; however, the caterpillars are somewhat different (see Note). The hindwings may offer a clue to the moth's identity; those of the Dark Dagger are usually, but not always, pure white rather than off-white. The forewings of both species have a complex pattern of black markings on a grey background, resembling and old and cracked tree bark.

"cracked bark" look

2 black dagger marks on forewing

black markings

off-white hindwing

grey ground colour

up to 4cm long

NOTE
The caterpillar of the Grey Dagger can be told from that of the Dark Dagger by the broad yellow stripe along the back, and the long black projection behind the head. These are the only obvious differences between the two.

WINGSPAN *3.5–4.5cm.*
TIME OF FLIGHT *Night.*
FLIGHT PERIOD *June–August.*
LARVAL FOODPLANT *Various trees.*
SIMILAR SPECIES *Blair's Shoulder-knot (right), The Sycamore (p.198), which has grey, mottled wings, Dark Dagger (A. tridens), which is very similar and not really distinguishable as an adult.*
STATUS *Widespread and common.*

Blair's Shoulder-knot

Lithophane leautieri (Noctuidae)

This subtly marked species, at rest resembling a piece of dead wood, has recently undergone a dramatic range expansion in Europe. This is thought to have been aided by the popularity of its foodplants (various cypresses) as garden plants. From its original range in southwest France, it has spread north, reaching southern England in 1951.

FOUND *wherever cypresses grow, especially in gardens and parks.*

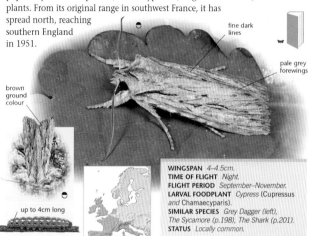

fine dark lines

pale grey forewings

brown ground colour

up to 4cm long

WINGSPAN *4–4.5cm.*	
TIME OF FLIGHT *Night.*	
FLIGHT PERIOD *September–November.*	
LARVAL FOODPLANT *Cypress (Cupressus and Chamaecyparis).*	
SIMILAR SPECIES *Grey Dagger (left), The Sycamore (p.198), The Shark (p.201).*	
STATUS *Locally common.*	

The Satellite

Eupsilia transversa (Noctuidae)

This moth gets its common name from the markings on its forewings, which resemble a planet with two satellites. These markings may be white, yellow, or orange. The adults emerge in September, and may be seen on mild nights through the winter until April. They are attracted to light, and feed on ivy blossom and blackberries, as well as sallow blossom in spring.

INHABITS *deciduous woodland, parks, and gardens; also moors in the north of its range.*

pale "satellite" marks

yellowish brown ground colour

FORM WITHOUT PALE MARKINGS

up to 5cm long

WINGSPAN *4–4.7cm.*
TIME OF FLIGHT *Night.*
FLIGHT PERIOD *September–April.*
LARVAL FOODPLANT *Various trees such as oak (Quercus), elm (Ulmus), sallow (Salix), and birch (Betula).*
SIMILAR SPECIES *None.*
STATUS *Widespread and common.*

Cabbage Moth

Mamestra brassicae (Noctuidae)

INHABITS *almost every possible habitat, as the larvae feed on a wide variety of plants.*

Despite its common name, the Cabbage Moth caterpillar feeds on many different plants, although it is partial to cabbages and other brassicas (and may be a pest in some areas). The adult moth is a rather nondescript brown, with darker mottling and pale marks on the forewings. It is attracted to light and may be found at night feeding at flowers such as red valerian.

white marks on forewings

pale margin

up to 5cm long

wavy light line on trailing edge

WINGSPAN *3.5–5cm.*
TIME OF FLIGHT *Night.*
FLIGHT PERIOD *May–September, but may be seen throughout the year.*
LARVAL FOODPLANT *Brassicas and many other wild and cultivated plants.*
SIMILAR SPECIES *Common Rustic (p.188).*
STATUS *Widespread and common.*

The Sycamore

Acronicta aceris (Noctuidae)

FOUND *wherever Sycamore grows; particularly common in urban areas where it has been planted.*

The Sycamore is more often noticed in the larval stage than as an adult, because of the caterpillar's extraordinary appearance, with brightly coloured hairs and black-ringed white spots along its back. The adult moth, by contrast, is well camouflaged in shades of grey with dark and light mottling. It flies after dark, and may be found feeding at flowers or on honeydew, and is also attracted to light.

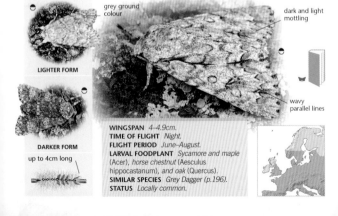

grey ground colour

dark and light mottling

LIGHTER FORM

wavy parallel lines

DARKER FORM

up to 4cm long

WINGSPAN *4–4.9cm.*
TIME OF FLIGHT *Night.*
FLIGHT PERIOD *June–August.*
LARVAL FOODPLANT *Sycamore and maple (Acer), horse chestnut (Aesculus hippocastanum), and oak (Quercus).*
SIMILAR SPECIES *Grey Dagger (p.196).*
STATUS *Locally common.*

Golden Plusia

Polychrysia moneta (Noctuidae)

Originally from southern Europe, the Golden Plusia has
spread over the last century to northern and western
Europe, even reaching the Arctic Circle. By day the mottled
ochre and brown adult is well camouflaged as
it rests among withered leaves. After
dark it feeds at flowers, and also
comes to light in small numbers.

FOUND *in gardens in
N.W. Europe; and in
mountainous areas in
other parts of its range.*

dark zig-zag line

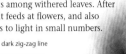

light wing spot

pale wing
tips

up to 4cm long

WINGSPAN *4–4.5cm.*
TIME OF FLIGHT *Night.*
FLIGHT PERIOD *June–September,
in two broods.*
LARVAL FOODPLANT *Delphinium*
(Delphinium).
SIMILAR SPECIES *Frosted Orange (p.193).*
STATUS *Locally common.*

Merveille du Jour

Dichonia aprilina (Noctuidae)

This beautiful species varies greatly in the markings of
the forewings: some individuals have a broad black band
across the wings, while others may be almost completely
black. The typical form has an intricate
pattern of green, black, and white
markings. This autumnal species
feeds at ivy blossom, and is
attracted to light.

OCCURS *mainly in
mature oak woodland,
also occasionally in
gardens and parkland.*

black and white
markings

green ground
colour

dark
hindwings

up to 5cm long

patterned
legs

WINGSPAN *4.2–5.2cm.*
TIME OF FLIGHT *Night.*
FLIGHT PERIOD *September–October.*
LARVAL FOODPLANT *Oak (Quercus).*
SIMILAR SPECIES *Scarce Merveille du Jour
(Moma alpium), which is smaller; Portland
Moth (Ochropleura praecox) has thin wings.*
STATUS *Widespread and locally common.*

The Herald

Scoliopteryx libatrix (Noctuidae)

The brightly coloured Herald may be found hibernating in buildings such as sheds and barns and in cellars during the winter months. In its natural habitat, its orange and brown coloration and the ragged outline of its forewings provide perfect camouflage against dead leaves. It is attracted to ivy blossom and blackberries, and also to sallow blossom in the spring, when it reappears after hibernation.

OCCURS *in damp woodland, waterside habitats, and wherever sallows grow. Also found in gardens, parks, and commons.*

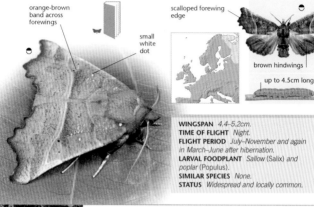

orange-brown band across forewings

small white dot

scalloped forewing edge

brown hindwings

up to 4.5cm long

WINGSPAN *4.4–5.2cm.*
TIME OF FLIGHT *Night.*
FLIGHT PERIOD *July–November and again in March–June after hibernation.*
LARVAL FOODPLANT *Sallow (Salix) and poplar (Populus).*
SIMILAR SPECIES *None.*
STATUS *Widespread and locally common.*

Angle Shades

Phlogophora meticulosa (Noctuidae)

The Angle Shades folds its wings in a unique way when at rest, giving it the appearance of a dried, dead leaf. The colour of the wings varies from olive-green to reddish brown, but the pattern is fairly constant. Some individuals migrate north each year, swelling the numbers of resident moths in northern Europe.

FOUND *in gardens, woodland, commons, and urban areas; not tied to any particular habitat as it feeds on a variety of plants.*

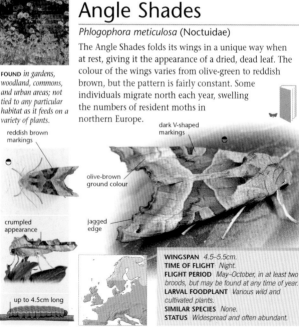

reddish brown markings

dark V-shaped markings

olive-brown ground colour

crumpled appearance

jagged edge

up to 4.5cm long

WINGSPAN *4.5–5.5cm.*
TIME OF FLIGHT *Night.*
FLIGHT PERIOD *May–October, in at least two broods, but may be found at any time of year.*
LARVAL FOODPLANT *Various wild and cultivated plants.*
SIMILAR SPECIES *None.*
STATUS *Widespread and often abundant.*

Dark Arches

Apamea monoglypha (Noctuidae)

This large brownish moth is very common throughout Europe, and is found in a wide variety of habitats. The forewings vary in colour from medium brown to almost black, the lighter forms having darker and lighter blotches and lines. Dark Arches is attracted to flowers such as red valerian, and is also attracted to light.

INHABITS *a variety of grassy areas such as meadows, moorland, downland, and commons.*

mottled wings

dark line at wing margin

blackish ground colour

DARKER FORM

up to 4.5cm long

WINGSPAN *4.6–5.4cm.*
TIME OF FLIGHT *Night.*
FLIGHT PERIOD *June–October, in two broods.*
LARVAL FOODPLANT *Various grasses (family Poaceae).*
SIMILAR SPECIES *Large Nutmeg (A. anceps), which is smaller.*
STATUS *Widespread and often abundant.*

The Shark

Cucullia umbratica (Noctuidae)

At rest, The Shark sits with its wings tightly folded around its body, its greyish coloration and subtle patterning providing good camouflage against tree trunks or fence posts. After dark, it feeds at the flowers of plants such as honeysuckle, thistles, and red valerian, but is not often attracted to light. The very similar Chamomile Shark (*C. chamomillae*) is usually smaller and flies earlier in the year, between April and June.

PREFERS *gardens and weedy places such as downland, commons, waste ground, and shingle beaches.*

wings folded around body

projecting crest on thorax

♂ ●

numerous fine lines

grey-brown ground colour

up to 5cm long

WINGSPAN *4.8–5.9cm.*
TIME OF FLIGHT *Night.*
FLIGHT PERIOD *June–July.*
LARVAL FOODPLANT *Sow-thistle (Sonchus) and wild lettuce (Lactuca).*
SIMILAR SPECIES *Blair's Shoulder-knot (p.197), several other Shark species.*
STATUS *Widespread and common.*

Silver Y

Autographa gamma (Noctuidae)

One of the great migrants of the insect world, the Silver Y sometimes arrives from warmer areas in vast numbers in spring and early summer to breed in northern Europe. The species cannot survive the severe northern European winters, and caterpillars, pupae, and adults are all killed by the first frosts. The adult moth is active by day and night, and can be found feeding at the flowers of clover, teasel, heather, buddleia, and red valerian, especially at dusk; it is also attracted to light.

FOUND *in almost every possible habitat in temperate climates, as the larvae feed on a wide variety of plants.*

double crest on thorax

mottled grey and brown ground colour

silver Y marking on forewing

scalloped wing margin

dark outer edge

up to 4cm long

NOTE

Silver Y moths that emerge later in the year are often darker and browner than those that arrive as migrants in the spring. An uncommon variety is almost entirely black in colour, and very small specimens can occasionally be seen.

WINGSPAN *3.5–5cm.*
TIME OF FLIGHT *Night and day.*
FLIGHT PERIOD *Successive broods, but May–October in N. Europe.*
LARVAL FOODPLANT *Feeds on a wide variety of wild and cultivated herbaceous plants.*
SIMILAR SPECIES *Beautiful Golden Y (Autographa pulchrina) is browner; Scarce Silver Y (A. interrogationis) is smaller and darker.*
STATUS *Widespread and often abundant.*

Copper Underwing

Amphipyra pyramidea (Noctuidae)

This moth forms a species pair with the very similar
Svensson's Copper Underwing. The main difference is in
the coloration of the underside of the hindwings, which is
very difficult to see on a live moth. On the Copper
Underwing, this area is pale yellow, while on Svensson's it

FREQUENTS *deciduous woodland; also parks, gardens, hedgerows, and other areas where there are trees and shrubs for the caterpillars to feed on.*

is orange-brown. The
colour of the
forewings ranges from
mottled brown to
almost wholly black.
The Copper Underwing
is attracted to sweet
substances such as ripe
blackberries and rotting
fruit, and is also drawn to
light in small numbers.

NOTE

The Copper Underwing may be found resting by day, sometimes in small groups, in dark places such as sheds and hollow trees.

orange-brown
hindwing

up to 4.5cm long

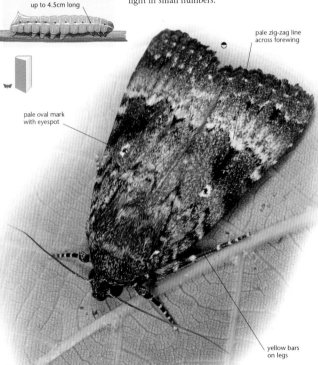

pale zig-zag line
across forewing

pale oval mark
with eyespot

yellow bars
on legs

WINGSPAN *4.7–5.4cm.*
TIME OF FLIGHT *Night.*
FLIGHT PERIOD *August–October.*
LARVAL FOODPLANT *Various trees and shrubs, such as oak (Quercus), ash (Fraxinus), hornbeam (Carpinus betulus), and privet (Ligustrum).*
SIMILAR SPECIES *Svensson's Copper Underwing (A. berbera), which is orange-brown on the underside of the hindwings.*
STATUS *Widespread and common.*

Large Yellow Underwing

Noctua pronuba (Noctuidae)

FOUND *in almost every possible habitat as the larvae feed on a wide variety of plants; a particularly common garden species.*

This is one of the commonest and most widespread moths in Europe, occurring in almost all habitats. In some years, numbers at light traps may run into hundreds, or even thousands. The forewing colour is variable, ranging from light brown with dark markings to a uniform dark brown, with males tending to have darker wings than females.

Although most large moths have to warm up their wings by rapidly vibrating them before taking flight, the Large Yellow Underwing is able to take flight instantly without doing so. This sudden flight exposes the yellow and black hindwings, which scare off potential predators.

black border to hindwing

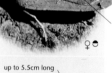

paler ground colour

♀ ◐

up to 5.5cm long

NOTE

The Large Yellow Underwing is the largest and commonest of several similar species with yellow and black hindwings. The Broad-bordered Yellow Underwing (N. fimbriata) has orange hindwings with broader black borders.

yellow and black hindwing

black mark near forewing tip

dark patches on forewing

WINGSPAN *5–6cm.*
TIME OF FLIGHT *Night.*
FLIGHT PERIOD *June–September.*
LARVAL FOODPLANT *Various plants including grasses.*
SIMILAR SPECIES *Lesser Yellow Underwing (N. comes), which is smaller; Broad-bordered Yellow Underwing (N. fimbriata), which has orange hindwings; several other Yellow Underwing species.*
STATUS *Widespread and often abundant.*

Old Lady

Mormo maura (Noctuidae)

The upper wings of this large moth are banded in mottled greys and browns and have a serrated fringe. The Old Lady flies at night, when it feeds on tree sap and honeydew, and it can be recognized by its slow, lazy flight with deep flaps of its broad wings. By day, it hides in dark places, such as sheds and outbuildings, or in hollow trees, especially near water. The caterpillar starts life feeding on low-growing plants such as dock and chickweed, before hibernating. In the spring, it feeds on a wide variety of trees and shrubs.

INHABITS *a wide variety of habitats, including open woodland, gardens, parks, commons, and open countryside.*

serrated wing edge

dark band across forewings

paler markings on wing tips

mottled grey and brown ground colour

NOTE

Smear a mixture of brown sugar, treacle, beer, and rum on to tree trunks to attract these moths, since they feed readily on sweet substances.

up to 7cm long

WINGSPAN *6.5–7.5cm.*
TIME OF FLIGHT *Night.*
FLIGHT PERIOD *July–August.*
LARVAL FOODPLANT *Dock (Rumex) and chickweed (Stellaria) at first; later hawthorn (Crataegus) and sallow (Salix).*
SIMILAR SPECIES *None.*
STATUS *Locally common.*

Red Underwing

Catocala nupta (Noctuidae)

At rest, the Red Underwing's grey-brown forewings camouflage it perfectly against tree trunks. If disturbed from its resting place during the day it may be seen in flight, when the vivid red and black hindwings are revealed. After dark it is found feeding on rotting fruit or tree sap, but is only drawn to light in small numbers.

FOUND *in damp woodland, waterside habitats, and wherever sallows and poplars grow; also in gardens, parks, and commons.*

grey-brown forewings

red and black banded hindwing

concealed hindwings

up to 7cm long

WINGSPAN *7–9.4cm.*
FLIGHT PERIOD *August–September.*
TIME OF FLIGHT *Night; occasionally by day.*
LARVAL FOODPLANT *Sallow (Salix) and poplar (Populus).*
SIMILAR SPECIES *Three species, which vary in the shade of brown on the forewings.*
STATUS *Widespread and common.*

Clifden Nonpareil

Catocala fraxini (Noctuidae)

This is the largest European noctuid, nearing some of the larger hawk-moths in wingspan. At rest, the mottled grey-brown forewings give it excellent camouflage against tree trunks. In flight, the hindwings are visible: these are dark brown with a band of a delicate lilac. Like the Red Underwing (above), the adults feed on sap and rotten fruit, but are not strongly attracted to light.

INHABITS *open deciduous woodland where aspen is present.*

grey-brown forewing

concealed hindwings

lilac band on dark hindwing

dark brown hindwing

up to 7.5cm long

WINGSPAN *8.5–11cm.*
TIME OF FLIGHT *Night.*
FLIGHT PERIOD *September.*
LARVAL FOODPLANT *Aspen (Populus tremula).*
SIMILAR SPECIES *None.*
STATUS *Widespread, but rather uncommon; rare migrant to Britain.*

Ghost Moth

Hepialus humuli (Hepialidae)

Also known as the Ghost Swift, this is a member of one of the most primitive groups of moths, characterized by long wings and very short antennae. The males, which are pure white, may be seen in large groups hovering in a ghostly fashion over vegetation at dusk. This is thought to be a display to attract females. The yellowish females are generally larger and have a distinctive pinkish brown pattern on the forewings. After mating, the female lays her eggs in flight, scattering them over the vegetation. The adults do not feed at flowers; they are attracted to light.

FREQUENTS *grassy places such as field margins, meadows, downland, commons, and gardens. Also found in arable fields.*

NOTE

The rather maggot-like caterpillar feeds inside the roots of the foodplants, often causing damage to crops. After feeding for about ten months, it pupates underground before emerging as an adult.

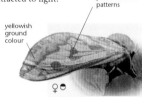

pinkish brown patterns

yellowish ground colour

♀

up to 3.5cm long

silvery white wings

yellowish thorax

wing veins on forewing and hindwing

♂

WINGSPAN *4.5–5cm.*
TIME OF FLIGHT *Dusk onwards.*
FLIGHT PERIOD *June–August.*
LARVAL FOODPLANT *Grasses (family Poaceae) and other plants, including crops.*
SIMILAR SPECIES *None.*
STATUS *Widespread and generally common.*

Leopard Moth

Zeuzera pyrina (Cossidae)

FOUND *in orchards, hedgerows, gardens, and open woodland, wherever there are trees for the caterpillars to feed on.*

This rather primitive-looking moth, has white wings boldly spotted with black and a densely furred, almost woolly head and thorax. The female is much larger than the male, and has a long ovipositor (egg-laying tube) that could be mistaken for a sting. The adults can sometimes be found during the day, resting on trees, fences, or on the ground. The larvae feed inside the trunks and branches of trees for two or even three years, boring into the wood. This can occasionally cause severe damage to the tree, making the Leopard Moth an unpopular species with gardeners and fruit growers.

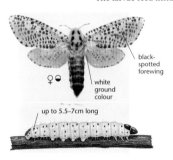

black-spotted forewing

white ground colour

♀ ●

up to 5.5–7cm long

NOTE

With its black-spotted, translucent white wings, the Leopard Moth is an unmistakable species. There is very little variation, but occasional specimens may be found with larger or smaller black spots.

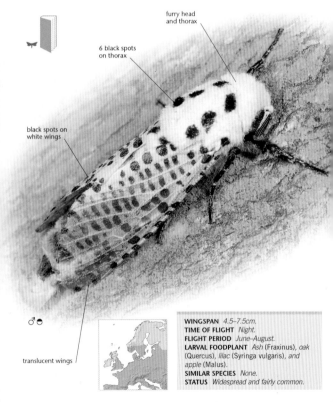

furry head and thorax

6 black spots on thorax

black spots on white wings

♂ ●

translucent wings

WINGSPAN *4.5–7.5cm.*
TIME OF FLIGHT *Night.*
FLIGHT PERIOD *June–August.*
LARVAL FOODPLANT *Ash (Fraxinus), oak (Quercus), lilac (Syringa vulgaris), and apple (Malus).*
SIMILAR SPECIES *None.*
STATUS *Widespread and fairly common.*

The Drinker

Euthrix potatoria (Lasiocampidae)

The caterpillar of this large and attractive moth supposedly drinks more frequently than other species, and may be seen drinking from drops of water on leaves or other surfaces. The adult female is larger and paler than the male, and has more pointed wing tips. Both sexes fly at night, and are drawn to light, although the male is more frequently attracted than the female.

SEEN *in woodland, commons, moorland, fens, and other grassy habitats.*

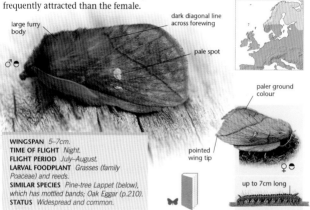

large furry body

dark diagonal line across forewing

pale spot

♂●

paler ground colour

♀●

pointed wing tip

WINGSPAN *5–7cm.*
TIME OF FLIGHT *Night.*
FLIGHT PERIOD *July–August.*
LARVAL FOODPLANT *Grasses (family Poaceae) and reeds.*
SIMILAR SPECIES *Pine-tree Lappet (below), which has mottled bands; Oak Eggar (p.210).*
STATUS *Widespread and common.*

up to 7cm long

Pine-tree Lappet

Dendrolimus pini (Lasiocampidae)

This is a common moth across Europe, but does not occur in Britain, except as a rare immigrant. It is a very variable species, but the males are usually a dark reddish brown, with darker bands and mottling. Females are larger, and usually paler and plainer grey-brown. Both sexes have white spots on the forewings. The caterpillar, which feeds on pine needles, may be a pest in commercial plantations.

OCCURS *in areas of natural and planted coniferous woodland, in both lowland and upland regions.*

white spot on forewing

grey and brown bands

lighter bands

♀●

♂●

reddish-brown ground colour

grey-brown ground colour

DARKER FORM

♂●

WINGSPAN *4.5–7cm.*
TIME OF FLIGHT *Night.*
FLIGHT PERIOD *May–August.*
LARVAL FOODPLANT *Pine (Pinus) and spruce (Picea).*
SIMILAR SPECIES *The Drinker (above); Oak Eggar (p.210), which has a buff band.*
STATUS *Widespread and locally common.*

up to 7cm long

Oak Eggar

Lasiocampa quercus (Lasiocampidae)

This species is extremely variable in coloration, ranging from pale yellow-buff to a very dark brown or almost black. Most forms have a pale spot on the forewings and a band of buff or lighter brown across both the forewings and hindwings. The female, which is more uniform in colour and much larger than the male, flies at night, and is sometimes attracted to light. The male flies with an erratic zig-zagging flight during the day in sunshine and is attracted to the female's scent.

FOUND *in a variety of habitats, including deciduous woodland, along hedgerows, commons, and moorland.*

PALER FORM ♀●

yellow-buff
ground
colour

♀●

dark and pale lines

up to 8cm long

NOTE

Northern forms of the Oak Eggar are often darker, and also have a two-year life cycle – the caterpillar lives for 15 months before pupating. This form is sometimes considered a separate subspecies, the Northern Eggar.

feathery
antennae

♂●

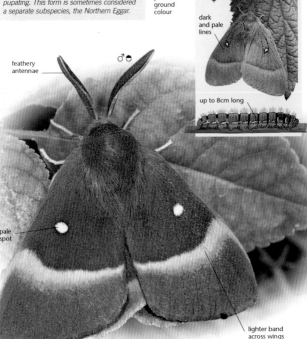

pale
spot

lighter band
across wings

WINGSPAN *5.5–10cm.*
TIME OF FLIGHT *Day (male); night (female).*
FLIGHT PERIOD *May–August.*
LARVAL FOODPLANT *Hawthorn (Crataegus), heather (Erica and Calluna), bramble (Rubus fruticosus), sallow (Salix), and bilberry (Vaccinium myrtillus).*
SIMILAR SPECIES *The Drinker (p.209), Pine-tree Lappet (p.209).*
STATUS *Widespread and locally common.*

Emperor Moth

Saturnia pavonia (Saturniidae)

The males of this spectacular moth may be seen flying in sunshine. The larger females fly at dusk, and are sometimes attracted to light. The males have feathery antennae and both sexes have large and conspicuous eyespots on all four wings. In the resting position, the hindwings of the Emperor Moth are concealed; the spots on the forewings, combined with the dark brown thorax, give the impression of the eyes and snout of a small mammal, which may deter birds from attacking it.

INHABITS *a variety of habitats such as heathland, moorland, and open woodland where the larval foodplants grow.*

feathery antennae

large furry body

large eyespots on all 4 wings

♂

DARKER FORM

♂

brown ground colour

red on forewing tip

lighter colouring than male

♀

up to 6.5cm long

NOTE

When ready to mate, the female releases a pheromone scent, which is detectable by the male, with its sensitive feathery antennae, from up to 2km away. Several males may be attracted to the same female – this behaviour is known as "assembling".

WINGSPAN *5.5–8.8cm.*
TIME OF FLIGHT *Day (male); night (female).*
FLIGHT PERIOD *May–August.*
LARVAL FOODPLANT *Heather (Erica and Calluna), bramble (Rubus fruticosus), hawthorn (Crataegus), sallow (Salix), and other plants.*
SIMILAR SPECIES *Great Peacock Moth (S. pyri) which is larger, and occurs only in S. Europe.*
STATUS *Widespread and locally common.*

Hummingbird Hawk-moth

Macroglossum stellatarum (Sphingidae)

This small, day-flying hawk-moth resembles a hummingbird as it hovers in front of flowers, feeding on nectar. It is particularly fond of fuchsia, jasmine, red valerian, and campion. A resident of southern Europe, it breeds all year round. Some migrate north in summer, and may turn up in northern Europe.

BREEDS *wherever bedstraws are present. Migrants found in places where flowers abound, such as parks, gardens, meadows, and wasteland.*

brownish forewings

dark wavy bands

up to 6.5cm long

long proboscis

white marks on black abdomen

orange hindwing

WINGSPAN *5–5.8cm.*
TIME OF FLIGHT *Day.*
FLIGHT PERIOD *Adults may occur in any month of the year.*
LARVAL FOODPLANT *Bedstraw (Galium).*
SIMILAR SPECIES *None.*
STATUS *Irregular migrant to N. Europe in summer, in varying numbers.*

Elephant Hawk-moth

Deilephila elpenor (Sphingidae)

This species gets its common name from the caterpillar, which vaguely resembles an elephant's trunk. The adult moth has buff forewings, banded with pink, while the underside is mostly pink; the hindwings have white fringes. This attractive moth flies at dusk and through the night, often feeding at flowers such as honeysuckle or red valerian.

FOUND *in woodland clearings, river valleys, meadows, commons, and gardens; also found in wasteland.*

pink and buff forewing

pointed forewing tip

up to 8.5cm long

pink and buff striped body

pink wing margin

WINGSPAN *6.2–7cm.*
TIME OF FLIGHT *Night.*
FLIGHT PERIOD *May–June.*
LARVAL FOODPLANT *Willowherb (Epilobium) and bedstraw (Galium).*
SIMILAR SPECIES *Small Elephant Hawk-moth (D. porcellus), which is smaller.*
STATUS *Widespread and often common.*

Lime Hawk-moth

Mimas tiliae (Sphingidae)

The ground colour of the Lime Hawk-moth's forewings is variable, ranging from lime-green to a delicate salmon-pink. The dark markings on the wings also vary, from dark green to brown. The adults have no proboscis, and so do not feed on nectar. The moth can be found even in urban areas, especially where lime trees are planted.

INHABITS *gardens, hedgerows, tree-lined streets, parks, and deciduous woodland.*

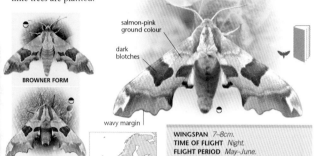

salmon-pink
ground colour

dark
blotches

wavy margin

BROWNER FORM

GREENER FORM

up to 6.5cm long

WINGSPAN *7–8cm.*
TIME OF FLIGHT *Night.*
FLIGHT PERIOD *May–June.*
LARVAL FOODPLANT *Lime (Tilia); also birch (Betula), elm (Ulmus), and alder (Alnus).*
SIMILAR SPECIES *Oleander Hawk-moth (Daphnis nerii) lacks wavy wing margin.*
STATUS *Widespread but locally common.*

Poplar Hawk-moth

Laothoe populi (Sphingidae)

Although quite closely related to the Eyed Hawk-moth (p.214), with which it can hybridize in captivity, the Poplar Hawk-moth has a very different resting position – it holds its hindwings at right angles to its body, projecting in front of the forewings. If disturbed, it flicks its hindwings forward, revealing a patch of orange-red.

FAVOURS *open woodland, waterside habitats, and wherever sallows and poplars grow. Also gardens, parks, and commons.*

large thorax
and abdomen

hindwings
project in
front of
forewings

short
hindwings

red
patch

grey-brown
ground colour

up to 7cm long

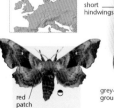

WINGSPAN *7.2–9cm.*
TIME OF FLIGHT *Night.*
FLIGHT PERIOD *May–June.*
LARVAL FOODPLANT *Poplar (Populus), aspen (Populus tremula), and sallow (Salix).*
SIMILAR SPECIES *None.*
STATUS *Widespread and generally common throughout Europe.*

Eyed Hawk-moth

Smerinthus ocellata (Sphingidae)

INHABITS *open woodland, orchards, gardens, and waterside habitats where sallows grow.*

When it is at rest, with its hindwings concealed, the mottled brown Eyed Hawk-moth resembles the bark of a tree. If disturbed, however, it will suddenly open its wings to reveal a startling pair of blue and black eyespots on the pinkish hindwings. These, combined with the sharply defined, dark chocolate-brown centre of the thorax, which resembles the snout of a small mammal, have the effect of scaring off predators. Like the Lime Hawk-moth (p.213), this species does not feed at flowers as an adult. It is attracted to light in small numbers.

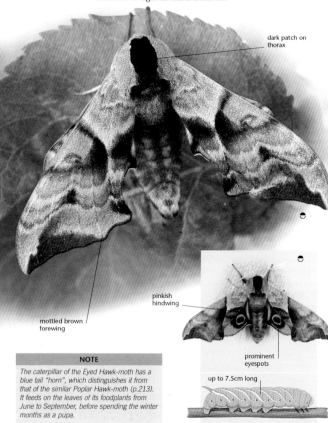

dark patch on thorax

pinkish hindwing

mottled brown forewing

prominent eyespots

up to 7.5cm long

NOTE

The caterpillar of the Eyed Hawk-moth has a blue tail "horn", which distinguishes it from that of the similar Poplar Hawk-moth (p.213). It feeds on the leaves of its foodplants from June to September, before spending the winter months as a pupa.

WINGSPAN *7.5–9.5 cm.*
TIME OF FLIGHT *Night.*
FLIGHT PERIOD *May–July.*
LARVAL FOODPLANT *Sallow (Salix), apple (Malus), and aspen (Populus tremula).*
SIMILAR SPECIES *None.*
STATUS *Widespread and locally common.*

Privet Hawk-moth

Sphinx ligustri (Sphingidae)

This is the largest hawk-moth resident in northern Europe, on average just a little smaller than the migrant Convolvulus Hawk-moth (below) and Death's-head Hawk-moth (p.216). An impressive insect, it has a large blackish thorax and long, pointed forewings. The hindwings have pale pink bands, and the abdomen is striped pink and black. It flies at night, visiting flowers to feed, and is attracted to light.

FOUND *in open countryside, gardens, woodland rides, hedgerows, and commons.*

black thorax

dark band across forewing

pink and black banded hindwing

up to 8.5cm long

WINGSPAN *10–12cm.*
TIME OF FLIGHT *Night.*
FLIGHT PERIOD *June–July.*
LARVAL FOODPLANT *Privet (Ligustrum), lilac (Syringa), and ash (Fraxinus).*
SIMILAR SPECIES *Convolvulus Hawk-moth (below), which lacks the black thorax.*
STATUS *Widespread and locally common.*

Convolvulus Hawk-moth

Agrius convolvuli (Sphingidae)

This large hawk-moth is mostly seen at dusk, hovering in front of flowers, especially of the tobacco plant, from which it takes nectar with its long proboscis. It is a strong migrant, and moths from Africa and southern Europe regularly reach northern Europe. At rest, it resembles a piece of wood, but when it opens its wings, two bright red spots at the rear of the thorax are revealed.

BREEDS *in fields, gardens, and waste ground. Migrants are most often seen in gardens or parks.*

black streaks

pink, black, and white bands

bright red spots

up to 10.5cm long

grey-brown wings

WINGSPAN *9.5–12cm.*
TIME OF FLIGHT *Dusk onwards.*
FLIGHT PERIOD *June–November.*
LARVAL FOODPLANT *Bindweed (Convolvulus).*
SIMILAR SPECIES *Privet Hawk-moth (above), which has pinkish bands on hindwings.*
STATUS *Migrant to N. Europe.*

Death's-head Hawk-moth

NOTE

The Death's-head Hawk-moth enters beehives to feed on honey. It uses its thick and strong tongue to pierce the wax and suck up its food.

Acherontia atropos (Sphingidae)

This impressive species is the largest European hawk-moth. It gets its name from the markings on the thorax, which resemble a skull, and it was traditionally considered to be a harbinger of danger. At rest, the dark brown forewings are held over the abdomen, which is yellow with a broad central blue stripe. The hindwings are bright yellow with a faint brown edge. If disturbed or handled, the Death's-head Hawk-moth has the alarming habit of squeaking, which it does by forcing air through its short proboscis. It is a native of southern Europe, Africa, and the Middle East, but some moths migrate north each year; it is an annual visitor to Britain in small numbers.

mottled, dark brown forewings

skull-like pattern on thorax

yellow, blue, and black bands on abdomen

light patches on forewings

black head and thorax

dark limbs

bright yellow hindwings

up to 12.5cm long

WINGSPAN *10–13.5cm.*
TIME OF FLIGHT *Night.*
FLIGHT PERIOD *May–October.*
LARVAL FOODPLANT *Potato (Solanum tuberosum).*
SIMILAR SPECIES *None.*
STATUS *Scarce migrant to N. Europe in varying numbers.*

Glossary

Many of the terms defined here are illustrated in the general introduction (pp.8–13). Words in *italics* are defined elsewhere in the glossary.

ABDOMEN The segmented, third section of an insect's body in which much of the digestive, excretory, and reproductive organs are located.

ANTENNAE Paired sensory appendages attached to, and projecting from, the head of a butterfly or moth.

BROOD A generation of individuals produced by a *species*. Some species produce more than one generation in a given year.

CELL A space on the wings of a butterfly or moth, defined and bordered by veins.

CRYPTIC Describes markings that afford the butterfly or moth a degree of camouflage when resting, for example, on tree bark or leaf litter.

EYESPOT A marking on the wing that resembles an exaggerated mammal or bird eye; its function can be to alarm and deter a potential predator.

FAMILY A category in classification, grouping one or more *genera* that are closely related; ranked at a higher level than the *genus*.

FORM A term applied to certain *species* that occur in two or more different colour variations across the species' range.

GENUS (pl. genera) A category in classification grouping together closely related species, whose relationship is indicated by the first part of the scientific name, e.g. Colias in Colias crocea.

HIBERNATION A period of dormancy undergone typically during the winter months.

LARVA The young stage in the life cycle of a butterfly or moth that follows on from the egg but precedes the *pupa*; it is often popularly referred to as the caterpillar.

LOCAL Having a distribution that is geographically restricted, be that as a continuous range or in isolated pockets.

LOCALLY COMMON A species that is common but only within a geographically restricted range, be that as a continuous range or in isolated pockets.

MACRO-MOTH A term commonly used to distinguish certain families of usually larger moths from the other families, called *micro-moths*, which are generally less easily identified.

MAQUIS A Mediterranean scrub habitat where the dominant vegetation comprises aromatic and often spiny shrubs and trees, typically growing to a height of 1–3 metres.

MICRO-MOTH A term commonly used to distinguish certain families of usually smaller, and less easily identified moths from the *macro-moths*.

MIGRANT A butterfly or moth species, members of which engage in long-distance and, to a degree, directional seasonal movements.

OVIPOSITOR The part of the *abdomen* of a female butterfly or moth that is used to lay eggs.

PALPS Sensory appendages associated with the mouth of a butterfly or moth, and concerned with taste and smell.

PHEROMONES Chemical 'messengers' released by an animal in order to attract a member of the opposite sex of the same species.

PROBOSCIS The coiled but extensible 'tongue' of a butterfly or moth.

PUPA The stage in the life cycle of a butterfly or moth that follows on from the *larva* and from which the adult insect emerges.

PUPATE The metamorphic process by which a caterpillar becomes a *pupa*.

RACE A *subspecies* of a butterfly or moth that is confined to a well defined and often isolated geographical region.

SCALE Tiny, flattened plates that cloak the wing surfaces of most butterflies and moths. They are arranged rather like roof tiles and are variously coloured.

SEX BRAND A patch or line of scent-emitting scales that is found on the fore-wing of a male butterfly.

SPECIES A unit of classification that embraces a group of genetically similar individuals, members of which are capable of reproducing with one another and of producing viable offspring.

SPECIES PAIR A pair of very closely related species that are difficult to tell apart on external features.

SUBMARGINAL Used in the context of a band of colour, or perhaps a row of spots, that are found on the area of the wing just inside the margin.

SUBSPECIES A group of individuals that are distinctly different in appearance, and often geographically separated, from other members of the same species.

THORAX The middle section of an adult insect's body and the one to which the legs and wings are attached.

Index

Acknowledgments

DORLING KINDERSLEY would like to thank Bridget Lloyd-Jones for her help with picture administration and editing, Erin Richards for additional administrative help, and Dr Kudrna for his kind permission to use the maps from his book *The Distribution Atlas of European Butterflies* as reference for the maps in this book.

PICTURE CREDITS

Picture librarians: Richard Dabb, Claire Bowers
Abbreviations key: a = above, b = bottom, c = centre, f = far, l = left, t = top, r = right.

Andrew Mackay: 33 bl, clb; 40 cla; 42 cal, cla; 49 bcr, cbr; 57 car, cra; 72 cla; 98 cra; 99 clb; 100 cla; 108 cbr, crb; 111 cfl, cla; 120 clb; 123 clb, cla; 127 car, cr; 128 cbl, crb; 131 bl; 134 crb; 152 cra; 153 cbr; 154 la; 155 cla, crb; 156 cla; 157 bl, cbr; 160 bl; 164 br; 169 ca; 171 cbr; 172 cal, cla; 182 crb; 183 bl; 184 cbl; 187 car; 189 clb; 191 cla; 192 bl; 193 br, ca; 195 cla; 205 bl; 213 car; 214 ca.
Chris Gibson: 151 bcr, br, ca; 152 cbr, clb; 155 cbl; 158 cal; 160 cal; 161 cbr; 162 cbr; 163 bcr, car; 168 bl, cbr; 174 cr; 177 cbr; 179 bl; 180 crb; 182 cla; 183 cbr; 185 clb; 187 cal; 189 cla; 191 br; 192 crb; 195 bcr; 197 cb; 199 car; 201 bl; 206 cal; 207 car, cb; 209 cal; 210 cr; 212 cbr; 213 cfl; 215 cra; 216 cbr.
Diego Reggianti: 14 br; 25 cla; 51 bl; 54 br; 96 cal, cra; 123 cal; 137 br.
Ilaria Pimpinelli: 14 bl; 15 bl; 20 cbr; 29 bcr; 30 cr; 31 car; 32 clb; 41 cbl; 43 cl; 78 bcr; 101 car; 112 cal; 115 bl.
Jeff Higgott: 152 ca; 194 crb.
Jens Schou: 14 bl; 15 bl; 20 cbr; 29 bcr; 30 cr; 31 car; 32 clb; 41 cbl; 43 cl; 78 bcr; 101 car; 112 cal; 115 bl; 153 cca, car; 154 bl, car, crb; 155 ca; 156 car; 157cla ; 161 car, cra; 163 cla; 164 cla; 165 crb; 166 cal, cra; 167 cla; 168 cra; 169 cla; 170 cal, cla; 179 cla; 183 cla; 186 cbr, crb; 190 cal, cla; 191 clb; 196 cbr; 199 clb; 203 cla.
Mario Maier: 17 ca, clb; 18 cal; 23 cfl; 24 cal; 25 bl, cb; 27 bcr, cal; 30 car; 32 bl, tr; 35 bcr, cbl; 40 crb; 44 cbl; 45 clb; 46 cbl; 47 car; 49 cbl, cla; 50 cal; 51 car, clb; 56 cbr; 57 bl; 59 cbr; 60 cbr; 61 cla; 67 car, cb; 68 cal, cbl; 71 ca; 72 cbr; 74 ca; 75 cbr, cla; 76 ca, cbl; 80 cbl, crb; 82 bl; 83 cbl; 85 bcr, ca; 87 car, cla; 88 ca, cbl; 90 cb; 91 cbr; 93 cbr, clb; 94 cal, cbr; 106 cbl; 107 bl, cbr, cla; 108 bcl; 111 br, cb; 120 bcr; 125 cra; 126 cal, cla; 130 cal, cra; 135 cbr; 136 bcl, crb; 138 cb; 144 car; 147 car, cr; 148 cbl; 149 bl.
Neil Fletcher: 15 tr; 16 cfl; 17 tr; 19 tr; 22 cfl; 27 cfr; 31 tr; 33 cfr; 37 cfr; 38 tl; 39 tr; 41 tr; 43 tr; 44 tl; 46 tl; 50 tl; 53 tr; 54 tl; 63 tr; 66 cfl; 82 tl; 86 tl; 87 tr; 88 tl; 92 tl; 93 cfr; 97 tr; 121 tr; 126 tl; 147 tr; 152 cfl; 153 tr; 167 tr; 183 tr; 200 clb; 216 tl.
Paolo Mazzei: 21 cb; 24 cl; 27 car, cra; 28 cra; 29 car, clb; 34 cb; 60 cl; 61 cbr, cfl; 66 crb; 69 ca; 73 ca, cra; 75 bl; 77 br, car, cb, cla; 81 ca; 82 car, cb; 83 ar, cr; 84 cra; 86 ca, cbl; 91 ca; 92 cb; 93 bl; 95 clb; 101 cal; 106 ca; 109 cbr; 117 br; 118 cra; 121 bl, ca, clb; 122 cra, crb; 130 cbl; 133 cla, clb; 135 cla; 136 cal, cra, tr; 139 car, cla; 141 bcr, car, clb, cla; 142 car, cla; 145 bcl, cfl, cla; 149 car, cla; 150 ca, cra, crb; 151 bcl; 156 bl, crb; 157 car; 158 cb; 162 cl; 163 cbl; 164 car; 165 bl, cla; 166 cbr; 167 bcr; 171 car; 173 ca, cfl, clb; 176 cal, car, cbl, cbr, cfl, cla, crb; 177 ca; 178 cbr; 179 ca, cbr, clb; 180 car, cbl, cla; 181 car, cb; 182 car, cbl; 183 car; 184 cal; 185 ca; 187 cb; 188 cb; 191 car, cfl; 192 car, cbr; 193 cbl, crb; 194 bcl, car; 195 car, cbl; 197 ca; 198 cbr; 199 cb; 200 bl, cal, cbr; 201 cal, cbr; 202 ca; 203 cb; 204 cbr; 205 ca; 206 car, cb, cabr; 208 cb; 209 br, cbl, crb; 210 car, cb; 211 ca, clb; 212 bl; 213 cbr, cla; 214 cbr; 215 car, crb; 216 ca.
Rob Petley-Jones: 164 cbl.
Simon Curson: 159 ca; 160 cbr, cra; 161 cal, clb; 163 cbr; 165 car; 167 car, clb; 168 cal, clb; 169 bl, cbr, clb; 172 clb; 174 cal; 176 cla; 177 cbl; 181 cr; 185 bl; 186 bl, ca, cla; 188 cal, cl; 189 car; 190 cb; 193 cla; 196 cal; 197 cla, clb; 198 bl, cal, clb; 199 cla; 201 car; 204 cl; 208 cra; 211 cfl; 212 cla.
Ted Benton: 14 bcl, bcr, ca; 15 cra, crb, cfr; 18 br, car, cbl, cla, crb; 19 bcr, car, cbl, cbr, cla; 20 cl, tl; 21 cfr, tr; 22 tl, bcl, cal, car, crb; 23 ca, clb; 24 cb; 25 ca, cbr; 26 bcl, cal, cra, crb; 27 cbl; 28 bcl, cal, car, crb; 29 ca, cra; 30 cbl; 31 cbl, cr; 32 cal, cbr, cra; 33 car, cbr, cla; 34 cal; 35 ca, cbr, cla; 36 ca, cb; 37 car, cra; 39 car, cbl, cr; 40 bcl, car; 41 car, cr; 42 bcl, car, cbr; 43 car, cr; 44 ca; 45 cr; 46 ca; 47 cbl, cr; 48 car, cbl, cr; 49 car; 50 cfl; 51 cal, cbr; 52 ca, cbl; 53 car, cb; 54 car, cbl, cla; 55 car, cbl; 56 ca; 57 cal, cbr, clb; 58 cal, cbr, cr; 59 bl, ca, car, cb, cra; 60 cal; 61 bl, car; 62 bcl, cal, cbl, cbr, cra; 63 bl, cal, ca; 64 cal, cb; 65 bcr, ca; 66 cal, car, cbl; 68 cbr, cra; 69 bcr, cbr; 70 cal, cbl, cra; 71 cbr; 72 bcl, cal, cra; 73 bcr, clb; 74 cbr; 75 car; 78 cal, cla, cra; 79 bcr, car, cbl, cbra, cla; 80 cal, car; 81 clb; 84 bcr, cal, cbl; 87 br, cbl; 89 car, cb; 90 cal; 92 cal, cl; 95 ca; 96 br, cal, cbl; 97 cb; 98 bcr, ca, cbl; 99 car, bcr; 100 bcr, cal; 101 cbr, clb; 102 bcl, cal, cbl, cbr, cra; 103 cbr, cfl, cla; 104 ca, cbr, cr; 105 bcl, ca, cal, cla; 106 bcl; 107 cal, car; 108 car; 109 cbl; 110 car, cla, cr; 111 car; 112 cb; 113 bcr, cal, clb, cra; 114 br, cal, cbl, cra; 115 car, cbr, cla; 116 bcl, cal, cra, crb; 117 car, cb, cla; 118 cal, cbl, cbr; 119 bl, car, cbr, cla; 120 cal, cra; 122 bcr, ca; 123 tr, cbr; 124 bcl, car, cla, crb; 125 bl, ca, cbr, bcr; 126 cra; 127 bcr, cal; 128 bcr, cal; 129 ca; 130 cbr; 131 ca, cbra, cra; 132 bcl, cal, car, crb; 133 bcr, car; 134 bcl, cal, car; 135 bcl, car; 137 clb; 138 br, cal; 139 bl, cbr; 140 cal, cbl, cbr, cra; 142 cbl, crb; 143 car, cb, cr; 144 br, cal, cbl, crb; 145 car, cb; 146 ca, cbl; 147 cb; 148 car, cla; 149 cb; 150 bcl; 153 cbl; 166 bl; 178 cal; 189 bcr; 208 cal; 212 cra; 215 cbl.
Tero Piirainen: 108 cal; 109 cal, car, cla; 138 cfr.

All other images © Dorling Kindersley